Beyond CO-TEACHING Basics

WENDY W. MURAWSKI
WENDY W. LOCHNER

Beyond CO-TEACHING Basics

A Data-Driven, No-Fail Model for Continuous Improvement

ASCD
Alexandria, Virginia USA

1703 N. Beauregard St. • Alexandria, VA 223111714 USA
Phone: 800-933-2723 or 703-578-9600 • Fax: 703-575-5400
Website: www.ascd.org • E-mail: member@ascd.org
Author guidelines: www.ascd.org/write

Deborah S. Delisle, *Executive Director;* Robert D. Clouse, *Managing Director, Digital Content & Publications;* Stefani Roth, *Publisher;* Genny Ostertag, *Director, Content Acquisitions;* Allison Scott, *Acquisitions Editor*; Julie Houtz, *Director, Book Editing & Production;* Joy Scott Ressler, *Editor;* Melissa Johnston, *Graphic Designer;* Mike Kalyan, *Director, Production Services;* Kelly Marshall, *Production Specialist;* Valerie Younkin, *Production Designer*.

All web links in this book are correct as of the publication date below but may have become inactive or otherwise modified since that time. If you notice a deactivated or changed link, please e-mail books@ascd.org with the words "Link Update" in the subject line. In your message, please specify the web link, the book title, and the page number on which the link appears.

PAPERBACK ISBN: 978-1-4166-2424-0 ASCD product #118007 n10/17

PDF E-BOOK ISBN: 978-1-4166-2425-7

Quantity discounts are available: e-mail programteam@ascd.org or call 800-933-2723, ext. 5773, or 703-575-5773. For desk copies, go to www.ascd.org/deskcopy.

Library of Congress Cataloging-in-Publication Data
Names: Murawski, Wendy W.
Title: Beyond co-teaching basics : a data-driven, no-fail model for continuous improvement / Wendy W. Murawski and Wendy W. Lochner (Authors).
Description: Alexandria, Virginia : ASCD, [2017] | Includes bibliographical references and index.
Identifiers: LCCN 2017022876 (print) | LCCN 2017036526 (ebook) | ISBN 9781416624257 (PDF) | ISBN 9781416624240 (pbk.)
Subjects: LCSH: Teaching teams. | Educational change. | School improvement programs.
Classification: LCC LB1029.T4 (ebook) | LCC LB1029.T4 M85 2017 (print) | DDC 371.14/8--dc23
LC record available at https://lccn.loc.gov/2017022876

26 25 24 23 22 21 20 19 18 1 2 3 4 5 6 7 8 9 10 11 12

We dedicate this book to a group of superior co-teachers who have truly committed themselves to continuous improvement:

The co-teachers at Granada Hills Charter High School in California.

We would like to highlight the supportive administration at GHCHS and give the most special shout-out to Mr. Marty Eisen, the GHCHS Co-Teaching Coordinator. Mr. E has gone above and beyond to not only co-teach physics to students with significant disabilities, but he also willingly piloted CTIME and gave hours and hours of support to his teams.

Dude, you rock!

Beyond
CO-TEACHING
Basics

Acknowledgments

The Wendys would like to thank all the teachers, administrators, and school districts that have committed themselves to co-teaching as a service delivery option for supporting all students. We especially thank those schools that welcomed us into their classrooms as we were piloting the CTIME model and collecting data. These include Granada Hills Charter High School and Blue Ridge Elementary. In addition, we thank our support network as we were working on this book. For Wendy Murawski, this includes Kathy Scott, Dani Lavoie, Tanya Hartley, Tamarah Ashton, Jessica Hanson, Brooke Blanks, and the freakishly awesome. For Wendy Lochner, this includes Chuck Hampton and Bill Furgason. We both also thank Allison Scott, Amy Marks, and Joy Scott Ressler, our editors on this book; we appreciate your input and guidance.

I would like to acknowledge my wonderful husband and children who fulfill me with their love and support each and every day. To my mom, my hero, rock, and stability through the years, and my dad, whose loving spirit invigorates and sustains me. For my twin brother, Curt, please stop setting the bar so high! And to grandmother Grace, whose inspiration continues throughout the generations of our family. ~ Wendy W. Lochner

I would like to acknowledge all of the educators who are constantly working too hard and burning themselves out. Take a breath—relax—you're doing great. Thank you to my friends who help me find balance and for whom I hope I do the same. To my son, Kiernan, who is made of sarcasm, pasta, and awesomeness, and my fiancé, D, who matches me with energy, positivity, and projects. To my mother, Susan Farrell, and my sister, Amy Weichel Casey, who are always on my side! ~ Wendy W. Murawski

1 An Introduction to CTIME and PDSA

Welcome to CTIME! The Collaborative Teaching Improvement Model of Excellence©

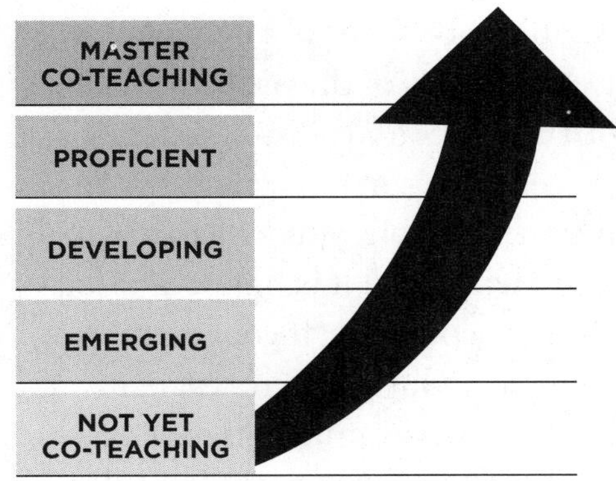

A Data-Driven Continuous Improvement Model

> We are what we repeatedly do. Excellence, therefore, is not an act, but a habit.
>
> *—William Durant (1991)*

The Collaborative Teaching Improvement Model of Excellence (CTIME) is a continuous improvement model that embraces personalized professional learning to ensure teachers meet the core competencies for co-teaching without burning out along the way. (We'll introduce those competencies in Chapter 2.) Co-teachers do not have to sit through hours of professional development that may give them little to take back to the classroom. The CTIME process helps the teachers themselves determine what is needed

Take-Aways

- *This book is for those who are ready to move beyond the question: What is collaborative teaching?*
- *CTIME is a continuous improvement model designed to help schools and co-teaching teams analyze data to determine how to improve practices.*
- *The PDSA cycle is a recursive loop that will be applied to co-teaching to help educators plan, act, reflect, and make changes based on that data.*

for their co-teaching team, addresses the competencies in the most time-efficient manner possible, and provides an opportunity for them to improve upon those competencies by receiving collegial feedback and support. CTIME allows schools to see immediate results in their co-teaching programs and makes it easy to generalize the improvements to the classroom level.

CTIME is the culmination of the best research in the field. It incorporates a systematic and systemic application of data analysis, feedback, collegial support, microteaching, and collaborative grouping. In this book, we describe each of the aspects of the CTIME process in detail, with a discussion of the supporting research. In a nutshell, co-teachers will spend more of their time focused specifically on their own situation and needs, which will accelerate and sustain improvement, and less of their time in a room away from students learning about strategies that they may or may not implement.

Note that we emphasize both the co-teaching teams at the classroom level and the overall systemic changes that might be made at a school level to help build capacity and lead to institutionalization of the process. That means we have written this book with both teachers and administrators in mind. We talk directly to all of you using second-person narrative, rather than using a more formal voice. Depending on your role, you may focus on some aspects of the process over others, but we feel that it is important for everyone to know about the whole CTIME protocol. Thus, if you are an administrator at the central office, you will read about what co-teachers should be doing at the classroom level and with their communities of practice. Similarly, classroom teachers will be able to read about what we tell administrators and those in school leadership positions that they can do to support this process. For the many of you who have a foot in both areas, please bear with us as we write to "you," regardless of whether your role is administrator or teacher. We believe all of you are important to this process!

We hope that you are intrigued by the CTIME process by now and would like to bring it to your own school. What exactly would you be bringing? The CTIME Professional Learning Expectations in Figure 1.1 describe what co-teachers and schools implementing co-teaching as a service delivery option for students should be able to do if they use the process with fidelity.

Getting Started

If you truly are ready to change co-teaching practices—and outcomes—at your site, then this is the book for you. If you choose (1) not to collect data or (2) to do nothing with your co-teaching observation results, then this will be a very short read; this is not the book for you. We plan to walk you from point A to point B step by step for co-teaching improvement, but this process does require the use of data. What do we need from you? Simple. We require teachers and administrators who want to get better at their craft of implementing true co-teaching. We know that most teachers want that and all students deserve it.

FIGURE 1.1

CTIME Professional Learning Expectations

Schools and teams engaged in the CTIME process will be able to

1. Identify individual and team strengths and limitations in co-teaching knowledge, skills, and actions.
2. Describe co-teaching domains, strands, and competencies and recognize the co-teaching core competencies.
3. Collaborate with colleagues in providing and receiving feedback on co-teaching practices.
4. Systematically analyze practice data using quality improvement methods and implement changes based on those data.
5. Incorporate observation feedback into the daily execution of co-teaching.
6. Make data-driven decisions on co-teaching at the school and team levels based on root cause and trend analyses.

Other books provide more detailed information on what co-teaching is or is not, how to schedule it in schools, how to address personality conflicts, and even strategies to use for engaging in differentiated instruction in a co-taught class (e.g., Conderman, Bresnahan, Teacher, & Pedersen, 2008; Murawski, 2009, 2010; Murawski & Spencer, 2011; Villa, Thousand, & Nevin, 2013). This is a different book. This book is designed to help schools and teams that are looking for a systematic way of building, honing, and institutionalizing co-teaching practices. It is not a Co-Teaching 101 book. It is perhaps a Co-Teaching 301 book. Is it for you? Let's find out. Start by answering the nine simple questions in Figure 1.2.

Our goal is to help you and your partner, school, district, or even your state move the needle on co-teaching implementation. Having worked with thousands of schools on their inclusive practices, we know that many schools are lamenting their lack of progress. We hear things like, "We did co-teaching years ago, but it went away for a while" and "We call it co-teaching, but it's really just 'one teach, one support' only" and "We have what we think is really good co-teaching, but we have no data to show what the teachers are doing in those classes." We have worked with teams that are strong but want to get better, and with teams that are weak and simply do not know where to start in order to improve. That is where this book comes in.

The CTIME process combines the best of what we know about professional learning and growth as educators with the best of what we know

FIGURE 1.2

Is This the Book for You?

1. Are you trying to find out what co-teaching is as a basic introduction?
   - ☐ Yes? We recommend you read *Co-Teaching: A Simple Solution That Isn't So Simple After All* (Friend, 2008).
   - ☐ No? If you already feel comfortable with what co-teaching is, read on.
2. Are you trying to get some practical strategies for co-teachers to use to improve their daily practices with students?
   - ☐ Yes? We recommend you read *Collaborative Teaching in Elementary Schools* (Murawski, 2010) or *Collaborative Teaching in Secondary Schools* (Murawski, 2009).
   - ☐ No? If you already feel comfortable with co-teaching strategies, read on.
3. Are you trying to learn more about scheduling and managing co-teaching logistics from an administrative perspective?
   - ☐ Yes? We recommend you read *Leading the Co-Teaching Dance: Leadership Strategies to Enhance Team Outcomes* (Murawski & Dieker, 2013).
   - ☐ No? If you already feel comfortable with co-teaching logistics, read on.
4. Are you hoping to learn the specific competencies required for true co-teaching and have a framework of expectations?
   - ☐ Yes? Read on.
   - ☐ No? Why not?
5. Are you looking for a way to collect meaningful data on co-teaching?
   - ☐ Yes? Read on.
   - ☐ No? Why not?
6. Are you looking for a step-by-step guide to help support and coach co-teaching teams?
   - ☐ Yes? Read on.
   - ☐ No? Why not?
7. Do you want to know how to set up professional learning communities (PLCs) and communities of practice (CoPs) to facilitate professional learning around co-teaching?
   - ☐ Yes? Read on.
   - ☐ No? Why not?
8. Are you looking for a systematic way to help teams at different levels improve their own co-planning, co-instructing, and co-assessing?
   - ☐ Yes? Read on.
   - ☐ No? Why not?
9. Do you want students to be in classrooms where their co-teachers have a "no-fail" mindset and are continuously working on improving their practices?
   - ☐ Yes? Read on.
   - ☐ No? Why not? Seriously . . . why not???

about co-teaching. The consolidation of a variety of best practices in professional growth led to the creation of a process geared to help teachers and teams effectively and efficiently build on their co-teaching skills in the classroom. The CTIME process is a way to avoid long, drawn-out professional development sessions that are general or broad in nature. It is a way to minimize the gap that often results between what we know we should be doing in schools related to collaborative teaching and what we are doing in daily practice (Pfeffer & Sutton, 2000). It is a way to sidestep hours of "marriage counseling" between two teachers who are unable to share the inclusive classroom (Murawski, 2010). It is a way to eliminate parents or students complaining that their teachers are unskilled, demonstrating ineffective practices, or not providing accommodations or differentiation as guaranteed in a student's individualized education program (IEP). In sum, it is a way to ensure "no-fail" co-teaching practices in the classroom.

CTIME emphasizes a process that includes teachers collaborating with, communicating with, and supporting each other in an environment that can at times be contentious and isolating. Most important, this process allows teams to make progress in co-teaching at a rapid pace because they will be focused, motivated, supported, and driven by data. So, roll up your sleeves because it's CTIME, and we will get co-teaching teams on their way to phenomenal co-teaching!

Overview of the CTIME Process

CTIME utilizes a continuous improvement model to monitor the entire process, ensuring that co-teachers and schools are getting the results they seek. This process is called the Plan-Do-Study-Act (PDSA) model (Deming, 1950, 1993), and it has been around for a long time, getting serious results in other fields such as health care (Cleghorn & Headrick, 1996; Taylor et al., 2014), project management (Ramaprasad & Prakash, 2003), and education (Tague, 2004), as well as innovation, science, and quality control (Moen & Norman, 2010). We apply it here to co-teaching and pair it with other best practices known to elicit positive results. For example, much of the work done to increase the use of core competencies in the classroom is addressed through a microteaching framework (Cinici, 2016; Ghosh, 2016), which reduces the complexities of working on too many skills at once in a traditional classroom. Microteaching alleviates the fear often seen as a barrier in the gap between knowing and doing (Ahmadi, Vogel, & Collins, 2016) that would inhibit the implementation of the competencies. Finally, feedback and collaboration are a major part of the professional learning community and community of practice groups (Hallam, Smith, Hite, Hite, & Wilcox, 2015; Kelly & Cherkowski, 2015), allowing teachers to share their experiences and learn from each other, while providing support and creating a more collaborative culture within the school. If you're starting to feel overwhelmed by all the jargon, research, and components, please don't be. We plan to walk you systematically through each of these pieces, tell you more about why they are considered evidence-based practices, and show you how to put them together into the CTIME process.

CTIME is a model that supports the acquisition of the knowledge and skills of co-teaching core competencies, which are then generalized into the classroom setting and sustained. Co-teachers are expected to execute the co-teaching competencies at a mastery level, which are monitored continually. Once the necessary skills are identified (that is, once the team determines what they need to work on based on their own data), microteaching allows them to practice and develop these essential skills. The PDSA cycle provides for continual monitoring of individual teams' progress, as well as overall improvement at the school level. CTIME was based on the premise that improvement comes from the application of knowledge—not from sitting around and chatting about what should be done, or venting about why things aren't getting done! Simply doing a "dog-and-pony" show for teachers will not change practices. A one-day professional development seminar might be motivating, but it does not result in sustained practices.

Educators need job-embedded professional learning (Shaffer & Thomas-Brown, 2015). They need to have buy-in that the change is needed and also in how change will be implemented. They need to be actively engaged in the "doing" for any real learning to stick. This is where the PDSA cycle comes into play. Let's jump into it!

Overview of PDSA

Walter Shewhart, a physicist, engineer, and statistician, came up with the concept behind what we now know as the PDSA cycle in 1939, although he called it the PDCA cycle, using the word *check* instead of *study* (Moen & Norman, 2010). Shewhart used this model for quality control in science. Think about the scientific method. You generate a hypothesis, test the hypothesis, analyze the data, and then disseminate your results. Those of you who are science teachers, please give us some leeway on our abbreviated and simplistic version of this. Shewhart was essentially encouraging others to (P) *plan* what they were going to do, including objectives and processes; (D) *do* their experiment, statistics, creation, and so forth; (C) *check* the results for accuracy and see if there were differences from their expectations; and (A) *act* on those differences. Seems pretty simple, right? It is.

Although Shewhart may have started the whole PDCA concept, it is W. Edwards Deming who gets the credit for popularizing it. (Isn't that always the case? One person comes up with an idea, but someone else knows how to market it better.) Deming changed the C for *check* to an S for *study,* because he felt that "checking" didn't emphasize the need to analyze the results sufficiently (Aguayo, 1991). The Deming model became popular in Japan in the 1950s, where the process was used to monitor quality control in many areas, most notably car manufacturing. Toyota is one of many companies that continue to use this process today.

We know you are fascinated by quality control for cars in the 1950s. We also imagine a few of you are wondering how this relates to you and the co-teaching process. Bear with us! It is this PDSA model that we now apply to co-teaching. PDSA is about continuous improvement. Cleghorn and Headrick (1996) wrote, "The Plan-Do-Study-Act (PDSA) cycle lies at the heart of continuous improvement and is a redefinition of the scientific method for application to the world of work" (p. 206). It is based on the premise that you're not just done/finished/*fertig*/*terminado* once you have acted. You need to learn from that act—whether you learn how to improve your practice or you have a clearer understanding of why that action yielded positive results. Positive, negative, and null outcomes all have information from which we can learn.

Let's apply the PDSA cycle methodology to collaborative teaching. Despite the real temptation to analyze how the method was applied to cars in the 1950s, we need to keep our focus on educational applications in inclusive classes. It's tough, but we can do it.

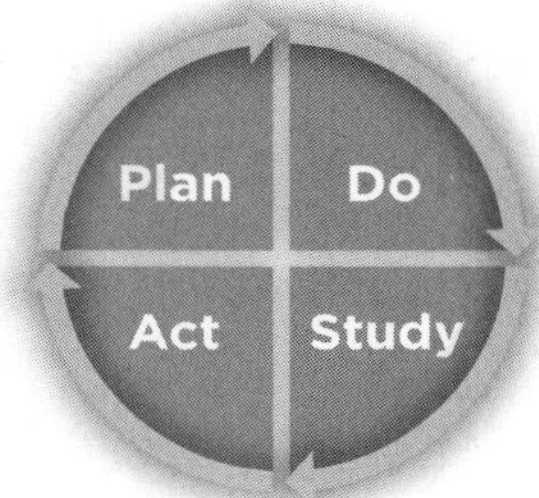

Plan: Establish the Objectives and Processes Necessary to Deliver Results

What would this look like for co-teachers? This is the time when school teams and co-teachers decide what they want to improve upon to help their students and their situations. Preferably, these decisions will be shared and will be data-driven, not just opinion-driven. Remember that PDSA is a recursive cycle, so you'll return to the planning phase again and again.

Who would do this? Decisions regarding what you will work on need to be shared decisions. That's what collaboration is all about. Can't decide? Don't worry. There will be plenty of time to work on various components of your collaborative teaching. You can pick one co-teaching core competency for the first cycle and save another for the next. Take baby steps.

Where and when would this occur? During co-planning. If you were about to comment on how you and your partner never plan together, rethink that quickly. Then let us remind you that true co-teaching requires

Get some help with co-planning by using the free template at www.2TeachLLC.com or use the Co-Teaching Solutions System (CTSS) Teachers' Toolbox software at www.coteachsolutions.com or Dieker's The Co-Planner: Two Professionals + One Plan for Co-Teaching *at www.knowledge-by-design.com.*

(yes, *requires*) co-planning between partners (Murawski, 2012). If you want results, you two need to plan together and determine what needs to be done to help your diverse group of students. This is also the perfect time to talk about any areas you both think you may need to improve upon as co-teachers.

Why would you do this? Think about the different outcomes you had when you planned a lesson thoroughly (maybe for student teaching) and when you just were winging it. Certainly, those off-the-cuff lessons worked well some of the time, but often they were not as effective as when you walked in knowing what you were doing and what your goals were. The same holds true here. If co-teachers just keep taking every day as it comes, they aren't able to systematically improve. We have so much on our plates that knowing what we are trying to accomplish will reduce the load and help us focus when we are together.

How would this occur? Hold on to that question, please. We intend to walk you through the entire process once you understand each element of CTIME. In fact, for the remaining elements of the cycle, we won't refer to the "who," "why," and "how." Just refer to the responses to those questions in this section.

Do: Implement the Plan, Execute the Process, and Collect Data

What would this look like for co-teachers? This is the time when co-teachers, well, co-teach. (Don't roll your eyes!) There is actually more to it than that. The idea here is that you two are not just teaching together as you always have. This time, you will have a plan of action. You will have a specific competency you are focused on, and both of you will focus on it at a particular time. This is the process called *microteaching* that we'll describe later. For now, just know that in the PDSA cycle, the "Do" phase is when you two engage in the particular co-teaching core competency that you jointly decided you wanted to improve upon.

Where would this occur? This will all depend on the competency or competencies you've selected to improve upon. It might be just the one classroom you both share, or it might be in multiple classrooms if you decide to use a regrouping approach and have students in multiple areas. For example, say you decided that using "*We*" language is important to you in order to demonstrate more parity between co-teachers in front of the students. Currently, one or both of you tends to say to students, "I want you to . . . .” This may not be a power play or out of spite or disrespect; it may simply be that the individual has taught in a solo class for years and is used to saying “I” instead of “we.” The data collection would then take place whenever the two teachers are teaching together during the “Do” phase of PDSA. On the other hand, if your competency of focus is the use of regrouping strategies, each of the teachers might be working with a different group of students in a different room. In that case, both venues would become the areas of observation for the “Do” phase of the PDSA cycle.

When would this occur? We will address microteaching and how it interplays with the PDSA cycle in Chapters 7 and 8, and this question will be addressed there more fully, especially as it relates to how often data should be collected. However, in a nutshell, this is up to you. We will give some suggestions for how often we think co-teachers should go through the PDSA cycle as a part of the CTIME process, but we also respect that teams, schools, and cultures are different. You and your partner might be veteran co-teachers who mainline caffeine and meet for two hours every night to plan; if you want to do a different competency every day, we won’t stop you! But you might be new to this whole co-teaching thing, have an infant at home, be working on your master’s degree, and take care of foster ferrets on the weekend. For you, this cycle might be daunting, and you and your partner may prefer to slow it all down a bit. Use our cycle as a guide, but work with your administrators to select a process that moves the needle forward and helps you with your students and your co-teaching relationship—but doesn’t kill you in the process. We are big fans of baby steps!

How would this occur? Okay, we know we said we wouldn’t address “how” again, but here it is. Though we’ll describe the data collection process when we discuss microteaching, we wanted to emphasize that this is the stage where data are collected. It is not enough to focus on a co-teaching competency for a short amount of time. You also need to have data that indicate whether there was a change based on this focused teaching. Data collection doesn’t have to be time-consuming or overwhelming—in fact, we hope that the CTIME process takes the fear right out of you—but it does need to include data. Otherwise, how do we get to that whole “data-driven decision making” thing?

Study: Study the Actual Results and Compare Them Against the Expected Results to Ascertain any Differences

What would this look like for co-teachers? This is the time when both of you look at what you planned to accomplish and the results you actually got. The results are the data you measured and collected during the "Do" phase. Naturally, it would be great if your results were what you expected or even better, but don't fret if they weren't. Every outcome (even those with no change) teaches us something. Reflect on what happened. Did the lesson go as expected? If not, why not? Were elements in your control, or not? The key here is that both of you sit together to analyze what happened, why you think you got the outcomes you did, and what both of you think should be done about it.

Where and when would this occur? There are a few different ways that the "Study" phase will occur. In our explanation of the CTIME process, we will discuss how small collaborative groups (called communities of practice or professional learning communities) get together to share observations and data collection. Together, these small teams will help one another analyze results, determine next steps, and identify any necessary resources. Ideally, this would occur once a month or so. Again, keep in mind our mantra of baby steps and doing what works for your situation.

Some larger districts and organizations get these collaborative groups together only once or twice a semester, due primarily to logistics, cost, and time. In that case, you and your collaborating partner may find yourselves self-reflecting on your results and then meeting to share with each other. These meetings often occur in conjunction with meetings to co-plan your lessons. Notice now why we call the PDSA cycle a recursive loop? As you discuss your findings and determine why you got the outcomes you did, you are also able to begin to move into the "Act" phase of setting goals for change. This goal setting, or professional learning actions, as we'll describe, also leads into the planning of the next microteaching lesson. This may all sound like a lot, but don't let it intimidate you.

Problem Solving

Can't find the time to get together with your community of practice every three weeks to a month? You can also

- *Meet less frequently.*
- *Meet via Skype, GoToMeeting, or another virtual platform.*
- *Share information asynchronously by uploading videos, feedback forms, data, and the like to Dropbox or a similar file-hosting service.*

Act: Develop Corrective Actions for the Significant Differences Between the Actual and Expected Results

What would this look like for co-teachers? We are right back to where we started, essentially. In this phase, we have analyzed the data and now we are going to do something about it. Together, either as a community of practice or as an individual team, co-teachers create a *professional learning actions plan* based on a root cause analysis (Okes, 2009). Don't let those words scare you. There is nothing "evaluative" or "punitive" about this plan. It's exactly what it says—a way for you two to take action so that you'll get the results you want. In the end, you will increase your own professional learning. Did your focused microteaching already result in what you wanted for students? Great! Your professional learning actions plan can state that you want to continue doing what you did, just on a more regular basis. And now you can start focusing on a different co-teaching core competency moving forward. Didn't get the results you wanted? No problem. You two create this plan to identify what you think you need to do instead. When you move back to the "Plan" phase, you'll figure out your objectives and processes for trying to address that same competency, but with a different method. That's why this is a systematic and sustainable process. You and your partner are able to focus on one thing at a time in a logical, practical, and "doable" way.

Where and when would this occur? Same answer as for the "Study" question. Ideally, you'll work with your community of practice to help create your professional learning actions plan. In fact, many larger organizations are able to get these small groups together only if they identify as a "work group" whose time together results in an actual artifact. In these cases, each team's plan for professional learning around co-teaching meets that criterion. These professional learning actions plans are well thought out by the group, include possible resources and strategies for teams to try, and therefore—though they were created with one particular team and class in mind—are often applicable and helpful for other co-teaching teams as well!

If you don't have a community of practice to meet with, we recommend meeting with at least one other co-teaching team in your school. If there is no other team, or if logistics simply won't allow that right now, it's partner time again. You and your co-teacher are the backbone of this endeavor, and it is your class and relationship that are the focus of this continuous improvement model, so it's up to you two to create your own plan of actions for professional learning! We would like to suggest, however, that you don't always try to do this alone. Work with an administrator or talk to an academic coach or consultant; it may be helpful for a new set of eyes to look over your plan and give you even more ideas for improvement. Murawski (2009, 2010) suggests that co-teachers identify one person on faculty or staff whom both of them respect to act as a "marriage counselor" when needed. Perhaps this same individual would be willing to look over your plan and give you additional suggestions. It might cost you a Starbucks once a month, but it'll be worth it!

Closing Thoughts

You've now had your CTIME and PDSA 101 introductions. You've jumped into the book, and we are excited to take you with us through this process.

As you read, please remember that this is a recursive loop, meaning that it is a process that goes round and round. That means it is also somewhat difficult to describe in a linear fashion. We promise that by the time you have finished reading this book, you will have all the components at your fingertips for a successful and productive CTIME experience!

2 Introducing the Co-Teaching Core Competencies

Demystifying Co-Teaching

Just as teaching requires educators to plan what they are going to do, to do it with students, and then to assess the effectiveness of the instruction, so too does co-teaching. Murawski (2003) boiled down other co-teaching definitions from over the years to a simple one, which we will use for the remainder of this book: Co-teaching requires two or more professional educators to "co-plan, co-instruct, and co-assess" (p. 10). Without all three of these components, educators are simply not co-teaching.

What we often see in schools these days is a call for co-teaching as an inclusive service delivery model for students—a call answered by the sharing of space by two educators. We recognize that teachers are sharing space more often, but we do not call that co-teaching in and of itself. National research on co-teaching has found that the majority of individuals who say they are co-teaching—or were told to co-teach by administrators—also admit that they use a "one teach, one support" model for most of their shared time together (Friend, Cook, Hurley-Chamberlain, & Shamberger, 2010; Scruggs, Mastropieri, & McDuffie, 2007; Weiss & Lloyd, 2002). Though co-teaching is supposed to be a way to provide for specially designed instruction in a general education setting for those students with identified disabilities who need it, studies have found that this area is still sorely lacking (Friend et al., 2010; King-Sears & Bowman-Kruhm, 2011; Murawski, 2006). Ideally, for true co-teaching to occur, we would see two or more educators bringing in their diverse areas of expertise to jointly create a universally designed lesson plan, instruct a diverse class using best practices, incorporate differentiation techniques and various co-instructional approaches, and assess students using multiple means of expression.

Take-Aways

- *Co-teaching requires co-planning, co-instructing, and co-assessing.*
- *The co-teaching competencies have been organized into domains, strands, and core competencies.*
- *Having clear competencies enables co-teachers and schools to know what they should be doing for effective, true co-teaching.*

Co-teaching: *when two or more professional educators "co-plan, co-instruct, and co-assess" (Murawski, 2003, p. 10).*

Simple, right? Maybe not, but we know it can be done, and this book is going to help you get there.

Now that we are clear as to what co-teaching is, let us also make sure we are clear on what it is not. It is not one teacher always in front leading, while the other is always in a support or "glorified aide" role. It is not teachers taking their own groups of students ("my kids" versus "your kids"). It is not one teacher telling the other to pull a group of students to the back of the room whenever they don't "get it." It is not two teachers disorganized, stepping on one another's toes, interrupting constantly, unaware of what is next, and unable to address students' academic, behavioral, and social needs. It is also not easy.

We stated in Chapter 1 that this book does not provide a detailed look at what co-teaching is and how to do it, nor is it a book of practical strategies to motivate and inspire co-teachers. We already created those texts for you (see Murawski's references). If you've picked up this book, then you should already be familiar with the basics of co-teaching. Even so, it's worth recapping some of the essentials and providing you with additional resources. In Figure 2.1, we provide the "Do's and Don'ts of Co-Teaching," which makes for a great discussion-starter at a faculty meeting. We also provide a list of "Commonly Used Co-Teaching Approaches to Instruction" in Figure 2.2. Many co-teachers like to print out and laminate this list as a quick cheat sheet for when they are co-planning. Finally, in Figure 2.3, we offer "Teacher Actions in Co-Teaching." This, too, gives co-teachers a nice reference guide for when they are struggling with how to share their classroom and maximize the use of two credentialed adults. Each of these documents is also available to download from www.2TeachLLC.com. With these resources in hand, you should be ready to move forward with actually *improving* the co-teaching occurring in your schools.

Problem Solving

Do you have a diverse group of teachers at your school, some with lots of co-teaching experience and knowledge and some with very little? Use the "Do's and Don'ts of Co-Teaching," "Commonly Used Co-Teaching Approaches to Instruction," and "Teacher Actions in Co-Teaching" to start a conversation about co-teaching so that teachers can learn from one another.

Identifying Co-Teaching Competencies

You know that you want to have teams co-teach. You recognize that co-teaching requires co-planning, co-instructing, and co-assessing (Murawski, 2010). This sounds good so far, but how do you know if teachers are *effective* in their co-planning, co-instructing, and co-assessing? What types of concrete feedback can you give to support their actions? This is where having clear competencies is essential. Let us now clarify the role of competencies and how they fit in the CTIME protocol.

There are many definitions of the word *competency*. Throughout this discussion, however, we will use the following definition: "A competency represents the skills, knowledge, and behaviors required to perform

Co-teaching competencies: *discrete behaviors or skills that can be witnessed or documented and rated by an observer.*

effectively" (Mind Tools, n.d.). The *Harvard University Competency Dictionary* (n.d.) states, "At the individual level, this focus on competencies enables people to take a proactive role in their own development by providing guidance in behavior change efforts" (p. 4). (Anyone else impressed that Harvard actually has a *Competency Dictionary,* for goodness' sake?) For the purpose of our application, we will reference competencies as they relate to the goals of developing true and successful co-teaching.

FIGURE 2.1

Do's and Don'ts of Co-Teaching

Co-Teaching Is...

- Two or more co-equal (preferably credentialed) faculty working together.
- Conducted in the same classroom at the same time.
- Conducted with heterogeneous groups.
- When both teachers plan for instruction together. The general education teacher (GET) is typically the content specialist, while the special education teacher (SET) is the expert on individualizing instruction and delivery to various learning modalities.
- When both teachers provide *substantive* instruction together—having planned together, the SET can grade homework, teach content, facilitate activities, etc.
- When both teachers assess and evaluate student progress. IEP goals are kept in mind, as are the curricular goals and standards for that grade level.
- When teachers maximize the benefits of having two teachers in the room by having both teachers actively engaged with students. Examples of different co-teaching models include team teaching, station teaching, parallel teaching, alternative teaching, and "one teach, one support" (see Friend & Cook, 2000).
- When teachers reflect on the progress and process, offering one another feedback on teaching styles, content, activities, and other items pertinent to improving the teaching situation.

Co-Teaching Is Not...

- A teacher and an assistant, teacher's aide, or paraprofessional.
- When a few students are pulled out of the classroom on a regular basis to work with the special education teacher (SET). It is also not job-sharing, where teachers teach on different days.
- Pulling a group of students with disabilities to the back of the general education class.
- When the general education teacher (GET) plans all lessons and the SET walks into the room and says, "What are we doing today, and what would you like me to do?"
- When the SET walks around the room all period as the GET teaches the content.
- When the SET sits in the class and takes notes.
- When the GET grades "his" kids and the SET grades "her" kids—or when the GET grades all students and the SET surreptitiously changes the grades and calls it "modifying after the fact."
- When teachers take turns being "in charge" of the class so that the other teacher can get caught up on grading, photocopying, making phone calls, creating IEPs, etc.—or when students remain in the large group setting in lecture format as teachers take turns "talking at them."
- When teachers get frustrated with one another and tell the rest of the faculty in the teachers' lounge or when one teacher simply tells the other teacher what to do and how to do it.

Adapted from Murawski, W. W. (2002). Demystifying co-teaching. *CARS+ Newsletter 22*(3), 19.

We use competencies to help define the expectations of what should be occurring when teachers co-teach. This can occur at the district, state, school, grade, and individual team levels. Schools need to know what should be occurring in order to determine if a team is an effective co-teaching unit, as well as how to make changes for improvement. It is much easier for individual teachers and co-teaching teams to assume responsibility for improvement if there are clear expectations for the co-teaching experience. When expectations are clear, teachers are more apt to be able to meet and even exceed expectations (Danielson, 2007).

FIGURE 2.2

Commonly Used Co-Teaching Approaches to Instruction

Co-Teaching Approach	Class Setup	Quick Definition
One Teach, One Support (OT/OS)	Whole Class B A	One teacher is in front of the class leading instruction. The other is providing substantive support (e.g., collection or dissemination of papers, setting up labs, classroom management). Both are actively engaged.
Team Teaching	Whole Class A B	Both teachers are in front of the class, working together to provide instruction. This may take the form of debates, modeling information or note-taking, compare/contrast, or role-playing.
Parallel Teaching	Regrouping A B	Each teacher takes half of the class in order to reduce student–teacher ratio. Instruction can occur in the same or a different setting. Groups may be doing the same content in the same way, same content in a different way, or different content.
Station Teaching	Regrouping B A	Students are divided into three or more small, heterogeneous groups to go to stations or centers. Students rotate through multiple centers. Teachers can facilitate individual stations or circulate among all stations.
Alternative Teaching	Regrouping B A	One teacher works with a large group of students, while the other works with a smaller group providing reteaching, preteaching, or enrichment, as needed. The large group is not receiving new instruction during this time so that the small group can rejoin when finished.

With author permission from Murawski, W. W., & Spencer, S. A. (2011). *Collaborate, communicate, and differentiate! Improving student learning in today's diverse classrooms.* Thousand Oaks, CA: Corwin.

FIGURE 2.3

Teacher Actions in Co-Teaching

If one of you is doing this...	The other can be doing this...
Lecturing	Modeling notetaking on the board/overhead
Taking roll	Collecting or reviewing last night's homework
Passing out papers	Reviewing directions
Giving instructions orally	Writing down instructions on board
Checking for understanding with large heterogeneous group of students	Checking for understanding with small heterogeneous group of students
Circulating, providing one-on-one support, as needed	Providing direct instruction to whole class
Prepping half of the class for one side of a debate	Prepping the other half of the class for the opposing side of the debate
Facilitating a silent activity	Circulating, checking for comprehension
Providing large-group instruction	Circulating, using proximity control for behavior management
Running last-minute copies or errands	Reviewing homework
Reteaching or preteaching with a small group	Monitoring large group as they work on practice materials
Facilitating sustained silent reading	Reading aloud quietly with a small group; previewing upcoming information
Reading a test aloud to a group of students	Proctoring a test silently with a group of students
Creating basic lesson plans for standards, objective, and content curriculum	Providing suggestions for modifications, accommodations, and activities for diverse learners
Facilitating stations or groups	Facilitating stations or groups
Explaining new concept	Conducting role-play or modeling concept
Considering modification needs	Considering enrichment opportunities

© Murawski, W.W. (2003). *Co-teaching in the inclusive classroom: Working together to help all your students find success.* Bellevue, WA: Bureau of Education & Research.

Using the Co-Teaching Competencies

Competencies focus on factors that contribute to the co-teaching team's and school's success. They provide a set of statements that may be used to show successful co-teaching and identify professional learning needs or gaps. By collecting and combining competency information, you can create a standardized approach that is clear and accessible to everyone in the school. The co-teaching competencies outline specifically what co-teachers need to do to be effective in their roles, and clearly establish how their roles relate to the school's goals and vision for success. The competencies described in this book ensure that true co-teaching is in place and that co-teachers are co-planning, co-instructing, and co-assessing (Murawski,

2009). We are purposefully repeating the definition of co-teaching here because we believe that if co-teachers are not doing these three things, they are not truly co-teaching.

Many administrators are familiar with the protocols of observation and evaluation of individual teachers. However, observing and giving feedback to two teachers who are sharing instruction is different and should be significantly so (Murawski & Lochner, 2011). Two teachers in the classroom should not simply be doing the same thing with different groups of students. Nor should one always be taking the lead as the other functions as a glorified paraprofessional. Their work now becomes intertwined and integrated. At the very core of co-teaching should be the essential question posited by Murawski and Spencer (2011): *"How is what the two teachers are doing together **substantively different** and **better for students** than what one of them would do alone?"* (p. 96; emphasis added). Simply having an additional set of hands and eyes does not constitute co-teaching. Simply mainstreaming students with special needs into a typical general education classroom with no specially designed instruction will also not constitute co-teaching—nor will it serve to provide the inclusive, differentiated classroom all students deserve. Later in this book, we address how administrators, peers, and other observers can use the competencies to observe teams and collect data for improvement. First, however, we must emphasize the need for the competencies themselves.

In this chapter, we introduce the *Co-Teaching Core Competency Framework,* which provides a way to focus on the multiple competencies that co-teachers should be able to demonstrate. Administrators, teachers, coaches, and communities of practice will be able to use the unique set of clear, well-communicated competencies provided in the framework to identify those areas in which co-teachers need assistance. This will enable them to hone their skills and become effective and true co-teaching teams. Not only can co-teaching team members work more effectively and achieve their own personal potential, but there is also a link between their team's performance and their school's vision or mission of an inclusive environment that provides a high quality education to *all* students. Being able to articulate the overall goal, as well as the specific actions needed to achieve that goal, will help everyone involved (teachers, administrators, parents, and even students) to work collaboratively to accomplish the shared goal.

The four co-teaching competency domains:

- *The Learner and Learning*
- *The Task at Hand*
- *Instructional Practices*
- *Professional Responsibilities*

The Four Competency Domains

The *Co-Teaching Core Competency Framework* is divided into domains, strands, competencies, and core competencies. It would benefit the school administration to clarify each of these different areas with co-teaching teams in order to avoid miscommunication. There are four domains in the co-teaching competencies. *Competency domains are simply broad categories under which the co-teaching competencies fall.* The four domains that incorporate all competencies are (1) The Learner and Learning, (2) The Task at Hand, (3) Instructional Practices, and (4) Professional Responsibilities (Figure 2.4). Let's consider each of these four broad categories.

FIGURE 2.4

The Four Competency Domains

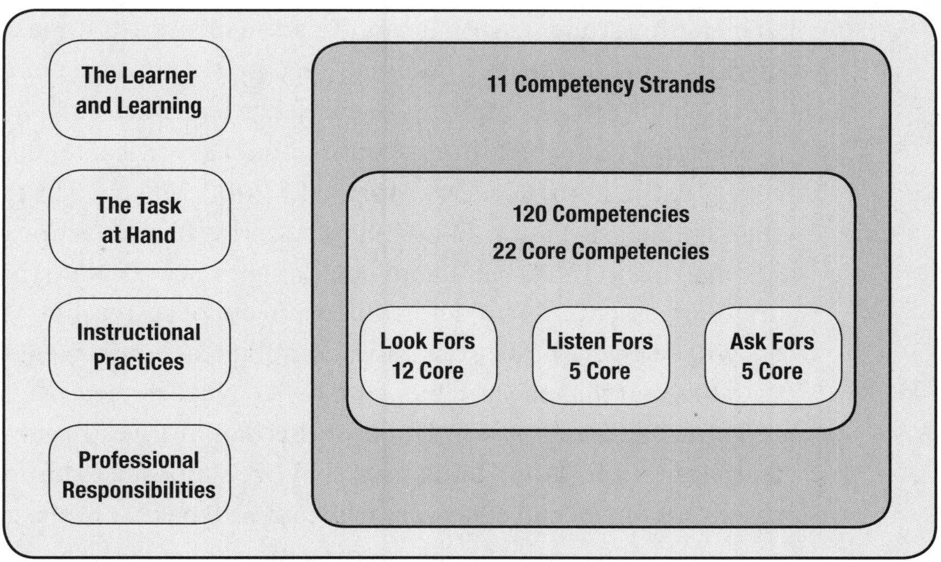

The Learner and Learning

The first domain, The Learner and Learning, deals with the students themselves and their individual learning profiles. Do some students have disabilities, are they English-language learners, or both? Perhaps some of the students in the class are twice-exceptional or have a 504 plan. What are their cultural backgrounds? What are their strengths and needs? As co-teachers, you need to be highly cognizant of the individual learners in your class and what they bring to the classroom. The competencies that fall under this domain relate to how co-teachers learn about and respect their shared students. Though students and their needs will change regularly, strong co-teaching teams have strategies in place to proactively take needs into account and differentiate for their inclusive group of students. They have set up a classroom environment that considers student needs physically, academically, behaviorally, and socially, and they are willing to adapt that environment as needed to benefit their students. For practical strategies on how to teach students with varying special needs, we recommend *What Really Works with Exceptional Learners* (Murawski & Scott, 2017).

The Task at Hand

The second domain, The Task at Hand, considers the curriculum that is being taught. It takes into account the specific content that co-teachers are trying to cover and teach to the varied learners in the class. In addition, this domain incorporates the "task" of following compliance issues related to including students with disabilities and meeting the goals and objectives identified in their IEPs. Finally, co-teaching itself is part of the task teachers are trying to accomplish. Research has identified certain components (e.g., supportive scheduling, planning time) as critical for co-teaching success (Austin, 2001; Dieker & Murawski, 2003; Mastropieri et al., 2005; Walther-Thomas, Bryant & Land, 1996). As a result, co-teaching teams should be engaging in those particular components as well. Note that these three areas are essentially predetermined and out of co-teachers' hands. Teachers will be given their curriculum, compliance requirements are nonnegotiable, and the research has established what strong co-teachers should be doing in the classroom. Thus, for this domain, we are emphasizing that teams are essentially "doing what they are supposed to be doing." Excellent resources for special educators who may still be new to the profession or struggling with really understanding their role are the best-selling *Survival Guide for New Special Education Teachers,* 2nd ed. (Martin & Hauth, 2015), and the new *A Teacher's Guide to Special Education* (Bateman & Cline, 2016). Both books are available through the Council for Exceptional Children at www.cec.sped.org.

Tech Tip

Looking for tons of resources for working with exceptional learners? Visit the Council for Exceptional Children (CEC) website—www.ced.sped.org—for books, conferences, webinars, and more.

Instructional Practices

In the third domain, Instructional Practices, co-teachers have far more flexibility and personal choice in terms of how they meet the competencies. As we've stated many times before, co-teaching requires co-planning, co-instructing, and co-assessing; this domain looks at how co-teachers engage in each of those activities. There is no one "right" way to co-plan. What is necessary, however, is that it is clearly happening. If an outsider were to enter the class, would it be evident that both teachers have had input in the lesson? That both of them were actively engaged in instruction? In this domain, we should observe universally designed lessons that provide multiple means of representation, engagement, and expression (see www.cast.org) to maximize student success. It should be clear that both teachers are committed to using the best evidence-based practices as they work with their shared class. For additional resources to help teachers get kick-started in this area, we recommend Ashton's chapter on universal design for learning, or UDL (Ashton, 2015); Novak's (2016) book *UDL Now!*; Hall, Meyer, and Rose's (2012) book on UDL; and Tomlinson's work on differentiation (e.g., Tomlinson & Murphy, 2015).

Professional Responsibilities

The fourth and final domain is Professional Responsibilities. Naturally, using best practices and following policies are the professional responsibilities of all educators, but additional responsibilities need to be expressly addressed when creating competencies for strong co-teaching teams. The first of these is the notion of collaboration, communication, and problem solving. Since co-teaching is often analogized as a professional marriage (Murawski, 2009, 2010), and research has found that the most important component of a solid marriage is communication (Cornell University, 2015), the most effective co-teaching teams communicate often. Interpersonal collaboration is defined as two or more co-equal individuals who share a common goal, responsibilities, resources, and decision making (Friend & Cook, 2016).

Clearly, strong communication skills are necessary for effective collaboration to occur. The same holds true for problem solving. There will be issues throughout a school year—with students, families, curriculum, technology, administrators, other teachers, and each other. How co-teachers manage those issues is critical to success. Other professional responsibilities relate to how co-teachers work with students' families and the broader educational community. A positive relationship between home and school can make the difference in the overall outcome for a student; for students with identified disabilities or those who struggle for other reasons, this is all the more reason to ensure that co-teachers are engaging with the students' support networks at home (McConnell & Murawski, 2017). Finally, teacher ethics must also relate to a co-teaching competency. Working with students who have IEPs or 504 plans means that an added level of confidentiality is involved, not to mention the need for positive behavior support and other practices that are important with all students but critical when working with students who have special needs.

The Competency Strands

As mentioned earlier, the four domains within the *Co-Teaching Core Competency Framework* are broad categorizations of major areas within which teaching teams should be focused. The 11 competency strands break up those areas even more. *Competency strands represent the topical areas within each domain and organize competencies into these manageable components.* Each domain has two or three strands to help organize and focus teams and those working with co-teaching teams.

Strands in The Learner and Learning Domain

The first domain, The Learner and Learning, has two strands within it: Learner Differences and Classroom Environment. *Learner Differences* (Strand 1) emphasizes that a classroom is a microcosm of our society and reflects that same diversity. Therefore, education is about teaching all students. Co-teachers should be sensitive to students and understand their strengths and weaknesses. Ultimately, the whole point of co-teaching is to be able to differentiate and meet students' diverse needs, regardless of ability or disability. *Classroom Environment* (Strand 2) recognizes that the environment in the classroom sets the tone for learning and for community. Co-teachers need to have agreed upon their rules, procedures, behavior management strategies, physical room arrangement, and support systems.

Strands in The Task at Hand Domain

The second domain, The Task at Hand, has three strands: Content Knowledge, Compliance Issues, and the Co-Teaching Construct. In terms of *Content Knowledge* (Strand 3), co-teachers are expected to ensure that all students have access to the content and curriculum. Both teachers need to be familiar with the content and the students so that they can ensure equal and meaningful access to the maximum extent possible. In dealing with *Compliance Issues* (Strand 4), co-teachers recognize that there are legal requirements when working in schools, especially with students who have identified disabilities. They work collaboratively with each other, students, families, administrators, and other service personnel to ensure they and the school continue to be in compliance with the law. The *Co-Teaching Construct* (Strand 5) emphasizes that, although many of the competencies that might be observed relate to quality teaching in general, some competencies relate specifically to the construct of co-teaching. These competencies relate directly to the literature and research on what is required for true co-teaching to occur.

Strands in the Instructional Practices Domain

The third domain, Instructional Practices, also has three strands, and they are the ones most overtly related to co-planning, co-instructing, and co-assessing. *Assessment* (Strand 6) is the cornerstone of good instruction. Co-teachers need to have assessed what the students know, need to know, and want to know. They need to assess themselves as instructors and share their own strengths and weaknesses pedagogically. Assessment occurs before, during, and after instruction. Strong co-teachers are aware of this and plan for it proactively to maximize their success and to know where to tweak, change, or stay the course. Strand 7 is *Planning*. Without co-planning, there is no true co-teaching. Both educators need to contribute to the proactive planning of what will occur in the classroom, as well as how students will be assessed and have their academic, behavioral, and social needs met. There is no one particular formula for planning, but both educators should contribute their own areas of expertise. Strand 8 is *Instruction*. The concept of co-teaching emerged from the philosophy that two teachers with different perspectives and professional backgrounds can bring a plethora of pedagogical strategies to the classroom (Friend & Cook, 2016). The experiences, brought by both teachers, are very powerful and necessary to meet the needs of all students. It should be obvious that co-teachers use numerous strategies for universal design and differentiation throughout the instruction to maximize learning and retention for all students.

Strands in the Professional Responsibilities Domain

The fourth domain, Professional Responsibilities, has three strands. Strand 9 is *Communication, Collaboration, and Problem Solving*. Co-teaching has been referred to as a professional marriage. As such, it requires continued communication, collaboration, and problem solving between educators. Professionalism and respect are keys to co-teaching success. Strand 10 is *Families and Community*. Every teacher will acknowledge how important communication with the family is for students to be successful. Co-teachers need to include parents and communicate with them as much as possible. Co-teachers also need to be aware of the entire community, including paraprofessionals and other special service personnel, and how these collaborations impact the learner. *Professional Practices and Ethics* (Strand 11) accentuates the expectation of teachers to focus on, among other things, the way in which they present themselves to students, colleagues, parents, and supervisors. At the forefront, both co-teachers need to continually remind themselves that they are working to ensure student success, even if they may disagree at times on how to accomplish that.

Emphasizing Individual and Core Competencies

The four domains and 11 strands organize the co-teaching competencies into manageable units. However, it is the competencies themselves that represent the skills, knowledge, and behaviors required to perform effectively in the role of true co-teaching around a particular practice. In a nutshell, *each of the co-teaching competencies describes a discrete behavior or skill that can be witnessed or documented and rated by an observer.* The expectation is that strong co-teaching teams will demonstrate all 120 of the co-teaching competencies to some degree. Though many of the competencies can be observed during a class session as a "Look For" or a "Listen For" (that is, an observer can see or hear evidence of the competency), others can be demonstrated by evidence provided by co-teachers (for more on observations, see Chapter 4). These permanent product data items are considered "Ask Fors" and are organized into the three key areas of co-planning, co-instructing, or co-assessing. The *Co-Teaching Core Competency Framework* may be downloaded from www.coteachsolutions.com.

The Importance of Co-Teaching Competencies

Why even have specific competencies for co-teaching? Without explicit and detailed behaviors identified, teams report feeling at a loss for how to meet the expectations for their collaboration (Hang & Rabren, 2009). In fact, many teams have stated that they have never had professional development on co-teaching and were thrown into the relationship, not knowing what to expect or what best practices were (Friend et al., 2010; Scruggs et al., 2007). Having clear, written, and widely disseminated competencies ensures that no individual, team, or school is asked to engage in co-teaching without a thorough understanding of the expectations for that service delivery option. In addition, these co-teaching competencies are expected to do the following:

1. Create a coordinated effort across co-teachers to embed essential skills in all co-taught classrooms.

2. Provide an opportunity for others to evaluate and monitor the competency in context.
3. Assist all educators in recognizing, understanding, and implementing the necessary skills for co-teaching.
4. Guide professional development approaches to achieve productive outcomes.
5. Provide the foundation for a learning continuum of competency development and the identification of attainable goals.
6. Prompt dialogue regarding team strengths and areas of need.
7. Be used to evaluate the effectiveness of collaborative practice in inclusive settings.

Having clear, written competencies is certainly a step in the right direction. We realize, however, that 120 competencies will seem overwhelming to some teams. We understand! The goal of this book is to result in "no-fail" co-teaching. Rather than having readers focus on all 120 competencies and then give up when it seems too much, we strongly recommend that schools start with the *core* competencies (Figure 2.5). *Co-teaching core competencies are the nonnegotiable competencies that must be performed at a high level for teachers to be truly co-teaching.* Since there are only 22 core competencies, this approach may seem much more manageable. These 22 competencies are the hallmark of true co-teaching: with a high level of implementation and fidelity, they allow co-teachers to provide a unique and deeply proficient learning experience for all students in their classroom.

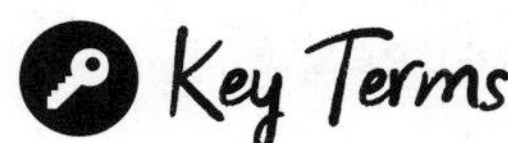

Co-teaching core competencies: *the nonnegotiable competencies that must be performed at a high level for teachers to be truly co-teaching.*

Determination of Core Competencies

As you consider the core competencies listed in Figure 2.5, you may wonder why some are considered "core" and others not. You may think that some competencies that are vitally important are not on the "core" list. Selecting specific competencies as core was an arduous task. Each of the 120 competencies could have qualified. We believe every one of the competencies is integral to co-teaching success. We are also realists and practitioners who recognize that often we need to focus on and emphasize a few major areas rather than trying to "do it all." In fact, as you will soon learn, that is the key to no-fail co-teaching and a way to move beyond basic co-teaching. As we have mentioned and will continue to mention repeatedly, we are huge proponents of baby steps and starting small.

Let's put this in context. Did you know that Marzano's research demonstrated that, to actually teach *all* of the state standards, it would take teachers 17 years (Scherer, 2001)? Seventeen years! We don't have that much time. So we pick and choose the most important standards and focus our efforts there, hoping that collateral improvement will occur across the board as students experience success in their content acquisition. The same holds true with us. We analyzed the research and practitioner literature on co-teaching (e.g., Kinne, Ryan & Faulkner, 2016; Murawski & Swanson, 2001; Scruggs et al., 2007; Strogilos & Stefanidis, 2015) and used content validity to help us select the core competencies—these are the competencies that will give you the biggest "bang for your buck!"

FIGURE 2.5

Co-Teaching Core Competencies

1.2	Co-Instruction: Evidence of differentiation
1.6	It is difficult to tell the special education students from the general education students.
1.8	Co-teachers phrase questions and statements so that it is obvious that all students in the class are included.
1.9	Students' conversations evidence a sense of community, including peers with disabilities and from diverse backgrounds.
2.7	Both teachers engage in appropriate behavior management strategies as needed and are consistent in their approach to behavior management.
3.7	Differentiated content and strategies, based on formative assessment, are used to meet the range of learning needs.
4.5	Two or more professionals working together in the same physical space.
5.7	A variety of instructional approaches (five co-teaching approaches) are used, including regrouping students.
5.9	Communication (both verbal and nonverbal) between co-teachers is clear and positive.
6.1	Ask Fors: Evidence of Co-Assessment
7.2	Ask Fors: Evidence of Co-Planning
8.1	Ask Fors: Evidence of Co-Instruction: Grouping
8.5	Ask Fors: Evidence of Co-Instruction: Parity
8.6	During instruction, both teachers assist students with and without disabilities.
8.8	Class instruction and activities proactively promote multiple modes of representation, engagement, and expression (universal design for learning—UDL).
8.13	Technology (to include assistive technology) is used to enhance accessibility and learning.
8.16	Co-teachers ask questions at a variety of levels (basic recall to higher-order thinking) to meet all students' needs.
9.5	Class environment demonstrates parity and collaboration (both names on board, sharing materials and space).
9.6	The class moves smoothly, with evidence of co-planning and communication between co-teachers.
9.10	Co-teachers use language ("we"; "our") that demonstrates true collaboration and shared responsibility.
11.3	It is difficult to tell the specialist from the general educator.
11.6	Both teachers begin and end class together and remain in the room the entire time.

Core competencies cut across domains and strands, ensuring that teams are addressing all critical areas. They, too, like all the competencies in the framework, are divided into Look Fors, Listen Fors, and Ask Fors. Once veteran teams have mastered the core competencies, they will feel more adept at identifying other competencies on which to improve. We identify all domains, strands, competencies, and core competencies in the *Co-Teaching Core Competency Framework* (www.coteachsolutions.com). Although the framework lays out all 120 competencies, schools that are just starting to collect data and work on improvement may choose instead to share just the co-teaching core competencies (see Figure 2.5) with their teams at the beginning of the process.

Figure 2.5 lists all the core competencies, without providing a description of each one. Consider asking teachers and administrators how they would envision each of the core competencies playing out in the classroom *before* you share additional information about them (Chapter 5 includes the "Co-Teaching Observation Checklist," which clarifies each competency and makes them measurable, observable, and objective). What would each item look like and sound like, or what type of evidence might demonstrate its attainment? Having school personnel analyze and discuss each of the 22 core competencies not only will help concretize and familiarize each one for participants, but also can build buy-in and help identify areas of concern early in the process.

Closing Thoughts

In Chapter 1, we gave an overview of CTIME and the PDSA continuous improvement model. In this chapter, we reviewed the definition of co-teaching and its role in supporting students with special needs in inclusive classrooms. We also introduced you to the domains, strands, and competencies comprised in the *Co-Teaching Core Competency Framework,* and clarified the role of the core competencies. Notice in Figure 2.6 how the co-teaching competencies and 11 strands are monitored through the PDSA process. Microteaching occurs as a method of job-embedded professional learning throughout the process as teachers work to improve their co-teaching skills and outcomes. Are you now ready to continue laying the foundation for CTIME? If so, please read on!

FIGURE 2.6

PDSA Applied to the Co-Teaching Framework

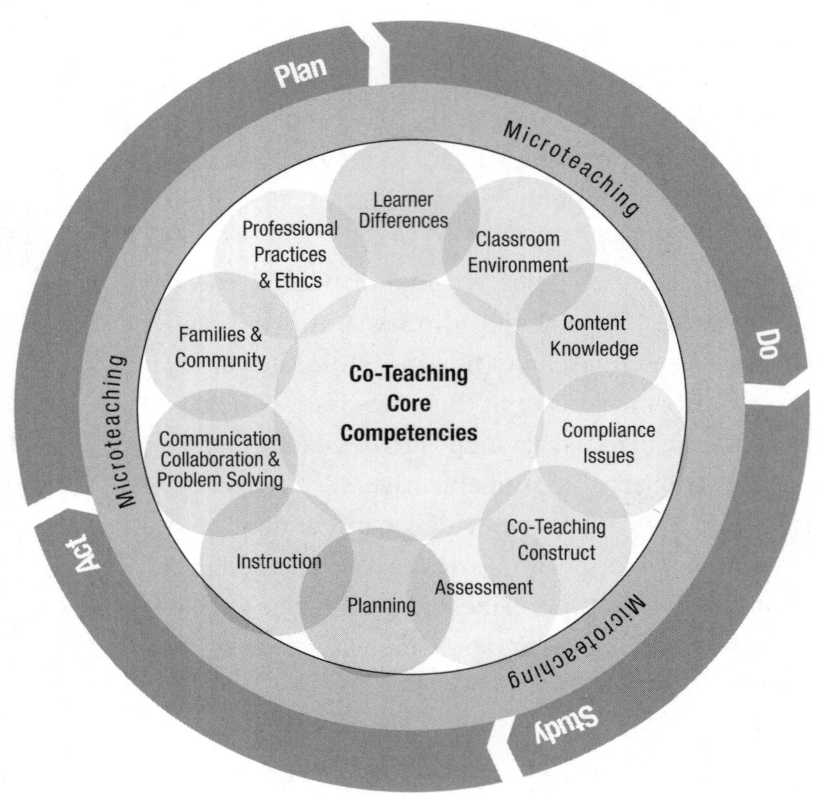

3 Laying the Foundation for CTIME: School Change, Professional Learning Communities, and Personalized Professional Learning

The Need for a Schoolwide Perspective

As consultants, we are often asked to help schools with the collaborative teaching process and outcomes. Administrators tell us that they want to use co-teaching to help with their at-risk students, but that they themselves were never trained. Or they share that a superintendent or other district administrator told them that they "needed" to incorporate co-teaching into their school as a service delivery option for special education students. Whatever the rationale, many administrators, department chairs, coordinators, or school leaders have not themselves engaged in or been trained in co-teaching—and yet they are expected to lead the charge! This is where having a school-level group focused on improving co-teaching outcomes comes in.

We wouldn't expect an administrator, instructional coach, department chair, or coordinator (especially those with little to no experience) to go into a co-taught classroom and immediately begin to give feedback on how co-teachers should improve. More important, we wouldn't expect that co-teachers would take that feedback to heart if the comments were made off-the-cuff or by someone who didn't understand the intricacies of co-teaching—even if that person were holding a copy of the Co-Teaching Core Competencies! Instead, we suggest that you take a good, hard look at your school's implementation of co-teaching—or lack thereof— to see what systemic changes might need to take place before you "drill down" to the individual team level. Also, from experience we can tell you that sometimes

Take-Aways

- *Professional learning communities (PLCs) help put teachers at the heart of change and improvement in a school, thereby increasing buy-in for an innovation such as co-teaching.*
- *Having a shared vision is one of the first steps for implementing schoolwide change.*
- *Traditional professional development does not result in sustained change. Successful professional development requires an ability to bridge the knowing-doing gap.*
- *Research has shown that practice, feedback, and collegial support are critical for real change to occur.*

teacher teams aren't ready to look at their own individual data right away. Having conversations about improvement at a schoolwide level seems much safer and less like a personal attack on a team that needs to improve.

How do you begin? First, consider that schools have often implemented co-teaching as a solution without really examining the problem that co-teaching is trying to solve! Nor have teachers, schools, or processes been prepared for co-teaching—much less methods planned for data collection. We hear a lot about data-driven decision making, but more often than not, we work with schools that have had absolutely no data collection related to their co-teaching or inclusive practices. It's understandable, then, that many teachers and other staff members may become frustrated. So, let's start with the basics here. You need to make sure that all participants know what you are doing and why you are doing it, before you start requiring teachers to make changes that aren't fully supported yet.

Professional Learning Communities (PLCs)

Nowadays, it feels like every committee in a school is called a PLC—professional learning community. For every teacher we hear talk about the positive change that his PLC is effecting, we hear another complaining that her PLC is simply an excuse for more meetings and paperwork. Let's take a moment to clarify what exactly PLCs are *supposed* to be.

Professional learning community (PLC): *a group of diverse individuals who share a learning vision and work to support one another to improve their practices and student outcomes.*

Stoll and colleagues (2005) defined a PLC as "an inclusive group of people, motivated by a shared learning vision, who support and work with each other to inquire on their practice and together learn new and better approaches to enhance student learning." That doesn't sound bad, does it? Unfortunately, those of us in education for a while know that there are often really good ideas that, with time and red tape, become lip service to the original idea. We want to get back to the original intent of PLCs and how they fit in the CTIME process.

Objectives of PLCs

A major objective of the PLC is to develop teacher leadership, in a teacher-driven culture, explicitly focused on building and sustaining school improvement efforts. Generally, PLCs are composed of teachers, although administrators and support staff routinely participate (Bolam et al., 2005; Huffman, 2011). In some schools, PLCs are extended to community members and students (Stoll, Bolam, McMahon, Wallace, & Thomas, 2006; Stoll & Louis, 2007). Through participation in PLCs, teachers enhance their leadership capacity while they work as members of ongoing, high-performing, collaborative teams that focus on improving student learning (Rentfro, 2007). Are you familiar with school site councils (SSCs)? SSCs enable teachers, students, staff, and community members to have input with the school's administration on the leadership and direction of a school. An SSC is typically a small group that meets regularly to discuss school issues and decisions, especially when they impact the budget (Great Schools, 2016). PLCs are like SSCs on steroids.

Breadth of PLCs

PLCs can focus on different topics, needs, and goals. They are not limited to a focus on big-picture items like school leadership or budgetary concerns. In fact, student achievement is typically the primary focus and—as you well know—student achievement can be addressed from a variety of areas (e.g., math, writing, athletics, test-taking). As schools grapple with improving across the board, it has become widely accepted that PLCs are the vehicle to build capacity to impact student achievement. Much of the work of DuFour and DuFour (2010) recognized that collaborative teams that have shared visions, missions, and values could accomplish more together for student achievement than they could alone. Through processes of collaboration, collective inquiry, and dialogue, members work side by side to clarify what each student must learn, monitor their progress, and provide the necessary supports or enrichment based on student need. Sounds exactly like what we need to do to ensure differentiation and student success in inclusive classrooms, doesn't it?

In a nutshell, PLCs are rooted in the following questions:

- What do we want our students to learn?
- How will we know when they have learned it?
- What will we do when we know?

PLCs were not created with co-teaching in mind. We are simply adapting and adopting this concept to our needs. The impetus of the PLC is to develop an interdependent culture that maintains a clear focus on student need and increasing student achievement. This collaboration is exactly the kind of culture needed to support and facilitate co-teaching! Waldron and McLeskey (2010) and Murawski and Spencer (2011) discuss how important it is for a collaborative culture to exist in schools that want to become more inclusive. Consider how much simpler it will be to encourage teachers to

Worried that your PLC experiences haven't been successful? Consider doing a book study on PLCs so that everyone is on the same page. We recommend Learning by Doing: A Handbook for Professional Learning Communities at Work (DuFour, DuFour, Eaker, & Many, 2010).

co-teach and work together to adapt for students in the same class if they are already used to working together in collaborative PLCs.

A Typical PLC

What does the typical PLC look like? If you were a fly on the wall of a typical, successful PLC, you would observe members discussing student results on both summative and formative assessments and making instructional changes as needed. You would see teachers sharing knowledge of best practices geared at obtaining positive student outcomes. You'd notice teachers improving their own teaching and learning as a result of working collaboratively. PLCs have helped reduce the isolation seen in so many schools, and they've created an opportunity for schools to build capacity for change through this distributive, shared, and collaborative model of educational leadership (DuFour & DuFour, 2010; Weißenreider, Roesken-Winter, Schueler, Binner, & Bioemeke, 2015). We know that not all PLCs are as successful as the one we've just described, but we've viewed enough good ones to know that this is happening nationwide. It is this type of student-focused, teacher-driven collaborative group that we incorporated into the CTIME process.

The Co-Teaching Leadership PLC

Co-teaching leadership PLC: *the group focused on identifying strengths and needs at the schoolwide level. The team is able to look at a macro level, determine a vision, review outcomes, and allocate resources.*

Professional learning communities are a foundation of the CTIME protocol and are apparent throughout the entire process. We want schools to create PLCs that are willing to look at co-teaching from a macro or big-picture level. This group will be focused on co-teaching for the overall school or district or organization. We'll have different groups committed to focusing on the more micro or classroom level of co-teaching. For now, we'll keep the focus on what we call a *co-teaching leadership PLC.*

Who should be on your co-teaching leadership PLC? Anyone who you think should have input at the macro level. We generally recommend the following participants:

- *The principal.* This person is always busy, but really needs to know and fully support co-teaching beyond lip service. Knowing the data will also help the principal make key decisions about resources and staffing, and use those data when branding, marketing, and promoting the school.
- *An assistant principal or two.* These people are often the ones working directly with co-teachers, especially those who are tasked with

overseeing special populations (e.g., special education, English-language learners). They are often able to add commentary to fill in the gaps when data seem confusing or specific trends are happening.

- *A school counselor.* We often forget to include counselors in our planning, but these individuals can really know the students. Counselors who are involved with master scheduling (which is the case in many schools) should definitely be included.
- *A co-teaching coordinator.* You may not have one of these, but consider creating the position. In our successful schools, there is usually at least one person who keeps his or her focus on co-teaching. If this is a working co-teacher, this person can attend the co-teaching leadership PLC meetings to add perspective, as well as facilitate the teacher-level community of practice (CoP) meetings (see Chapter 7).
- *Teacher and paraprofessional representatives.* You don't want to have too many people on this leadership team, but choose strategically. If there is a strong, vocal teacher (general or special education) who would help the team or whom it would help to include because he or she is in the teachers' union or would influence other teachers, then invite that teacher! If you have numerous paraprofessionals in inclusive classes and you think their input would help, as the "eyes and ears on the ground," then invite one to join. Paraprofessionals do not co-teach per se, but they do support students in inclusive classrooms and they could help explain data trends they are seeing.

Other possibilities include an individual at the district level to help with data management and resources; a parent to help provide perspective and share your efforts with parent groups; and a student, depending on the grade level. As the data begin to reveal needs, other individuals can be added, like a math coach to provide professional development if it appears that math co-teachers are struggling the most. Let the data lead you.

What is the role of the co-teaching leadership PLC in the overall CTIME process? Remember, the overall goal is to provide a bird's-eye view of how co-teaching is happening in the school and to be able to make decisions and take actions that help improve co-teaching based on the data. Let's look at the flowchart in Figure 3.1 to see how it all fits together.

Don't worry if your eyes are crossing at this flowchart. We will break it down for you throughout the book. Note that at the inception of the CTIME protocol (see the top left corner of the figure), the co-teaching leadership PLC kicks off the process by determining their "preferred state" for co-teaching—we call this their vision. Next, they begin scheduling and conducting co-teaching observations. Using those observations, the PLC

FIGURE 3.1

Collaborative Teaching Improvement Model of Excellence CTIME©

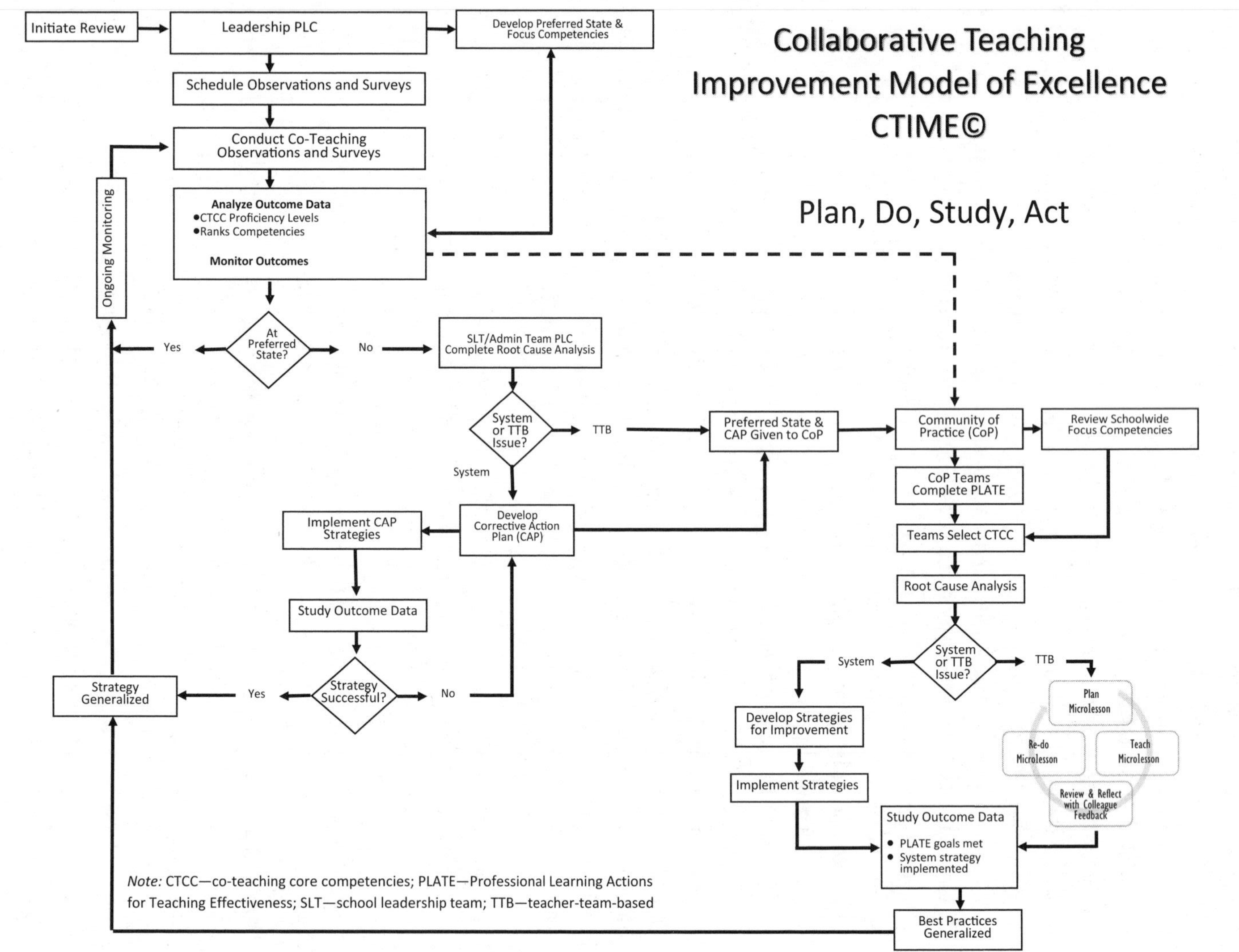

Note: CTCC—co-teaching core competencies; PLATE—Professional Learning Actions for Teaching Effectiveness; SLT—school leadership team; TTB—teacher-team-based

analyzes the data to determine the level of effective co-teaching at the macro (schoolwide) level. If the results are not where they are supposed to be (and when are they, really?), then the PLC gets to do some problem solving and root cause analysis. The co-teaching leadership PLC must ascertain if the identified deficiencies are primarily due to a systemic problem or to a teacher-team-based problem. For example, does it appear that teams are not successful due to a lack of common planning time (a systemic problem) or due to a lack of parity between teachers because one teacher still wants to be "in charge" (a team problem)? Depending on the answers, the co-teaching leadership PLC may decide to investigate the issues further themselves, or they may determine that another entity would be better suited for problem solving. Typically, if the issue is primarily with co-teaching teacher teams, the problem solving will be given over to the CoP team for isolated introspection and work. Wait, what? Another collaborative team? Yes, indeed. Bear with us. We'll explain about communities of practice in Chapter 7.

Remember when we introduced the Plan-Do-Study-Act (PDSA) cycle in Chapter 1 and discussed how it is integral in the CTIME model? Here is where it comes back into action. The overall PDSA cycle establishes a structure for adapting the PLC's knowledge and putting it into practice in a supported, systematic way. It is really a recursive loop that continues to build on itself (as we've depicted in Figure 3.2).

For those of you who might prefer to follow a structured checklist, check out Figure 3.3. It lists the five steps the schoolwide co-teaching leadership PLC will want to follow. Don't worry if you don't feel comfortable with all the terms included in the five steps yet. You will!

Envisioning Successful Co-Teaching

What's your vision? Seriously. Do you have one? We don't just mean a "We will be the best middle school in the state" kind of vision. We don't mean a general "We will improve all of our state assessment scores" kind of vision. This book is titled *Beyond Co-Teaching Basics,* and we emphasize that our goal is no-fail co-teaching. It will be difficult to move beyond co-teaching basics if you don't know what you are striving to accomplish. We want to know your vision for what co-teaching and inclusive practices will look like at your school. As part of your "envisioning," utilize the three components of co-teaching (co-plan, co-instruct, co-assess) and the 22 co-teaching core competencies as the underlying foundation.

Creating the vision requires a team process that includes various stakeholders. We've worked with schools whose vision, it became abundantly

Working with a large group to craft a vision can be frustrating. Use technology to help! Project your document on a screen so that everyone can see what's written and use track changes so that you don't lose language. Or put a basic statement into a Google Doc and let everyone work on recrafting it simultaneously.

clear, was created solely by one administrator. We strongly recommend that you get more buy-in than that and that you include different frames of reference. You know that your co-teaching leadership PLC should comprise a variety of representatives, so they are a great group of people to start creating a vision for co-teaching at your school. Feel free to invite others who are not always at your co-teaching leadership PLC meetings. For example, since IEPs will be written with co-teaching included, you might also consider inviting your school psychologist and other special services personnel who would be affected. You can certainly craft your vision with your entire school faculty if you'd like, but you need to know your school. Are you in a situation where too many cooks spoil the broth, or if you don't include everyone, will it come back to haunt you? We're flexible and we recognize the importance of school culture.

Let's assume that your co-teaching leadership PLC is together, and you're ready to start crafting your vision. Here's how you do that:

FIGURE 3.2

PDSA with Co-Teaching PLCs

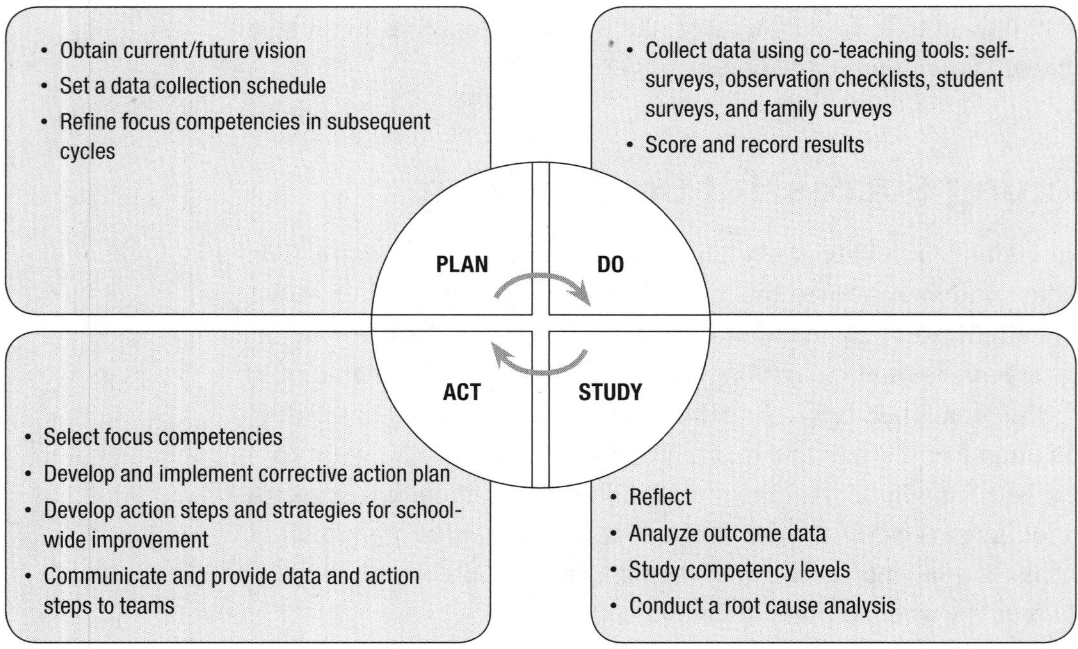

1. Set up a collaborative environment where you have chart paper, a whiteboard, or another recording device. It's time to get everyone's input.
2. Have members provide responses to the driving question in an open forum. Here's a quick tip: *When crafting a vision, answer the following question from the point in the future when the vision has been achieved.* That's right. Let's assume you have already achieved your co-teaching success! Here's your driving question: What is our school famous for when it comes to co-teaching? (Supporting questions: What is our purpose? What values guide our choices and daily actions? How will we measure success?)

Crafting Our Vision for Co-Teaching: An Example

The leader presents the driving question to the team: What is our school famous for when it comes to co-teaching?

Team members' responses:

- *High expectations for both teachers to bring their "A" game.*
- *Our co-teachers co-plan, co-instruct, and co-assess so that students have the best opportunities for academic growth.*
- *All students are included and are succeeding academically, behaviorally, and socially.*
- *We provide the time and support needed to differentiate in the class with two teachers.*
- *All students feel included and receive the best education possible.*
- *Our co-teaching teams are communicating and collaborating.*
- *Students are receiving a quality education from both educators.*

3. As a group, come to a consensus on your vision statement by compiling all of the responses and crafting the final vision statement. Here is a sample:

Co-Teaching Vision Statement: *Teachers will work collaboratively to co-plan, co-instruct, and co-assess in order to differentiate and provide universally designed lessons so that all students in our school will be engaged and successful academically, behaviorally, and socially.*

FIGURE 3.3

Five Easy Steps to Co-Teaching Success

PLAN
Step 1: Craft your vision for co-teaching and determine focus competencies.

DO
Step 2: Prepare the data collection schedule and PIE—Performance, Impact, and Ease—scores.

Step 3: Conduct observations and collect data on the corrective action plan.

STUDY
Step 4: Analyze the data and conduct a root cause analysis (as needed).

ACT
Step 5: Develop action steps and strategies and celebrate successes.

Using the Bone Diagram to Identify the Current State of Co-Teaching

It is now time to describe how your current practices support this vision. Be honest! Are these things occurring now? If not, why not? You can use any of a number of reflection tools to determine your school's desired state, but we find the Bone Diagram method (see Figure 3.4) to be effective in the schools with which we have worked. We include a Bone Diagram template (see Figure 3.5) for you to use, but let's walk you through it. The Bone Diagram is a simple reflection and planning tool that a school-level team can use to clarify co-teaching schoolwide, particularly where the team is currently, where the team wants to be in the future based on the vision they just created, and what actionable attributes and barriers will have an impact on reaching this desired vision.

Here are the steps for completing the diagram:

1. The leadership team begins by brainstorming ideas that describe the school's current level of co-teaching implementation. The team must be as descriptive as possible. This should be relatively easy because you have likely had a similar conversation when creating your school vision, but now need to get more specific. These statements are placed in the lower circle of the Bone Diagram. For example: *Students are in the classroom but not participating; no buy-in that students are everyone's students; no co-planning time in the schedule.*
2. Have the team brainstorm the ideal co-taught classroom, based on their school's vision. Remember to specify the necessary actions to

get you to the desired results. For example: *Cannot tell the general ed from the special ed students in a classroom; all students are engaged in higher-order, deeper thinking skills; co-teachers have adequate planning time.*

3. The team identifies the positive forces that support improvement and the negative forces that inhibit improvement.

Congrats! You now have your vision and your current and future state clarified and aligned. It is time for the true work to begin. You know where you want to go, but how do you get there? CTIME is going to take you there.

FIGURE 3.4

Sample Bone Diagram

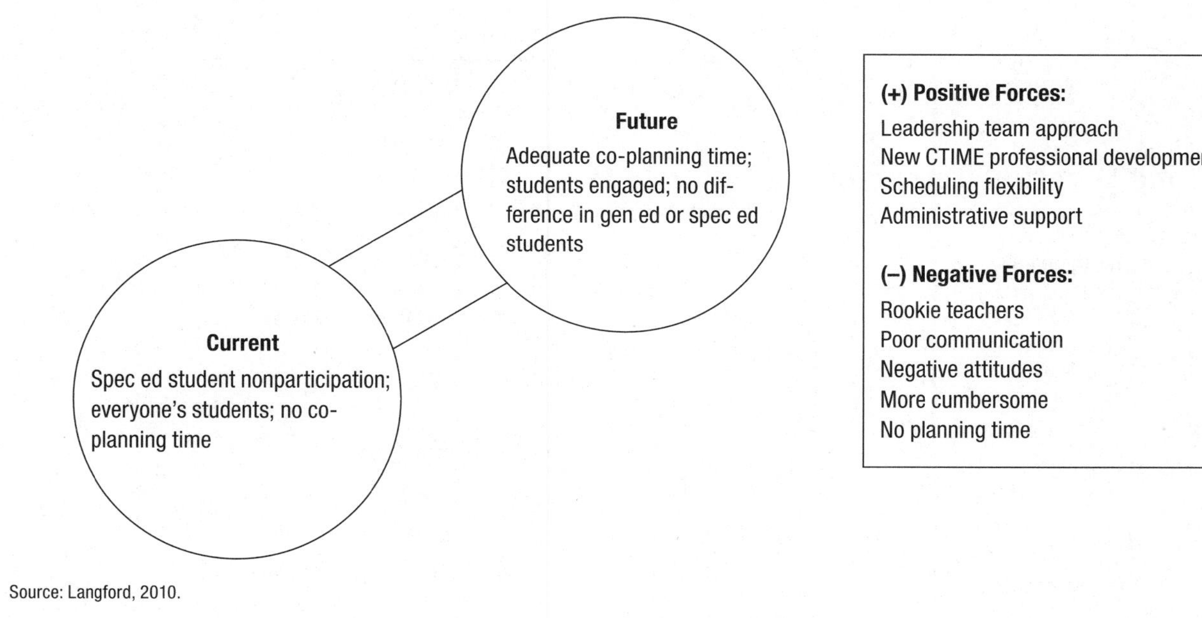

Source: Langford, 2010.

Selecting Focus Competencies for the School Level

The planning phase of the PDSA cycle allows the co-teaching leadership PLC members to truly understand the role of co-teaching and determine where it fits in their current and future vision for their school. The plan for the school is to have highly effective co-teaching that is evidenced by the implementation of the co-teaching core competencies in daily teaching. You might be assured of phenomenal co-teaching if all the core competencies were successfully implemented regularly, but it is also important for your team to determine those competencies that align most closely with your school's vision. (You *did* craft your co-teaching vision, right? That was Step 1.) Now it's time to start addressing and improving those competencies that are the most meaningful to your school. This is like a triage experience. Each school is different, and the level of experience in co-teaching, as well as the needs of the school, will determine your starting point. Don't forget that baby steps are key. Everyone, including you, will be overwhelmed if you try to take on too much too soon. That's the beauty of the CTIME method. You can see all 22 co-teaching core competencies and you know the method to achieve them, but the process allows for individualization and differentiation in (1) which competencies you address first and (2) how much time you take to get there.

FIGURE 3.5

Bone Diagram Template

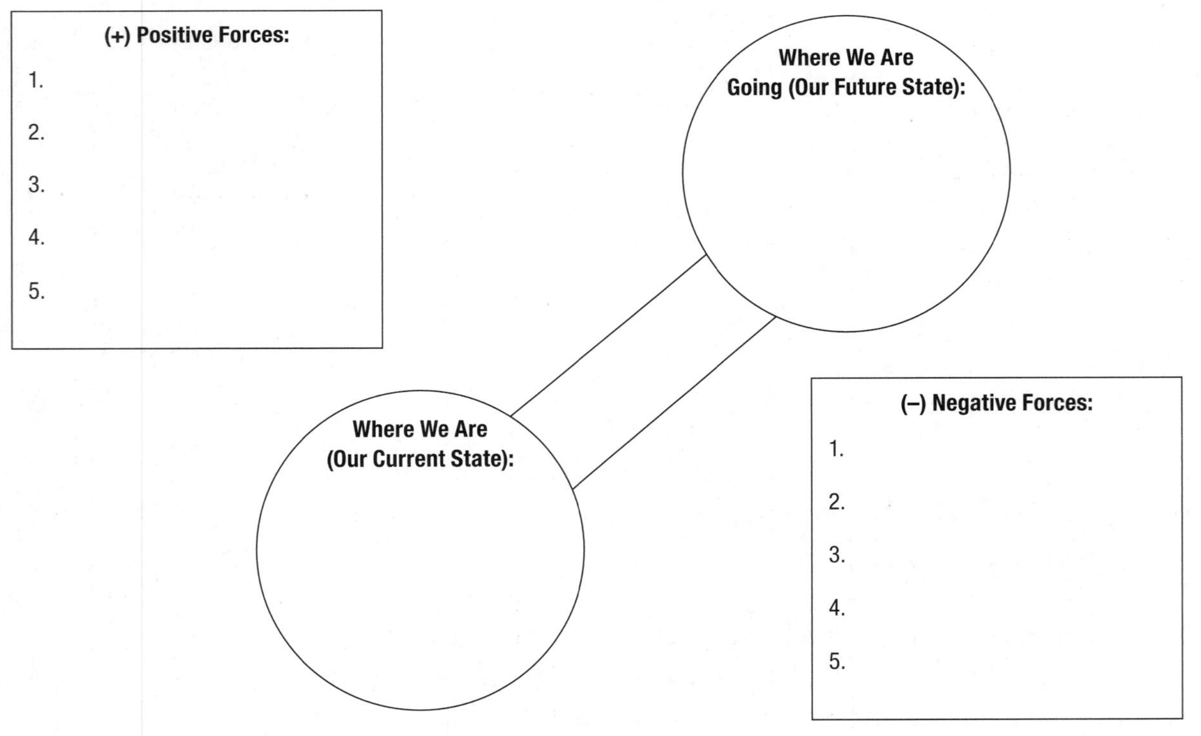

You've created your Bone Diagram. Now let's use it. Your team compares this diagram to the co-teaching core competencies. What competencies correlate to the ideal schoolwide co-teaching environment that the team has identified as being a priority? Write down between one and three focus competencies using the Focus Competencies Worksheet (see Figure 3.6).

FIGURE 3.6

Sample Focus Core Competencies Worksheet

Co-Teaching Vision Statement: *Teachers will work collaboratively to co-plan, co-instruct, and co-assess in order to differentiate and provide universally designed lessons so that all students in our school will be engaged and successful academically, behaviorally, and socially.*

School Future Co-Teaching Description: Adequate co-planning time; students are engaged 95% of the time; observers can not tell the difference between the general education and special education students because differentiation is embedded seamlessly.

Focus Core Competencies:

Co-planning time

Communication/Collaboration:

9.6 The class moves smoothly, with evidence of co-planning and communication between co-teachers.

7.2 Team co-plans its lessons and integrates both teachers' area of expertise to the maximum extent possible.

Students engaged

Instruction:

8.16 Co-teachers ask questions at a variety of levels (basic recall to higher-order thinking) to meet all students' needs.

No difference in general education and special education students

Cultural Diversity:

1.6 It is difficult to tell the special education students from the general education students.

1.8 Co-teachers phrase questions and statements so that it is obvious that all students in the class are included.

Congrats! Your team has now selected a focus for co-teaching by looking at the overall vision for co-teaching, and you've determined priorities for your school in terms of which competencies to focus on first. Don't worry. As your school moves through the PDSA cycle, teams can always add or change the focus. The process is flexible, and most important, it is data-driven! At this point, you haven't collected any data yet. You have selected these focus core competencies based on your vision and your current state of co-teaching. Once you have data, you may decide to change those focus competencies, and that is perfectly acceptable. Those changes may occur at the end of the first semester or after monitoring reveals that goals are being met or new goals need to be added. What keeps this entire process positive and forward-moving is that the co-teaching leadership PLC and all related individuals continue to communicate and set expectations for fabulous co-teaching throughout the school. Keep in mind that the focus competencies you set are ones that you are working on from a *systems-level approach*. These are the competencies that the school-level co-teaching leadership PLC will be working on collaboratively to address on behalf of all teams. That might mean changing schedules, working with administrators, bringing in consultants, or providing additional professional development or resources. Your selection of these competencies means that your co-teaching PLC is committed to making changes to benefit co-teaching systemically. There will be plenty of additional work from each individual co-teaching team as they use the PDSA process at the team level to improve. Think about how supported they will feel when they know they are not working in isolation!

Personalized Professional Learning

Let's take a moment to review where we are in this process. We have now introduced you to the PDSA cycle, the CTIME process, and the various domains, strands, and co-teaching core competencies. We have discussed the need to create a school-level team geared at looking at data from a macro level and working collaboratively to craft a vision for where you would like your school to be. You have even selected the competencies that you want to work on schoolwide. Excellent! What's next? At this point, your focus is on using the CTIME process as a tool for personalized professional learning, as a way to improve your co-teaching practices on an ongoing basis. We have seen many schools create vision statements, mission statements, goals, and objectives, only to let those documents sit and gather dust. In this section, we emphasize the need for a different type of professional development or, as we will explain, professional *learning*.

Think back to the last professional development session you attended. Mentally look around at the participants of that workshop. Do you see teachers grading papers, cutting construction paper, and basically disengaging from the presentation? We see that often (not, of course, when *we* are presenting. Never then...). Teachers are often the most difficult audience because (1) they feel that they already know the content and (2) they have extremely high expectations for what "good teaching" should look like. Professional development presenters only add insult to injury if the session is not results-driven, and there is no assessment or outcomes at the end to determine retention. Teachers typically report that they feel professional development is a waste of time and money (Strauss, 2014). Then why is so much of both spent on professional development? Because we still have a need for improvement! Unfortunately, just as many of our classrooms still appear stuck in the 19th century, so, too, does our professional development.

This is in part why the Every Student Succeeds Act (ESSA), the reauthorization of the Elementary and Secondary Education Act signed into law by President Barack Obama in 2015, includes an improved definition of professional development. In ESSA, professional development now has to be "sustained, intensive, collaborative, job-embedded, data-driven, and classroom-focused." Whoa! Anyone else thinking that CTIME fits in perfectly with this? Stephanie Hirsh, executive director of Learning Forward, is quoted as saying that they have long advocated for a definition in professional development that aligns with the Standards for Professional Learning (Learning Forward, 2015). In addition, there is an increased change of language for many schools, districts, and even states that call for "professional learning" for educators instead of "professional development." The name change alone emphasizes that there is a renewed sense of urgency for teachers to *learn*, in the same way we expect students to learn. In line with that, you will see that CTIME is designed as personalized professional learning that integrates those aforementioned criteria (sustained, job-embedded, and so on).

Let's get back to what we traditionally have seen—and continue to see—in most schools related to professional development. There has definitely been an increased push to tie professional development to student achievement, which is a positive move. However, to accomplish this, teachers are still typically presented with information about a theory or new practice that they should incorporate into their teaching repertoire to help students. The "really good" presenters provide some visuals or a demonstration of how to implement these techniques, but that is usually where it stops. There is rarely an opportunity to practice these new techniques, to apply them, reflect on them, and determine how to master them. These are exactly the actions required to create change in implementation. Joyce and Showers (2002) showed that it can take up to 20 separate instances of practice to change a skill—and the more complex the skill, the more practice attempts will be required! Certainly, these traditional lecture-style trainings do not provide for actual practice. Further, there is not time for feedback or collaboration among peers. We need to change this antiquated system.

Want to know more about the Standards for Professional Learning and professional learning opportunities? Visit https://learningforward.org/standards and www.edutopia.org.

Knowing: *comes from doing and then teaching others what one has learned—not merely talking about something.*

The Knowing-Doing Gap

In their nationally acclaimed book, *The Knowing-Doing Gap,* Jeffrey Pfeffer and Robert Sutton (2000) discuss how organizations have a very difficult time turning knowledge into action. Much time is spent on determining the right steps and best practices, which are presented to organizational staff but never put into practice. Clearly, education is not the only arena where training implementation is a struggle. A few main points are derived from their work:

- Knowing comes from doing and then teaching others what one has learned—not merely talking about something.
- Learning will be inhibited if it is not grounded in real-life experience.
- Organizations need to develop a learning culture in which failure is conducive to learning. It is better to try and fail than not to try at all.
- Fear widens the knowing-doing gap; thus, a supportive and collaborative culture is necessary.
- Knowledge can turn into action if you are specific in stating how you will measure what matters.

Though Pfeffer and Sutton's work was not geared specifically toward schools, their findings clearly translate across multiple settings. Just because you introduce students to a mathematical formula or grammatical structure does not mean they have internalized it or will be able to use it for years to come. The same is true of learning, hearing, or reading about co-teaching. We want to embed opportunities for teachers to reduce the knowing-doing gap around inclusive practices in their schools.

We know that the knowing-doing gap issue relates to the education industry as well, thanks to a substantive review of educational research carried out by Joyce and Showers (2002). They studied more than 200 in-service education and training programs whose stated goal was to change a classroom practices. The overall results determined there was no effect on the participants' classroom practices. That is not to say that some participants did not try some of the changes; they did. Unfortunately, the changes were not lasting, and the teachers always reverted back to their old methods and comfort zones.

So how do we get co-teachers to transfer and sustain change in their daily practices? Joyce and Showers (2002) looked at five components of staff training and how incorporating those components would impact the implementation and sustainability of the practice when transferred to the classroom. Figure 3.7 lists those five critical components and describes how each would look when applied to co-teaching. (*Spoiler alert:* As you read on, you'll notice that each of these five components becomes a major factor in the overall CTIME process.)

FIGURE 3.7

Five Components of Professional Development

Component of Professional Development	Explanation	Co-Teaching Application
Theory	Explain and justify the new approach.	Describe what co-teaching is and is not; explain its role in supporting inclusive practices as a service delivery option.
Demonstration	Show/model how it can be done in practice.	Have the professional development co-taught so that co-teaching is modeled; have participants watch videos of co-teaching in action; find ways for teachers to visit successful co-teaching teams.
Practice	Let the teachers try doing it the new way.	Create opportunities for participants to try co-teaching; ask them to create co-taught lessons; allow them to co-teach a class or unit; encourage them to co-present an instructional strategy at a faculty meeting; create pilot teams at a school.
Feedback	Give the teachers feedback on their use of the new way.	Use the co-teaching competencies to give concrete and specific feedback to teachers; have teachers video-record and reflect on their own lessons; encourage teachers to watch each other and give each other feedback; give teachers opportunities for more practice.
Collegial Support	Help teachers work out what to do next to improve their new approach.	Gather small groups of co-teachers to share successes and failures; provide time for them to meet, reflect, share resources, and determine next steps; ask them to identify goals and measurable objectives for improvement and find out how the school might provide additional support to meet those goals.

We doubt any of you will think these components are *not* helpful, but we're not sure if you realize just how critical they are! In fact, since so many schools spend their professional development money on bringing in experts for the "say and spray" or "sit and get" or "merely motivational" presentations, we have to imagine that those who hold the purse strings simply are not aware of this research. Incorporating each new component has a great impact on a teacher's ability to know and understand the practice (knowledge), execute the practice (skill), and then implement the practice in the classroom (transfer). Transfer is our goal. We want co-teaching to be an institutionalized part of your school's culture—a way that you can better meet the needs of all students in an inclusive class. Certainly it is not your only option; we recognize that. It is, however, one of the most common ways that schools are trying to support students in general education classes (Nierengarten, 2013; Scruggs et al., 2007). If this is the plan, then we want to be sure that teachers' time isn't wasted, that students are not frustrated and failing, and that administrators are not shaking their heads in confusion. How do you get to that transfer? You make sure all components are a part of your process. Luckily for you, CTIME has you covered.

Concerned that the professional development at your school hasn't led to any substantive change? Start by changing your language! Call it "professional learning" and let teachers help identify how they will demonstrate their learning, beyond merely sitting and listening to a speaker all day!

Figure 3.8 illustrates how each component of staff training affects knowledge, skill, and transfer, based on the research of Joyce and Showers (2002). Research has found that staff training without practice, feedback, and collegial support is rarely transferred to the classroom (Garet, Porter, Desimone, Birman, & Yoon, 2001; Joyce & Showers, 2002; Lumpe, 2007; Van Driel, Beijaard, & Verloop, 2001). Look closely. That presentation might be chockful of content, data, examples, and theoretical underpinnings for co-teaching. Over time, however, no matter how good that presentation was, your teachers might be retaining only 10 percent of the information. Their own skills have improved by only 5 percent, if that. Generalized transfer into the classroom long-term is 0 percent. For those of you who aren't strong in math, 0 percent means that there is *no* transfer into the classroom. It means that teachers will resort to their typical, comfortable practices; in co-teaching, we know that means we will see a lot of "one teach, one support" and very little differentiated instruction (King-Sears & Bowman-Kruhm, 2011; Magiera & Zigmond, 2005; Murawski & Dieker, 2004; Weiss & Lloyd, 2002).

FIGURE 3.8

Staff Development Outcomes

Staff Development	Knowledge	Skill	Transfer
Theory	10%	5%	0%
Demonstration	10%	5%	0%
Practice and Feedback	60%	60%	5%
Collegial Support	95%	95%	**95%**

Source: Joyce, B.R., & Showers, B. (2002). *Student achievement through staff development* (3rd ed.). Alexandria, VA: ASCD.

Even allowing teachers to see co-teaching in action only helps minimally with knowledge and skill—and doesn't result in transfer to daily practice. With practice and feedback, the skill is developed. It is only with the addition of collegial support, however, that co-teachers are able to transfer the skill into their everyday practice. Use whatever mantra will help you remember the importance of that final critical component: "It takes a village," "There's no 'I' in team," "Better together." Make signs and post them all over your teacher workstations; whatever it takes. We can't emphasize enough how it is this final piece—collegial support—that needs to be embedded in your professional learning if you want to see real and sustainable results.

Co-Teaching Competency Progression Pyramid

In 1990, a physician named George Miller developed a framework for assessing levels of clinical competence. To ascertain these levels of competence, he developed "Miller's Prism," also known as "Miller's Pyramid" (see Figure 3.9). Dr. Curtis Whitehair, program director of MedStar Georgetown University Hospital/MedStar National Rehabilitation Hospital—Physical Medicine & Rehabilitation Residency Training Program, shared that Miller's Pyramid remains the model they use today with medical students in those critical years of residency, before students are considered accomplished doctors and allowed to practice on their own. Miller's research demonstrated that the "cognition zone," or what someone knows or knows about, does not directly relate to their "behavior zone," particularly what they "show" or "do." "Just because someone can tell me about a surgical procedure doesn't mean I trust him to do it on me," said Whitehair (personal communication, September 21, 2016). "Miller's Pyramid emphasizes the need for our students to progress from learning about content, to seeing and discussing it, to applying it themselves, before we can ever trust that they will be competent on their own."

This is huge! Think about it. Just because a student tells us about the Pythagorean theorem doesn't mean that he or she can solve mathematical problems involving it or generalize the need for that theorem to a real-world setting. Now relate this to co-teaching (or even teaching in general). We all know that some individuals can tell us all about best practices, but are not always implementing those practices themselves—either because they cannot or do not want to. Now link back to professional development: The most important part of professional development and *learning* is that educators put into practice what they have learned; otherwise, it would be pointless. We want educators to develop the co-teaching core competencies into daily best practices. Therefore, professional learning methods must foster this progression from knowing to doing in order to reduce the knowing-doing gap.

FIGURE 3.9

Miller's Prism of Clinical Competence

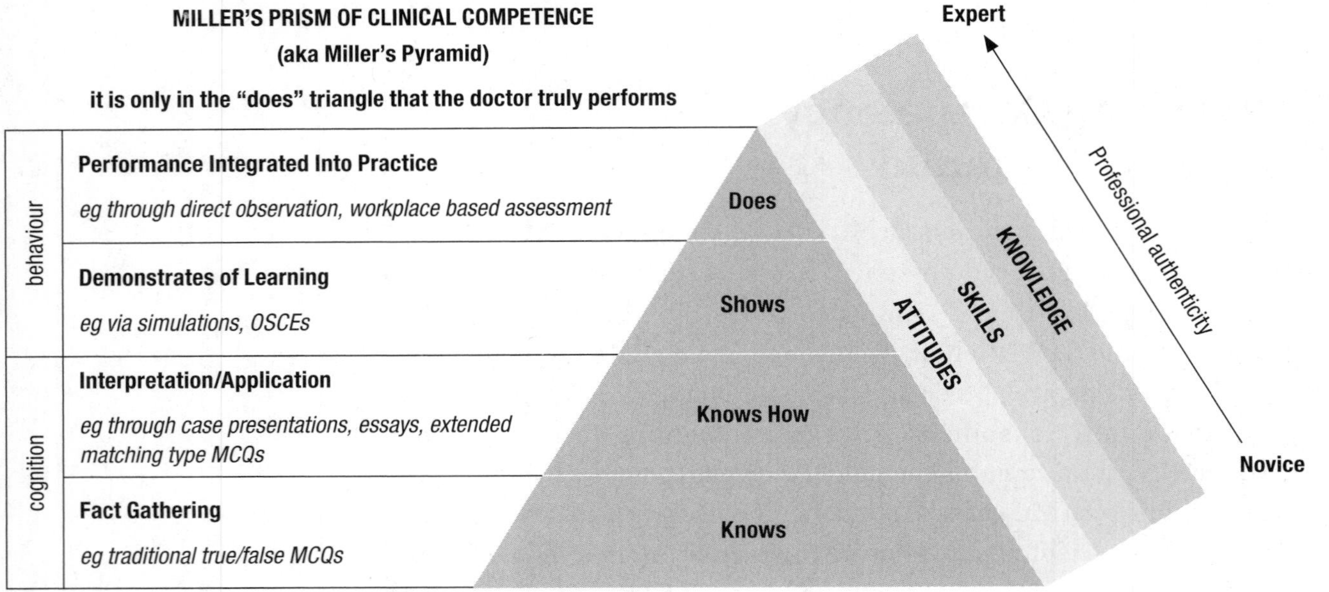

Note: MCQs – multiple choice questions; OSCEs – objective structured clinical examinations.

Attitudes and Skills

Take another look at Miller's Pyramid. Note that Miller included not just knowledge, but attitudes and skills as well. Consider the impact that a bad attitude can have on a pedagogical initiative. We all know that one teacher who just rolls out of his bed on the wrong side every morning, or perhaps has a poster up on her bathroom wall reminding her to "Be Negative Today!" Luckily, most people we have worked with are either positive or at least have healthy doses of skepticism, resistance, and sarcasm. With all the regular change happening in schools on a daily basis, it makes sense to question new initiatives coming down the educational pike. However, when the decision has been made to use co-teaching as a service delivery option for students in an inclusive environment, we hope that the educators involved will give it their best. We promise that skills will develop over time and that a positive attitude begets more positive experiences.

Miller's Pyramid and the Structure of This Book

Once more we bring you back to Miller's Pyramid. We want to tie Miller's ideas about competence development not only to the CTIME process, but also to how we structured this book. Note that basic "fact gathering" is at the bottom of the pyramid. Teachers are smart; they want to know what they are getting into and what the research base is behind a new initiative. The first chapters provided you with basic information on co-teaching itself (Chapter 1) and the competencies and how they were formulated (Chapter 2). This chapter (Chapter 3) shares how to build PLCs, create a vision, and change the way you engage in professional development. Next, the pyramid calls for a focus on interpretation and application. For clinicians, this is where they might demonstrate in an essay or presentation that they understand the facts they were provided. Chapters 4 and 5 relate to other ways to demonstrate an understanding of our basic facts—by conducting observations, collecting co-teaching data, and starting to craft action plans. On Miller's Pyramid, we now move out of the cognition zone and into the behavior zone.

Although we love to hear educators defining co-teaching correctly or administrators identifying the key elements of setting up for co-teaching success, these behaviors are not nearly as important to us as seeing that these elements are actually in place in the school. In Chapters 6 and 7, the rubber hits the road. Chapter 6 describes how schoolwide teams can get together and analyze the data they have collected. We describe how a co-teaching leadership team will get together to make critical decisions, collect resources, and make changes to more systematically support co-teaching. Ultimately, they have to *show* that they can improve co-teaching at the school level. Chapter 7 addresses communities of practice and microteaching to implement the continuous improvement model at the individual team level. Co-teaching teams use the resultant data to further improve their own practices. Small groups of like-minded educators come together in communities of practice to observe and give feedback to one another, definitely meeting the goal of "demonstration of learning" (Miller, 1990). That brings us to the top of Miller's Pyramid.

We want to be sure that our hard work won't simply fall to the wayside when a new administrator comes in, or a teacher moves, or there is a new "initiative-of-the-day." In Miller's Pyramid, this is the "Performance

Integrated into Practice" phase—the time when the individual learning a new skill performs that skill on his or her own at a level of mastery. Miller even includes "observation and workplace-based assessment" as his examples of how one can show attainment of this level. There's an easy connection here to co-teaching, isn't there? This is the point at which co-teachers are observed meeting the co-teaching core competencies. More important, their workplace-based assessment is the success of their students! Watching co-teachers who are truly successful engage in their craft—that of teaching, differentiating, grouping, and engaging learners—is a thing of beauty. Chapter 8 addresses the application, capacity-building, and institutionalization stages of the CTIME process through facilitation and continuous feedback. In addition, Chapter 9 provides a plethora of forms and helpful templates for you to use in your own practice of the CTIME process.

Closing Thoughts

We thank Miller for his pyramid and, with the appropriate recognition given, we have adapted it to our own devices. In Figure 3.10, we offer the Co-Teaching Competencies Pyramid. This illustrates the progression necessary for co-teachers to move from simply knowing the co-teaching approaches, competencies, and expectations, to actually being able to apply them. We are ready—as we are sure you are—for schools and teams to move out of the cognition zone of knowing about differentiation, universal design for learning (UDL), and the various approaches into which they might group students for lower student-teacher ratios, and into the behavior zone, in which they demonstrate the competencies daily. Only through regular behavior will they ultimately be able to integrate all the competencies and have them become daily practices in the co-taught classroom. This process emphasizes baby steps...but it does require forward movement!

FIGURE 3.10

Co-Teaching Competencies Pyramid

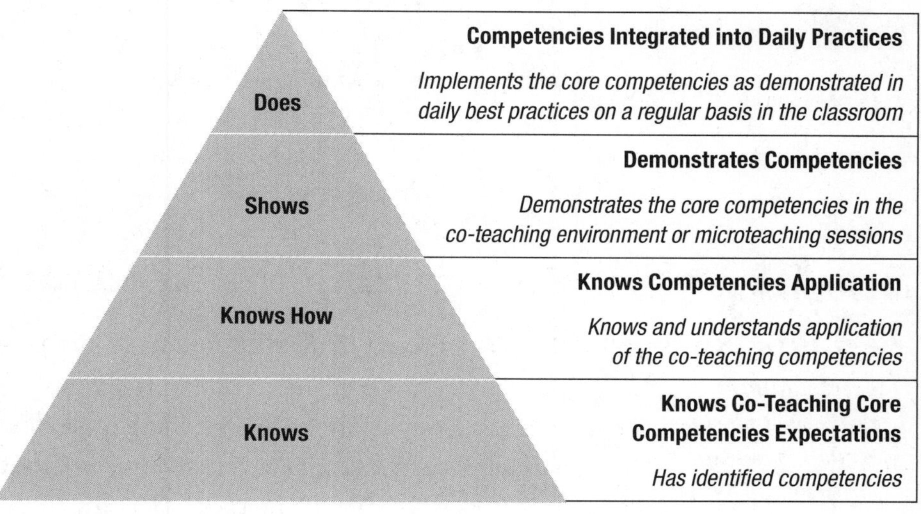

4 Collecting Data on Co-Teaching

Take-Aways

- *Most schools do not collect data on co-teaching, despite the fact that there is a consistent call for data-driven decision making.*
- *Observers need to know what to "look for, listen for, and ask for" when conducting co-teaching observations.*
- *Students and families should have a forum for sharing their feedback as well.*

Recognizing the Need for Data

With 61 percent of all students with identified disabilities spending 80 percent or more of their time in the general education setting (U.S. Department of Education, 2013), "the antiquated mindset of placing a student with a disability in a separate classroom, without consideration for their unique abilities, is a thing of the past" (Kramer & Murawski, 2017, p. 153). Instead, students with special needs are increasingly being provided with collaboration and co-teaching as the service delivery option identified on their IEPs. That said, although more and more schools are using co-teaching as their model for supporting and providing specially designed instruction for students with disabilities, as well as for other students who are exceptional learners (e.g., English-language learners, gifted learners, twice-exceptional learners, students on 504 plans, and students in tiers two or three of the Response to Intervention process), there continues to be a shortage of data demonstrating that this model is truly successful (Murawski & Goodwin, 2014; Scruggs et al., 2007). In a recent review of the research on co-teaching, Murawski and Goodwin (2014) reported that "[w]hat is known about co-teaching...can ultimately be viewed as a 'three c's conundrum' related to research and practice: confusion, contradiction, and cautious optimism" (p. 293). This doesn't mean that schools should go back to excluding and stigmatizing students. Quite the contrary! Zigmond, Magiera, Simmons, and Volonino (2013) clarified that "the lack of empirical support for co-teaching is not surprising; co-teaching may be a service, but it is not a 'treatment' that can be imposed with fidelity on an experimental group and withheld with equal fidelity from a control group" (p. 116). Without this type of experimental research, then, should schools give up on the notion of data-driven decision making when it comes to co-teaching?

We answer with a resounding, "NO!" Data are critical. They allow us to know if what we are doing is working. Nowadays, evidence-based practices are essential. The CTIME process, as explained in this book, will help schools and teams use co-teaching core competencies to determine, with actual data, how teachers are progressing in their inclusive classes. Partners will be able to work collaboratively to jointly determine where to improve and then work with a small, supportive team to ensure that improvement occurs. Only with real data and a true commitment to the process will schools and teams know if what they are doing to help students is worth continuing.

Go online and check out the Council for Exceptional Children's Standards for Evidence-Based Practices in Special Education: *https://www.cec.sped.org/~/media/Files/Standards/Evidence%20based%20Practices%20and%20Practice/EBP%20FINAL.pdf*

Lamenting a Lack of Data

Back in 2001, Murawski and Swanson conducted the seminal meta-analysis on co-teaching research and asked the question, "Where are the data?" Since that time, researchers continue to question the lack of empirical data on collaborative teaching in schools (Friend, 2008; Scruggs et al., 2007). Two large-scale reviews have purported to synthesize the research data on co-teaching. Solis, Vaughn, Swanson, and McCulley (2012) conducted a review of the empirical data available on co-teaching and inclusion. Their review included articles from 1990 to 2010. In that 20-year period, they only found one meta-analysis (Murawski & Swanson, 2001) and one meta-synthesis (Scruggs et al., 2007). In a nutshell, a meta-analysis includes all research articles that have numbers or quantitative data, and it allows researchers to create what is called an *effect size;* by contrast, a meta-synthesis includes all research articles that use qualitative data, and researchers use that information to identify *trends.* Both of these studies found mixed results for co-teaching effectiveness.

Hattie (2012) also has received a lot of press with his book *Visible Learning: A Synthesis of over 800 Meta-Analyses Relating to Achievement,* a text that synthesizes meta-analyses on a variety of educational practices related to achievement. Though Hattie questioned the effectiveness of co-teaching by giving it an averaged effect size of .19, his results were based on a limited data set. In fact, Hattie used a definition of co-teaching from 1977 (which did not include today's use of co-teaching between general and special educators), and though one of his two meta-analyses was the Murawski and Swanson (2001) one, the other was from 1983 and focused purely on instructional systems used in science (Willett, Yamashita, & Anderson, 1983). Clearly these two articles do not accurately reflect the state of co-teaching today. However, by looking at these two syntheses (Hattie's and Solis et al.'s), some observers might conclude that little data on co-teaching are available or that the available data are old. Either of these conclusions would be quite inaccurate.

Consistent Data Collection

We have found a plethora of data on co-teaching. In just the past few years, there have been co-teaching research articles on student outcomes in math (Harris, Pollingue, Hearrington, & Holmes, 2014; Nash-Aurand, 2013), language arts (Aliakbari & Nejad, 2013; King-Sears & Bowman-Kruhm, 2011), and science (King-Sears, Brawand, Jenkins, & Preston-Smith, 2014); co-teaching in foreign countries (Frey & Kaff, 2014; Loertscher & Koechlin, 2015; Tzivinikou, 2015); co-teaching at elementary (Mensah, 2011), middle school (Conderman, 2011; Strieker, Gillis, & Zong, 2013), and high school (Nierengarten, 2013) levels; and even co-teaching in professional development schools (Allen, Perl, Goodson, & Sprouse, 2014) and for social justice (Cobb & Sharma, 2015). It's not that we don't have data; it's that we do not have a consistent, systematic method for data collection on exactly what co-teachers are doing in schools. This points to a need for consistent data collection using a common language, methodology, and tool. We can't continue to compare apples and oranges when it comes to co-teaching implementation and outcomes.

Collecting Data from Students and Teachers

Overwhelmed by the options for data collection? Don't try to do everything. Get your co-teaching leadership PLC together and find out what you want to know. This becomes your research question and guides your decisions regarding what data you need to collect.

At the 2016 Council for Exceptional Children conference, Marilyn Friend coordinated a strand on co-teaching, and we were asked to present the session on data. In our presentation, entitled "Don't forget the data: Improving co-teaching student outcomes and evaluating program effectiveness" (Murawski & Lochner, 2016), we shared ways in which schools can collect data to assess academic, behavioral, social, and programmatic outcomes. We emphasized that data can be collected from both students and teachers. Figure 4.1 shares the different ways that schools might target specific areas. Though all of these options are potential areas to determine the impact of co-teaching in a classroom, we remind you that co-teaching has many variables that play a role in its success. Thus, we posit the co-teaching core competencies (see Chapter 2) and the Co-Teaching Core Competencies Observation Checklist (which we introduce later in this chapter) as concrete and consistent ways to ensure the reliability and validity in your data collection on what teachers are doing together in the co-taught classroom.

FIGURE 4.1

Areas for Data Collection in Co-Teaching

Looking to collect more data on co-teaching? Consider these areas:	
Students	**Teachers**
Academic	
Curriculum-based assessments	Special educator: Knowledge of content
End-of-course exams	General educator: Knowledge of strategies
Standardized measures	Use of universal design for learning
Grades	Creation of rigorous lessons
Pre-test/post-test	Lessons that provide differentiation
Comparison of classes	Percentage of passing/failing students
Behavioral	
Attendance/tardies	Use of co-teaching approaches
Expulsions/suspensions	Use of "we" language
In-class infractions	Use of questioning
PBIS: Schoolwide or classroom	Time spent on co-planning
Individual student behaviors	Time spent on co-instruction
Asking for help	Time spent on co-assessment
Social	
Friendships	Parity between teachers
Extracurricular activities	Use of heterogeneous groups
Social skills	"Our kids" vs. "your kids"
Empathy/patience	Working with all students
Self-concept	Self-efficacy
Programmatic	
Master scheduling	
Administrative support	
Planning time	
Creating partnerships	
Culture change	
Building capacity for co-teaching	

Note: PBIS—Positive Behavior Intervention and Support.

Source: Murawski, W. W., & Lochner, W. W. (April 2016). *Don't forget the data: Improving student outcomes and evaluating program effectiveness.* Presented at the Council for Exceptional Children national conference, St. Louis, MO.

Data Collection and Data-Driven Decision Making

Collecting data systematically is only the first step in the process, however. The next step is to use the information collected to result in data-driven decision making (Murawski & Hughes, 2009; Wischnowski, Salmon, & Eaton, 2004). We have worked with hundreds of schools that have collected abundant co-teaching data on students, teachers, outcomes, schedules, and the like, but they simply do not do anything with that information. Teachers and administrators are often too busy to make meaning of all the data they have. The CTIME process will help schools identify what information to collect, the tool to use to maximize efficient data collection, and a process for using data to improve co-teaching success for teachers and students.

Needs Assessment

We know you want data on co-teaching. We have you covered there. But we also respect that every school has its own culture, strengths, and needs related to inclusive practices (Waldron & McLeskey, 2010). Co-teaching is about developing relationships, and communication and buy-in are key (Friend & Cook, 2016; Murawski & Spencer, 2011). Rather than immediately telling teams that they are going to be observed and that data will be collected on the fidelity with which they are co-teaching, why not first investigate how faculty and staff feel regarding using co-teaching as a method for supporting students in the general education classes? Joyce and Showers (2002) write about the importance of conducting needs assessments prior to any professional development. Though data will be collected throughout this process, the ultimate goal of CTIME is for professional learning and growth, not to provide a one-shot presentation.

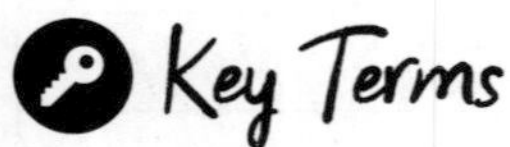

Needs assessment: *a systematic way of identifying the gaps between what currently exists and what the audience or participants want.*

Needs assessments do not need to be overly formal. Administrators can use strategies with their faculty that are often used with students. For example, a principal might use a K-W-L chart (Ogle, 1986) to find out what faculty and staff know, want to know, and have learned about co-teaching. Discussions at faculty meetings can help communicate concerns and misunderstandings. Short surveys or questionnaires with targeted questions will also help educators share the issues of concern to them and the areas in which they will need additional support, guidance, or clarification. Figure 4.2 illustrates a sample needs assessment.

What do you do with the information you gather? Put it in a pile on a desk and forget it? No. You communicate it back to your teachers and other school staff. Let them know that this process is about addressing those

FIGURE 4.2

Sample Co-Teaching Needs Assessment

Rate the following:	0-low					5-high
Your knowledge of co-teaching	**0**	**1**	**2**	**3**	**4**	**5**
Your attitude regarding co-teaching	**0**	**1**	**2**	**3**	**4**	**5**
Your skills in co-teaching	**0**	**1**	**2**	**3**	**4**	**5**
Your experience with co-teaching	**0**	**1**	**2**	**3**	**4**	**5**

What are your greatest needs for assistance in co-teaching?

Infrastructure

_________ Observing co-teaching
_________ Starting professional learning communities (PLCs)
_________ Co-planning process
_________ Parent/family communication
_________ Administrative support for co-teaching

Professional Development

_________ Clear co-teaching expectations for ALL
_________ Assessment in the co-taught classroom
_________ Co-teaching strategies and approaches
_________ Behavior management
_________ Communicating with my co-teacher

Best Practices

_________ Differentiated instruction
_________ Universal design for learning (UDL)
_________ Formative assessment
_________ Use of technology

Other: Please tell us what you think we can do to support effective co-teaching at this school—for you individually or for the school as a systemic change.

____

____

____

____

____

____

specific needs. Rather than bringing in outside experts for a one-day dog-and-pony show, you are going to have job-embedded professional learning activities designed to meet their specific needs (Shaffer & Thomas-Brown, 2015). In addition, let them know that you, or a fellow administrator, coach, mentor, teacher leader, or the like, will be coming into classes to observe co-teaching in action. Emphasize that the purpose is not to evaluate or criticize, or to make them uncomfortable. On the contrary, the goal of observations is to add more data to the needs assessment to give a clearer picture of the school's—and each team's—needs. You can make teams more comfortable by sharing information about the upcoming co-teaching observations.

Data Collection

We've mentioned the importance of data-driven decision making, but now it's time for the nitty-gritty. What data? How do you collect it? What does it look like, and how do you make sense of it? How often do you need to collect it? This chapter will clear up all of those questions. We'll start with what data to collect, then address when and how often to collect it, and finally how to make sense of it all.

Current Level of Performance

You now know where you want to be—but do you know where you *are*? As part of the PDSA continuous improvement process, your school will need to determine your current state of co-teaching so that you can compare it to the desired state you will define in the Plan phase of the PDSA cyle. Too often, this determination of this current level of performance relies on anecdotal evidence. Administrators and teachers share how they "feel" co-teaching is going, or what they "think" is happening in most of the classes. Instead, the CTIME process brings in data right away. Just as a reminder, the PDSA (Plan-Do-Study-Act) cycle involves the five steps identified in Figure 3.3. Because this is a recursive cycle, you may sometimes feel your "actions" and your "planning" are overlapping. That's completely normal. At this beginning stage, however, we are most interested in the use of a needs assessment to help you "Plan." Your school will want to "Do-Study-Act" as you are moving forward in this endeavor.

Current Level of Implementation

To determine the current level of implementation of co-teaching at the schoolwide or teacher-specific level, you will want to go back and look at the co-teaching core competencies we introduced in Chapter 2. You may have already done this as you were crafting your vision and, if you did, wonderful! We bring it up now to reiterate that the competencies can be used to help conduct a school's needs assessment, should you feel you would like to conduct one. If your Co-Teaching Leadership PLC has already ascertained the competencies to work on, you can move on; however, if you want to get further input from other stakeholders and want to give them guidance on what feedback to provide, the competencies can help. This reduces the chance that you will hear general feedback (e.g., "our co-teaching needs work") and increases the more specific feedback that can lead to outcomes.

Data Collection Tools

In the next few chapters, we will explain the process of selecting specific focus competencies that will have the most immediate value in addressing your overall vision. We will get you there step-by-step. For now, however, we want to introduce you to the tools that will help you collect your co-teaching data. We've provided the following tools to help you with this endeavor:

- Co-Teaching Core Competencies Observation Checklist
- Co-Teaching Core Competencies Observation (Teacher) Self-Survey
- Co-Teaching Team Classroom Family Survey
- Co-Teaching Team Classroom Student Survey

You might look at this list and say, "What?! Families and students, too?!" Don't worry. We know it can be daunting to include all stakeholders, but remember that this is a process. If you are able to use all of these assessment tools, then the rating of your site's overall co-teaching effectiveness will be much more valid and reliable. The observation checklist and surveys from various sources generate performance levels to help identify successful or unsuccessful co-teaching. It's no longer about what you "think." It's about what the data show.

We've already mentioned that CTIME is flexible and that we are huge proponents of baby steps. Some teams may think that they'd prefer not to include families and students as they are beginning this process. You certainly do not have to use *all* the assessment tools, but let us make a case for doing so. First, these tools will give you a clear picture of the overall effectiveness of co-teaching in your school. In addition, there is value in getting input from different frames of reference. Finally, this type of data collection provides what we refer to as "triangulation of the data" (Hussein, 2009, p. 1). Triangulating data essentially means that you are using more than one method of collecting data to ensure the validity of what you've found. It helps to cross-validate the findings, but even more important, it gives you a way to "use multiple methods... in studying the same phenomenon for the purpose of increasing study credibility" (Hussein, 2009, p. 1). For example, teachers may be focused on the way in which they collaborate during planning and instruction, whereas students may be more interested in how they are helped in the classroom, and parents are concerned about student achievement or communication between home and school. All of these elements are critical for co-teaching excellence, and so we strongly encourage you to collect data from all three, particularly when creating baseline data. You want to have the most valid, big picture possible of your current status. So, consider putting your best foot forward right from the beginning of the process and reach out to all stakeholders.

Co-Teaching Observations

There are two types of tools to use for data collection in the CTIME process: observations and surveys. Let's start with the observation tool first. The premise behind the Co-Teaching Core Competencies Observation Checklist, created by Wendy Murawski in 2002, was that it was intended to be a tool for administrators to utilize with their co-teaching teams to aid in their improvement. It started as a paper-and-pencil checklist and has grown from there in the past decade and a half. First published in *Intervention in School and Clinic* (Murawski & Lochner, 2011), it is now available as the primary hub of the online program called Co-Teaching Solutions System (CTSS; www.coteachsolutions.com). With the CTSS, the checklist was moved from paper and pencil to an electronic format that made it easier to provide accessible data to teams, schools, and districts that were eager to support co-teachers. The computer-based observations can be done on any smartphone, tablet, or computer and provide easily automated reports. The Co-Teaching Core Competencies Observation Checklist has been implemented by hundreds of schools and teachers to provide feedback on the state of co-teaching in their classrooms. It has been the tool used for multiple doctoral dissertations on co-teaching, and it is even being used for a national, multi-state study on the fidelity of co-teaching (Murawski, Ashton, & Scott, in progress). "Regardless of whether a school chooses to use an electronic or paper observation system, it is critical that data be collected, analyzed, and discussed so that schools can continue to identify the best practices for serving the needs of students with disabilities in their inclusive settings. *Without data, results are merely conjecture*" (Murawski & Lochner, 2011, p. 182, emphasis added). Streamlining the expectations and having transparency between observers and co-teaching teams has provided many opportunities for improvement.

This book is about developing superior co-teaching through systematic data collection and reflection. The Co-Teaching Core Competencies Observation Checklist is the tool that drives that improvement. Such a powerful tool has multiple uses. The checklist, revised in 2014 to reflect the co-teaching core competencies, is used predominantly to collect data by administrators, coaches, and teachers. The checklist is organized such that observers know immediately what to look for, listen for, and ask for in order to determine co-teaching quality. Whatever your preference (hard copy or electronic), the process launches with the co-teaching observation. Using the Co-Teaching Core Competencies Observation Checklist, the observer provides a rating score based on the rubric for each competency (see Chapter 9—Figure 9.1—for the full checklist). An observation is conducted for each co-teaching team multiple times throughout the year.

The checklist need not be limited to observations for evaluative or formal purposes, however. As part of the CTIME process, you will see that the Co-Teaching Core Competencies Observation Checklist is also used as a guide for teachers to observe how other teachers are implementing the co-teaching core competencies in the classroom. These peer-to-peer observations are often called professional practices observations. Luczak, Rubalcaba, and Frades (2014) write,

> Classroom observations are an essential component of all rigorous teacher evaluation systems. But in far too many schools, observations are treated as a compliance exercise rather than an opportunity to improve teacher practices.... We offer four main recommendations: (1) Ensure a system-wide understanding of effective practice; (2) build credibility by certifying observers and providing teachers with high-quality feedback; (3) make observations useful and manageable for teachers and observers; and (4) monitor observation results for quality and build a system of continuous improvement.

That is exactly what the CTIME process does!

Scoring the Observation Checklist

The Co-Teaching Core Competencies Observation Checklist is organized into three sections: *Look Fors*, *Listen Fors*, and *Ask Fors*. By using these three sections, data can be obtained to determine if co-teachers are truly co-planning, co-instructing, and co-assessing. Conversations can be held around data that assess if co-teachers appear to be working with "their own" students or with all students. Strategies can be developed to help improve areas such as differentiation, use of technology, shared responsibilities, and the implementation of specially designed instruction for individuals with special needs. Rather than relying on conjecture, teachers and observers can discuss what was seen, heard, or analyzed.

Look Fors are those items that observers can walk into a room and see for themselves. On the checklist, a rubric is provided to support observers in determining to what extent a team met that particular objective. *Listen Fors* relate to the ways in which teachers talk to each other and their students, as well as how students communicate with one another. Does it feel like everyone is a welcome and included part of the classroom? Are teachers respectful of one another? Finally, the *Ask Fors* section is provided to help observers know what products they can request in order to collect hard evidence of co-planning, co-instructing, and co-assessing. Each competency listed has a rubric with it to aid observers in their reliability in scoring. A 0 means "I didn't see it," whereas a 3 means that the item was observed at a mastery level. For each item, the rubric provides an example of what that competency would look like at the mastery level. Figure 4.3 gives examples of a Look For, a Listen For, and an Ask For. Look at the descriptors. Do you feel like you have a clear picture of what you would want to see and hear in a co-taught classroom? We hope so.

After completing the observation and giving each item a numeric score, the observer computes the grand total on the observation form, as well as subtotals for each of the three components: Look Fors, Listen Fors, and Ask Fors.

Note that underneath the grand total are the *Growth Ranges* for co-teaching teams. These scores let teams know where they are in their co-teaching, as determined by the implementation of the core competencies. Teams that score between 0 and 29 are considered "Not Yet Co-Teaching." These are often teams that are still following a model that looks more like a teacher and an assistant or aide. It is also possible that teachers are just taking turns delivering instruction. Teams then progress through "Emerging Co-Teaching" (30–45), "Developing Co-Teaching" (46–52), "Proficient Co-Teaching" (53–59), and "Master Co-Teaching" (60–66). For administrators who have read the book *Leading the Co-Teaching Dance* (Murawski & Dieker, 2013), consider how this progression mimics the progression from an elementary level dancer who is just learning the steps to a professional dancer who is now able to teach others. The CTIME process does not expect every team to be a master team—at first. However, it does help teams know where, objectively, they stand in terms of clear and concrete expectations. They will see exactly where they can focus their energies on improving their relationship in the shared classroom.

FIGURE 4.3

Examples of a Look For, a Listen For, and an Ask For

1.6 It is difficult to tell the special education students from the general education students.	*0 = Observer could easily determine who were the general education or students with special needs by their lack of integration (e.g., students at back or separated from class).* *1 = There was some inclusion of most students in most activities.* *2 = There was a clear attempt at inclusion of all students for most activities.* *3 = All students were included and integrated seamlessly into all activities, even when adaptations were needed.*	**2**
	LOOK FORS TOTAL	**16**

8.16 Co-teachers ask questions at a variety of levels (basic recall to higher-order thinking) to meet all students' needs.	*0 = Adults do not use questions and most instruction is directive.* *1 = Questions are almost all geared just to one level (to the middle or "watered down").* *2 = Teachers use closed and open questions at a variety of levels in a general manner.* *3 = Closed and open questions are asked at a variety of levels in a way that demonstrates they are able to differentiate for specific students in order to ensure maximum (appropriate) levels of challenge.*	**0**
	LISTEN FORS TOTAL	**7**

6.1 Co-Assessment	*0 = There is no evidence that this team co-assesses. One teacher is in charge of the grades and gradebook.* *1 = Teachers talk about assessments at times, but each teacher is primarily in charge of her "own" students.* *2 = Teachers use differentiated assessments occasionally and are willing to share responsibility for grading.* *3 = Teachers share responsibility for creating assessments, grading, and for students' overall success. Differentiated assessments are created when needed and both teachers are comfortable with adaptations.*	**1**	**Grade Book: Modified Assignments** **Individual Grading Reports** **Other:**
Notes:		**ASK FORS TOTAL**	**9**
		GRAND TOTAL	**32**
0–29 **Not Yet Co-Teaching** 30–45 **Emerging Co-Teaching** 46–52 **Developing Co-Teaching** 53–59 **Proficient Co-Teaching** 60–66 **Master Co-Teaching**			

Many administrators who have worked with us have said that, although they are fans of the Co-Teaching Core Competencies Observation Checklist and use it regularly, they find themselves not "Asking For" items regularly. Does that change the outcomes? It most certainly does. That is not to say that you can't still use the checklist, though. You should know us better than that by now. Even if you are planning to collect data in its ideal form, the Ask Fors are not ones you need to obtain every single collection period. We find that it is helpful to collect lesson plans regularly, though not all co-teachers write down their lesson plans unless they are asked for them. Go figure! However, many of the other items can be collected or viewed once a year. For example, if you know that co-teachers engaged in a conversation about the S.H.A.R.E. Worksheet (Murawski & Dieker, 2004; provided in Chapter 9 as Figure 9.2), then there is no need to ask to see it every nine weeks. The items that you ask for and the frequency with which you ask for them is up to you and the co-teaching team.

The scoring for the Growth Ranges is impacted by Ask For scores, though. So if you are not using the Ask Fors section at all (maybe you have decided this is a baby step for you, and you'll start to include them next year), then you will need to use the *adapted Growth Ranges* with your teams. You don't want them to feel penalized just because you haven't asked to collect their permanent product data. See Figure 4.4 for the adapted Growth Ranges.

FIGURE 4.4

Growth Ranges and Adapted Growth Ranges

Growth Range Descriptor	Observation Checklist Growth Ranges	Adapted Observation Checklist Growth Ranges (for Observations Without Ask Fors)
Not Yet Co-Teaching	0–29	0–20
Emerging Co-Teaching	30–45	21–35
Developing Co-Teaching	46–52	36–41
Proficient Co-Teaching	53–59	42–46
Master Co-Teaching	60–66	47–51

Conducting Co-Teaching Observations

Who should conduct co-teaching observations? Anyone. Truly anyone. This might be an administrator, a university supervisor, a coach, a consultant, a mentor, or a coordinator... but it can also be a fellow teacher, a paraprofessional, a parent, or a student. A huge benefit of having a clear, well-articulated tool for observations is that almost anyone can use it with a strong degree of reliability.

There are a few things that any observer should consider, however. First, when attempting to get an overall picture of a co-taught class, it is best to observe an entire co-taught session. This might be a whole period at the secondary level or a full lesson at the elementary level. Can you use the observation tool for walk-throughs or short observation snippets? Most definitely, but then you will want to have more of these observations to get a more detailed and accurate picture of what is occurring in the class (Luczak et al., 2014).

Second, observations can be planned or impromptu. Some observers prefer that co-teaching teams know when they are coming to observe so that (1) they are not surprised and (2) they can plan to present their very "best" lesson. Others prefer to go in unannounced in order to observe a more "typical" lesson. There are also those who choose to do a combination of the two. Whatever the case, remember that teachers are people too and that "things happen." Work to make the team you are observing feel comfortable with the observation; the more comfortable they are, the more likely they will do their best work with students.

Third, even with a tool that describes each of the co-teaching competencies, it is still important that observers be familiar with co-teaching and its critical components, and that they know the goal of the observation (Hopkins, 2006). Unfortunately, as Murawski and Lochner (2011) observe, "[W]hile the teachers themselves are struggling to understand their collaborative role in the classroom, many supervisors also have not received sufficient instruction on what they should be seeing in the effective co-taught classroom—despite the fact that their role is to observe, document, give feedback, and be instructional leaders" (p. 176). The entire January 2016 issue of *Educational Leadership* (Volume 73, Number 4) was dedicated to co-teaching practices. In it, Murawski and Bernhardt (2016) wrote to the administrator's role in supporting and maintaining co-teaching. Clearly, then, to use the data collected in a meaningful way, observers need to be familiar with the overall goal of co-teaching.

Co-Teaching Surveys

Co-Teaching Self-Survey

The next tool is the Co-Teaching Core Competencies Observation Self-Survey. Because we want you to have complete access to all of these resources and be able to access them easily, many of the longer forms are provided for you in Chapter 9. The self-survey is offered as Figure 9.3. This self-survey gives teachers a voice and enables them to share how they feel their co-teaching experience is going. Each teacher from the team is asked to complete the survey independently. It is important for teachers to complete it independently first, rather than as a team, so that each will be honest about his or her personal experiences and frame of reference (Murawski, 2010). When teachers complete the self-survey as a team, it is simply too easy for one person's opinion to dominate the others. This way, when teachers come together to share their responses, they can see where they are already in alignment and where they conflict. They can then use the data in the self-reflecting portion of their problem-solving sessions.

The self-survey has the exact same content as the Co-Teaching Core Competencies Observation Checklist so that teams are evaluating themselves and can compare their self-identified scores with those provided by observers. However, there is an added component on the self-survey: *the ease score*. The ease score is a rating determined by the team itself regarding how "easy" or "difficult" each individual competency will be to implement: *0 means the competency will be very easy to implement, whereas 3 means it will be extremely difficult to implement.* This is an excellent opportunity for teachers to identify where some of their barriers may be, while they are reflecting on how they will rate the competency in terms of their current status. For example, some teams may rate a particular competency as "difficult" because they feel achieving it is out of their hands. Because teams' strengths, situations, and needs differ, these scores also often differ. Some teams may feel like just being present on time will be a challenge, while others are ready to tackle differentiation strategies. Having to determine how easy or difficult a competency will be to master ensures a good discussion between co-teachers. We will bring up ease scores again in Chapter 5 and share how they contribute to the team's selection of competencies to focus on for improvement. For now, suffice it to say that having a team discuss how easy or difficult a particular competency will be to master is an excellent conversation starter.

For each co-teaching situation, teachers should complete the self-survey, considering the specific interaction with that particular partner. For example, if a special educator co-teaches with three different partners

	LOOK FORS	Rating Score	Ease Score
For the competency rating score, use the provided rubrics to rate each competency. The ease score is determined by how easy (0) to difficult (3) it will be to implement the competency into your daily co-teaching practices.			
4.5 Two or more professionals working together in the same physical space.	*0 = Only one adult; two adults not communicating at all; class always divided into two rooms.* *1 = Two adults in same room, but very little communication or collaborative work.* *2 = Two adults in same room; both engaged in class and each other (even if not perfectly).* *3 = Two adults collaborating together well in the same room.*	**0**	**3**
9.5 Class environment demonstrates parity and collaboration (both names on board, sharing materials and space).	*0 = No demonstration of parity/collaboration; room appears to belong to one teacher only.* *1 = Some attempt at parity; both adults share a few materials and general space* *2 = Parity exists; adults share classroom materials.* *3 = Clear parity; both names on board/report card; two desks or shared space; obvious feeling from teachers that it is "our room."*	**1**	**2**
11.6 Both teachers begin and end class together and remain in the room the entire time.	*0 = One adult is absent or late; adults may leave room for times not related to this class.* *1 = One adult may be late or leave early or may leave for brief time.* *2 = One adult may be late or leave early, but for remaining time they work together.* *3 = Both adults begin and end together, and are with students the entire time.* *Note: if adults have planned to use a regrouping approach (e.g., "parallel") and one adult takes a group of students out of the room (e.g., to the library), that is perfectly acceptable.*	**0**	**1**
8.6 During instruction, both teachers assist students with and without disabilities.	*0 = Adults are not helping students or are only helping "their own" students.* *1 = There is some helping of various students, but at least one adult primarily stays with a few of "their own."* *2 = Both adults are willing to help all students, but students seem to have one adult they prefer to work with.* *3 = It is clear that both adults are willing to help all students and that students are used to this.*	**1**	**2**
9.6 The class moves smoothly, with evidence of co-planning and communication between co-teachers.	*0 = Little to no prior planning is evident.* *1 = All planning appears to have been done by one adult.* *2 = Minimal planning is evident; most appears to have been done by one adult.* *3 = It is clear that both adults are comfortable with the lesson and know what is supposed to happen.*	**1**	**3**
8.8 Class instruction and activities proactively promote multiple modes of representation, engagement, and expression (universal design for learning—UDL).	*0 = There is no evidence of universal design; all students are expected to do the same thing.* *1 = There is minimal evidence of universal design: limited opportunities for choice in how students learn, engage, and show what they've learned.* *2 = There is some evidence of universal design: some opportunities for choice in how students learn, engage, and show what they've learned.* *3 = The class was universally designed; opportunities for choice in how students learn, engage, and show what they've learned were well selected.*	**2**	**2**
3.7 Differentiated content and strategies, based on formative assessment, are used to meet the range of learning needs.	*0 = There is no evidence of differentiation of instruction in the classroom.* *1 = There is minimal differentiation; most differentiation appears to be focused on groups rather than individuals.* *2 = Some differentiation is evident for individuals or groups.* *3 = It is clear that adults consider individual students' needs and regular use of differentiation is evident.*	**2**	**3**

over the course of five classroom periods, then she would receive three surveys—one for each partner. (We do not recommend more than two co-teaching partners if you want to see actual co-planning, co-instructing, and co-assessing.) We know that each team creates its own dynamic, and partners will mostly likely have different experiences based on the different teacher, content area, group of students, or even varying times of the day. Once co-teachers have completed the self-surveys, they turn them in to whoever is responsible for compiling the data for the school's co-teaching leadership PLC. Once the data are compiled, the surveys are returned to the co-teachers. They are going to need to use them during the CTIME process. The self-survey is typically conducted two times per year—around week 9 and week 27 of the school year. These are just general guidelines, so don't worry if those particular weeks don't work with your calendar. The idea is that teachers have an opportunity to share their personal frame of reference toward the beginning of the year and later in the year, and that those reflections are meaningful and shared.

Having individually scored themselves, co-teaching partners can then come together and compare their self-survey competency ratings and the ease scores. This communication begins an open and frank dialogue, which often saves the team from being frustrated in the classroom. We have found that partners are sometimes surprised by their colleague's different reflections on how well they might be doing on specific competency areas. Being able to use descriptive, rather than judgmental or evaluative, language is key to strong communication (Friend & Cook, 2016; Murawski & Spencer, 2011) between teams when sharing self-surveys. Teams that need additional support in communicating and asking one another questions in a more structured way should also consider Dieker's *The Co-Planner: Two Professionals + One Plan for Co-Teaching* (2016), which integrates questions and scenarios throughout the year-long text.

Help co-teachers with planning by getting them Dieker's The Co-Planner: Two Professionals + One Plan for Co-Teaching *(www.knowledge-by-design.com) or the Co-Teaching Solutions System (CTSS) Teachers' Toolbox (www.coteachsolutions.com).*

Having teachers complete self-surveys on how they feel they are doing on each individual core competency allows observers, such as administrators and coaches, to compare their observational data with the co-teachers' individual and team self-ratings. For example, look at the sample survey comparison form in Figure 4.5 to see how an administrator might meet with a team to discuss their perceptions of what they are doing compared to the data being collected during observations. Is there a big disparity? If there is, this would prompt a worthwhile discussion about the source of the disparity. For example, an observer might rate teams low on "11.6 Both teachers begin and end class together and remain in the room the entire time," while co-teachers rate themselves rather high on that competency. Why would that be? Perhaps the administrator is scoring what he or she sees—which is that one teacher is late or doesn't stay all the time. On

FIGURE 4.5

Sample Co-Teaching Core Competencies Observation Checklist: Self-Reflection Comparison

General Educator: *Heaven Hashtag* Special Service Provider: *Sochialle Media* Date: 11/30

Observer: *Bob Boberson* Grade: 7 Content Area: Math Pd/Rm: 4th period/Rm 33

School: Sierra Middle School Term: 2017-2018

	LOOK FORS	Gen Ed Rating	Specialist Rating	Admin Rating
4.5 Two or more professionals working together in the same physical space.	*0 = Only one adult; two adults not communicating at all; class always divided into two rooms.* *1 = Two adults in same room, but very little communication or collaborative work.* *2 = Two adults in same room; both engaged in class and each other (even if not perfectly).* *3 = Two adults collaborating together well in the same room.*	3	2	2
9.5 Class environment demonstrates parity and collaboration (both names on board, sharing materials and space).	*0 = No demonstration of parity/collaboration; room appears to belong to one teacher only.* *1 = Some attempt at parity; both adults share a few materials and general space.* *2 = Parity exists; adults share classroom materials.* *3 = Clear parity; both names on board/report card; two desks or shared space; obvious feeling from teachers that it is "our room."*	2	1	0
11.6 Both teachers begin and end class together and remain in the room the entire time.	*0 = One adult is absent or late; adults may leave room for times not related to this class.* *1 = One adult may be late or leave early or may leave for brief time.* *2 = One adult may be late or leave early, but for remaining time they work together.* *3 = Both adults begin and end together, and are with students the entire time.* *Note: if adults have planned to use a regrouping approach (e.g., "parallel") and one adult takes a group of students out of the room (e.g., to the library), that is perfectly acceptable.*	3	3	1
8.6 During instruction, both teachers assist students with and without disabilities.	*0 = Adults are not helping students or are only helping "their own" students.* *1 = There is some helping of various students, but at least one adult primarily stays with a few of "their own."* *2 = Both adults are willing to help all students, but students seem to have one adult they prefer to work with.* *3 = It is clear that both adults are willing to help all students and that students are used to this.*	3	2	1
9.6 The class moves smoothly, with evidence of co-planning and communication between co-teachers.	*0 = Little to no prior planning is evident.* *1 = All planning appears to have been done by one adult.* *2 = Minimal planning is evident; most appears to have been done by one adult.* *3 = It is clear that both adults are comfortable with the lesson and know what is supposed to happen.*	1	1	1

the other hand, the team knows that the special educator is coming from across the building and has to return there to start a class directly after the co-teaching situation; thus, they have agreed to a certain situation and have adjusted to what they feel are circumstances that cannot be changed. Having the discrepant scores will enable them to discuss this situation with the administrator. As a result, it is possible the administrator (1) will take that into account when scoring, (2) will consider moving the special educator's classroom in the future to be closer to the general educator's, or (3) will change the master schedule in the future to accommodate for the co-teaching needs. We have participated in some powerful meetings in which teachers were able to be honest with one another about how they felt the co-teaching was going, especially when their scores differed from one another's. We have also attended meetings wherein teachers were able to jointly express to an observer why their scores did not reflect what they were doing as a team on a daily basis. Being able to request additional observations or explain certain actions lets teachers know that the goal of these observations is truly to collect valid data on what they are doing. A template for the Self-Reflection Comparison is provided in Chapter 9 as Figure 9.4.

Family and Student Surveys

The other tools that CTIME incorporates in order to build a more complete picture of co-teaching are the family and student surveys (see Figures 9.5 and 9.6 in Chapter 9). The results of these surveys are incorporated into the data analysis when schools are ready and when it is appropriate to do so. As we've mentioned previously, including both student and family perspectives adds to a more complete, macro-level picture of the school's co-teaching success overall; however, not all schools are prepared to ask for—or receive—feedback from families and students in their first year of the CTIME process. We defer to you.

The research is clear, however, that teachers who are able to collaborate with families are more successful with students (Auerbach, 2015; Sileo & Prater, 2012). We all know this—but that doesn't make it any easier! Time, communication styles, cultural differences, and past experiences all play a role when collaborating with families (McConnell & Murawski, 2017). Collecting data from students' parents, caregivers, or family members can be daunting. That said, we cannot give up.

Collaboration and communication with families. Acknowledging that it can be difficult to obtain information from families, we also need to remember that collaboration and communication with families is a strand of the co-teaching core competencies! It is just too important not to do. We challenge schools and individual teams to reach out to the families of their students at least once or twice per year. Our Co-Teaching Team Classroom Family Survey provides a way for families to have a voice in what we are doing in the inclusive classroom. At the same time, these surveys provide another perspective on how teams are doing on the co-teaching competencies. They also encourage family conversations about what is happening in the classroom and let families know that co-teachers are eager to keep them involved in their students' educational experience.

Don't forget the students! Regardless of age, the student's voice is crucially important when determining how effective co-teaching is in the classroom (Embury & Kroeger, 2012; King-Sears et al., 2014). The learning environment is critical to student achievement. Co-teachers may feel they are providing what students need, but it is also important for them to ascertain the students' perspective of the learning environment. According to Embury and Kroeger (2012), "When teachers' roles are reduced to that of an assistant or aide in the classroom, the students show an awareness of that power differential and status.... [P]arity in co-teaching was in the best interest of the teachers and students" (p. 102). Do students see both teachers as co-equal? Or are they viewing one teacher as an assistant?

Incorporating family and student feedback. When you are ready to incorporate family or student feedback, you will notice that there are 22 indicators on each survey. That is because the surveys are closely aligned to the co-teaching core competencies. Brilliant, right? The rubric used is a Likert scale with possible scores on a scale from 0 to 3 for each competency. This makes it easy for participants to select their answers. The student survey usually is taken starting in 3rd or 4th grade and used through 12th grade. It is also completely acceptable, and in many cases encouraged, for teachers to read the questions aloud to their classes, in an effort to make the survey more accessible to students with special needs who are in the co-taught classroom.

Logistical tips for sending out surveys. We have found it helpful to send out a memo informing teachers of when family and student surveys will be sent out and collected, as well as the deadline dates for survey return. Teachers can choose to have students complete the student surveys on paper or electronically by putting the survey on SurveyMonkey or Google Surveys. Surveys can be sent home as homework or completed in class; naturally, the return rate is higher if it is done in class. Completed surveys can then be given to the person or persons assigned to the co-teaching leadership PLC who are going to compile the data.

As with the student surveys, family surveys may be sent home and provided in paper-and-pencil format, or the school may use a computer application. In some schools, we have seen teachers provide an incentive (e.g., extra recess, free dress pass, free homework pass) for the return of the family surveys and the completion of student surveys. It should come as no surprise that the return rate was higher in those classes than in the ones in which teachers did not offer an incentive. Other schools have had families complete the surveys as part of their parent-teacher conferences. Using this approach not only increased the return rate, but also enabled teachers to use these questions as a helpful communication and discussion tool with family members.

Aggregating surveys. In Chapter 9, we provide forms to aggregate the student and family surveys by averaging the responses for each competency. Co-teachers first receive averages for their own classroom data on families and students, and then the school PLC can collect those results and get averages for the whole school (see Figures 9.7–9.10). These data are used as part of the CTIME data analysis protocol. The information collected from the observation checklist, self-survey, family survey, and student survey is the basis of this book. It is what drives improvement and allows co-teaching teams to validate and improve their co-teaching. You may not be ready to use all of the tools right away, but you have them at your fingertips when you are.

What if you have other tools ready to go? Certainly some schools have tools already in place to collect co-teaching data or may want to select still other tools to collect data. If you already have measures in place, good for you! The most important considerations are (1) that you are collecting data from a variety of sources and (2) that you use the same tools throughout the process. These tools will be used throughout the school year to assess the ongoing status of the competencies, so their selection is critical. *A word of caution:* Other co-teaching assessment tools may not include all of the co-teaching core competencies or be as comprehensive as the ones we provide here. Be certain that your tools are those that measure the skills that will move you toward your vision, and not just tools that are easy to implement.

Setting Up a Collection Schedule

Now that you have your tools selected, it's time to actually use them! Ideally, observation cycles will occur every nine weeks. Try to have four collection cycles a year, though you might start with fewer. Research has shown, however, that when educators have just one set of observation data per year, there is usually no notable change in competency (Valentine, 2012). Valentine's research concluded that two observations per year resulted in some awareness, but little change. By contrast, when teams were observed and then met to collaboratively study their feedback three times per year, significant changes began to occur. Optimum results were found with four observations and the subsequent feedback sessions between faculty who were collaborating and supporting one another (Valentine, 2012). Why do you think that was? Because there was data. Teachers and school teams were able to look and see what was working and what wasn't and then make choices and changes accordingly.

Surveys, such as the self-survey or the family or student survey, do not need to be collected four times a year. That seems like too much even to us! Two administrations of the survey (once during the second quarter and once during the fourth quarter) allow teachers, parents, and students to have experienced the environment sufficiently to provide feedback. Naturally, the first observation and survey collection will serve as the baseline to compare the subsequent observations and surveys.

You are now familiar with the tools you will use to collect data. You can use them as much or as infrequently as your school finds appropriate. You can pick and choose which tools you will use regularly and which you will build up to using. Don't overwhelm your teachers, family members, students, or administrators. Get a sense of your community prior to rolling out this new plan to collect data and improve co-teaching practices systematically.

It is a best practice for your school to craft a data collection schedule early on in the process. *Collection* refers to the various concrete data we are assembling on each team or on the school in general. Dates for each of the collection periods should be established and communicated to all stakeholders. By having a document that stakeholders can refer to throughout the year, everyone involved is more able to plan proactively and meet deadlines to keep the CTIME process moving. In addition, participants will be less overwhelmed (which is a major goal of ours) if they know what will be required of them, how, and when. Figure 4.6 provides a sample schedule.

Closing Thoughts

You now are familiar with co-teaching, its competencies and goals, and the tools for data collection. Excellent! You are ready to do this data-collecting thing, right? Not so fast. Though you know what data you want to collect and how to collect it, you will need a system in place that won't change when your principal or lead teacher does. In Chapters 5 and 6, we discuss how to collect and analyze the data onto a structured and systematic form at both the school and individual team levels. Stick with us, friends. You are well on your way to no fail co-teaching!

FIGURE 4.6

Sample CTIME Collection Schedule

Date	Process	Who	Format/Time
September 12–16	Co-teaching team self-surveys	Individual teachers from co-teaching teams	Paper/CTSS
September 12–16	Student surveys	Students	During 1st period
September19–23	Co-Teaching Core Competencies Observation Checklist (Observation 1)	All co-teaching teams; observed by coordinator	CTSS
October 17–21	Family surveys	Family members	During parent-teacher conferences/SurveyMonkey
November 7–11	Co-Teaching Core Competencies Observation Checklist (Observation 2)	All co-teaching teams; observed by coordinator	CTSS
January 16–20	Co-Teaching Core Competencies Observation Checklist (Observation 3)	All co-teaching teams; observed by coordinator	CTSS
March 20–24	Co-Teaching Core Competencies Observation Checklist (Observation 4)	All co-teaching teams; observed by coordinator	CTSS
April 24–28	Family surveys	Family members	During parent-teacher conferences/SurveyMonkey
May 22–23	Student surveys	Students	During 1st period
May 29–31	Co-teaching team self-surveys	Individual teachers from co-teaching teams	Paper/CTSS

5 Action Planning: A Blueprint for Improvement

Data Tracking Forms: Put on Your CAP and Take Out Your PLATE

We hope you are convinced that no-fail co-teaching is a process that requires buy-in and baby steps. Given teachers' busy schedules and the diverse needs of their students, it is easy to understand why some might give up on change and just want to maintain the status quo in order to survive. But once teachers realize that they will be able to work together and focus on the areas that *they* determine to be important for success, they will be more willing to keep moving forward. With support, tools, and a data collection schedule in place, it's time to move to the next phase: making the data work for you!

In this chapter, we introduce two action planning forms for collecting, analyzing, and making sense of your data. Although the forms look exactly the same, they are used by two different groups for two different levels of analysis, so we gave them two different names. The Corrective Action Plan (CAP) Form is used throughout the entire year to analyze, track, and problem solve at the macro or schoolwide level. Remember from Chapters 3 and 4 that it is the co-teaching leadership PLC that looks at the schoolwide data. Looking at data at a schoolwide level could include viewing the data by grade level or content area, or it could involve identifying trends within particular areas or with certain individuals. It means having sufficient information at your fingertips to see where co-teaching is working and where it is not working in your school. Need a visual? Imagine your leadership team putting on their thinking CAPs to determine what needs to be done at a systems level to improve the environment so that co-teaching can occur.

Co-teaching teams will use the Professional Learning Actions for Teaching Effectiveness (PLATE) Form to document their co-teaching observation scores at the classroom level and then use those performance

Take-Aways

- *The PLC will use the Corrective Action Plan (CAP) to collect, rank, and analyze data on schoolwide co-teaching.*
- *PIE scores help teams prioritize their focus competencies.*
- *Co-teaching teams use the PLATE (Professional Learning Actions for Teaching Effectiveness) to hold their data, goals, and PIE.*
- *It is important to celebrate wins as teams improve their co-teaching skills.*

scores to determine where they need to improve. We chose the acronym, in part, because mnemonics really do help with retention, and, even though the last thing teachers want is for one more thing to be added to their plate, it means they're more likely to remember the name of this form. Ultimately, though, we want to emphasize that the CAP and the PLATE are both action plans. Teachers will use these forms to take action, based on their ongoing professional learning, to improve teaching effectiveness.

Let's start with the schoolwide Corrective Action Plan. The CAP is a comprehensive form that will give the co-teaching leadership team a complete picture of the impact, progress, and improvement of co-teaching. Although the use of the term *corrective* might make one think that this form is used for punitive measures, we want to emphasize that a mainstay of no-fail co-teaching is that we continue to correct our own actions in order to always be improving. The purpose of the CAP form is to have everything in one easy-to-review location. Co-teaching leadership PLCs will be taking a macro view of the school and its progress, while co-teachers will be taking a micro view of their individual co-teaching teams. As a result, some of the activities related to data tracking and decision making may differ. More on that later. For now, we introduce the CAP as a way for the co-teaching leadership PLC to track observation results, as well as any aggregate data obtained from self-surveys and student and family surveys, to see overall schoolwide progress.

The PLATE form is where co-teachers keep their own data. This is where they will compile their observation scores, their goals for improvement, and their ratings of individual competencies. This is also where they will document their plans for improvement and which core competencies they intend to focus on in a particular time period. When co-teachers meet to plan, when they reflect on observation scores they receive, and when they problem solve with peer groups, these PLATEs will be very helpful. Because the CTIME process is about continual improvement, we think that the actions co-teachers take based on their ongoing professional learning will result not only in their own improved teaching effectiveness, but ultimately in the increased success of the students in their inclusive classes.

Some Key Terms

Before we introduce you to the CAP and PLATE forms, let us acquaint you with all of the terms and concepts you will find on these forms. Here we describe each of the components of the CAP and PLATE and clarify what they are. That way, once you see them on the forms themselves, you'll be clear on their purpose (or you can just flip back to this section if you need a quick refresher).

- *Corrective Action Plan (CAP) Form.* A document to track, monitor, analyze, and record action steps to enhance implementation of the co-teaching core competencies at the schoolwide level.
- *Professional Learning Actions for Teaching Effectiveness (PLATE) Form.* A document to track, monitor, analyze, and record action steps to enhance implementation of the co-teaching core competencies at the individual team level.
- *Collection Period.* CTIME recommends four collection cycles, typically conducted each 9 weeks, but the cycle may be determined by your scheduling. Cycles include observation data collection and may also include (less often) self-surveys, family surveys, or student surveys.
- *Co-Teaching Observations.* Observations are conducted by administrators, coaches, coordinators, or even peers using the Co-Teaching Core Competencies Observation Checklist. This form is available on paper (see Figure 9.1 in Chapter 9) or electronically through the Co-Teaching Solution System (CTSS; www.coteachsolutions.com).
- *Self-Surveys, Family Surveys, and Student Surveys.* Directly aligned with the core competencies, these surveys ensure that teachers', families', and students' voices are incorporated into the process.
- *Goals:* Leadership and co-teaching teams use performance data to help set goals for each of the competencies for the next data collection.
- *Ease Score.* This is a team-defined score, one that the team has determined based on how "easy" the team feels the competency will be to implement. This team input helps to personalize the professional learning in the process as teams better understand their individualized barriers and strengths.
- *Impact Value.* The core competencies each come with an impact value. Core competencies have already been identified as imperative for true co-teaching, which means that teams should be trying to address all of them. With that said, sometimes teams will benefit from some "triage" to help them determine which competencies to address first. We have found that the competencies have a hierarchical logic behind them. Thus, each competency has been given a value score of 0–3. Those with a value of 3 have the most impact on the implementation process of the competencies.

- *PIE Score.* The PIE score is a quick calculation that can be done on each of the competencies, making it easy to rank and prioritize them. The score takes into account the team's performance (P), the competency's impact value (I), and the ease (E) with which they think they can achieve mastery of the competency. P-I-E, get it? PIE scores help facilitate team discussions regarding what competency will become a "focus" competency.
- *Competency Priority Ranking.* Once PIE scores are obtained, teams use those scores to rank the competencies in terms of priority. Because we value individual input in this process, teams are not required to use the rankings to select their focus competencies, but the ranking process will help them see which competencies might be an "easy win" and which may require more work.
- *Focus Competency.* Based on the initial analysis of the school's vision, the co-teaching leadership team identifies focus competencies for the school at large and documents them on the CAP. These are competencies that will be given the most attention throughout the entire process. In addition, co-teaching teams will be encouraged by their communities of practice to work on their own focus competencies in their rounds of microteaching sessions and as they prepare for the next observation cycle. Focus competencies are documented on the PLATE.
- *Next Steps.* These are the actions the team will take to research, obtain resources, or make infrastructure changes that are necessary to improve the designated focus competency.

Now, it's all clear to you, right? Don't worry if it's not. Take a few minutes to look at the forms themselves in Figure 5.1 and locate each of the above-mentioned components. We want you to be very familiar with the CAP and PLATE forms, as they will be at the heart of most of your data collection, analysis, and goal setting. We have provided blank CAP and PLATE forms for you in Chapter 9 as Figures 9.11 and 9.12.

Summarizing the Data

Once you have collected all of the observation results—as well as data from the self-survey, family survey, and student survey, if those were given—it is time to compile and summarize the data (see Figure 5.2).The CAP is where all information will be entered from the schoolwide level, and the PLATE is where teacher-level data are collected. These forms pull the information you have available back together and help teams develop a focus for their

FIGURE 5.1

Corrective Action Plan (CAP) and Professional Learning Actions for Teaching Effectiveness (PLATE) Forms

Co-teaching core competencies and rubrics provided for each observation.

Correlating collections for self-survey (SS), observations (Obs), student surveys (S), and family surveys (F).

Teams identify focus competencies to track and monitor and mark them with an "X."

What will we do to get better? This goes in Next Steps.

Area to put performance scores and develop goals

Team-defined ease score

Impact of a competency

PIE score

Priority ranking of competency

CAP and PLATE Forms												
Focus	Team		Content Area									
	School Term		Grade					Period				
X	LOOK FORS		SS 1	SS 2	Obs 1	Obs 2	Obs 3	Obs 4	S1	S2	F1	F2
	4.5 Two or more professionals working together in the same physical space.	*0 = Only one adult; two adults not communicating at all; class always divided into two rooms.*										
		1 = Two adults in same room, but very little communication or collaborative work.	**Goals:**									
		2 = Two adults in same room; both engaged in class and each other (even if not perfectly).	**PIE:**									
		3 = Two adults collaborating together well in the same room.	**Ease:**		**Impact:**		**Rank:**					
	Next Steps:											
	9.5 Class environment demonstrates parity and collaboration (both names on board, sharing materials and space).	*0 = No demonstration of parity/collaboration; room appears to belong to one teacher only.*										
		1 = Some attempt at parity; both adults share a few materials and general space.										
		2 = Parity exists; adults share classroom materials.										
		3 = Clear parity; both names on board/report card; two desks or shared space; obvious feeling from teacher that it is "our room."										

work. *Note:* If teachers are co-teaching with multiple partners, they will want to have multiple PLATEs. This is about personalized professional learning for each and every team. Situations differ and so will your desire to differentiate your focus areas.

FIGURE 5.2

PLC and Team Responsibilities: Collecting and Summarizing Data

Co-Teaching Leadership PLC: CAP	Individual Co-Teaching Teams: PLATE
Summarize the Observations: The PLC calculates the averages from the Co-Teaching Core Competencies Observation Checklist from all co-teaching teams in the school.	**Receiving Your Team's Observation Data:** Co-teaching teams will receive their feedback from the observer. The observation checklist has their rating score for each of the 22 core competencies.
Summarize the Self-Surveys: Calculate the average competency rating scores and average ease scores from the self-surveys completed by teachers. *Note:* This step is completed regardless of whether or not teacher teams have identified their ease scoring.	**Summarize the Self-Surveys**: When you have completed the self-survey, simply average your and your co-teacher's self-rated competency rating scores and enter the average score on your PLATE for each competency. An alternative may be to discuss each competency with your co-teacher and come to consensus on your rating. Then the co-teaching team will discuss and agree on an ease score for each competency. The team can simply note the ease score right on the PLATE, as shown in Figure 5.1.
Summarize Family and Student Surveys: If family and student surveys were completed, get the scores from each team. For a schoolwide snapshot, calculate the average score for each competency with Did Not Know (DNK) coded as a score of 0. Enter the average score on the CAP.	**Compile Family and Student Survey Data:** Average all the responses from your family or student surveys if you gave them. If teams are co-teaching multiple classes together, they can compile all data into just one PLATE, averaging the responses from all families and students.

Here we provide a step-by-step guide on how to use these action forms to prepare for your data analysis. Even though we both like data and recognize its need, neither of us is a professor of mathematics, so we promise to keep the calculations to a minimum. We also promise that this will take as little time and paperwork as possible! Let's start.

Summarizing the observations and survey results involves finding averages. You'll simply add up the rating scores for each competency, and then divide the sum for each competency by the total number of observations completed. We know that most of you can calculate averages, but we are special educators at heart, so we'll also provide a few visuals and additional examples for those who may find math onerous. Figure 5.3 illustrates an example for the PLC schoolwide summary.

The co-teaching leadership PLC will do the same calculations for all the self-surveys. If there are 16 co-teaching teams at the school—and for purposes of simple math, let's assume that each teacher has only one partner—then they would be collecting 32 self-surveys. Once those are collected, the PLC will simply add up the scores and divide by 32. These averages help the school see how it is doing schoolwide. Naturally, you will also want to note any outliers (for better or worse), see how they impact your final scores, and discuss why they may be an anomaly compared to the other team or individual responses. You then use the same approach to average the ease scores: Just select a competency, add up the ease scores, and divide by 32.

Save yourself some time! Schools that use the Co-Teaching Solutions System (CTSS; www.coteachsolutions.com) will be able to complete these calculations, sort data, and generate reports with a click of a button!

FIGURE 5.3

PLC Schoolwide Summary: An Example

Assistant Principal Sanchez has conducted 13 observations of co-teaching teams in the school and Academic Coach Brown has conducted 3. That is a total of 16 observations. We want to get the average overall.

For each competency (starting with the first one, 4.5), add up all the scores from each of the 16 observations. The school's scores might look like this on competency 4.5:

0, 1, 0, 3, 1, 2, 2, 0, 3, 2, 0, 1, 1, 1, 2, 1 = 20

20 (total score for that specific competency) / 16 (number of observations completed) = 1.25

1.25 is the average score for competency 4.5. (Feel free to round up or down as needed.)

The results of the family and student surveys will also have to be summarized and their results entered onto the CAP. If you choose not to use them in the first year as a way to ease into the process, that's fine. In that case, just leave those areas of the form blank. Our goal is to help you collect data; we want you to be able to include all stakeholder perceptions when you are ready.

Let's talk logistics. In Chapter 4, we discussed how co-teachers can get family and student data back. We recommend identifying one individual to compile the survey results. This is typically a member of the co-teaching leadership PLC. Thus, each co-teaching team submits its returned surveys to that individual, who will then create a summary sheet for the collected surveys for each team. Preferably, this summary sheet is returned with the surveys to the co-teaching teams so that the teachers do not have to compile the data themselves. We have found teachers to greatly appreciate this assistance. Back to the math. Again, you are simply finding the average scores for each competency from all the family or student surveys collected by a team:

Competency 4.5 Two or more professionals working together in the same physical space.

16 family surveys were returned from Co-Teaching Team A with the following scores:

2, 2, 1, 3, 3, 3, 2, 0, 1, 3, 1, 1, 0, 2, 1, 3 = 28

28 (total sum of scores) / 16 (total number of scores) = 1.75 (average competency score)

After the summary sheets have been completed on the family or student surveys for each co-teaching team, and the teams have received those scores and put them on their own PLATEs, it is time to calculate the schoolwide averages from all the summary sheets for each competency. These averages are recorded on the schoolwide CAP. Let's look at an example:

Competency 4.5 Two or more professionals working together in the same physical space.

10 co-teaching teams' summary sheets with the following scores:

2, 2, 1, 3, 3, 3, 2, 0, 1, 3 = 20

20 (total sum of scores) / 10 (total number of summary sheets) = 2 (average competency score)

Entering Observation and Survey Data on the CAP and PLATE

You've collected your data, and you've averaged your results. If you are part of a co-teaching team, you have also discussed each competency with your partner and determined how difficult or easy each item would be to master, and you've attached an ease score to each competency. You are now ready to use your action forms to put all your data in one place (see Figure 5.4).

Don't forget to complete the Look Fors, Listen Fors, and Ask Fors subtotals and the Grand Totals! (See Figure 5.5.)

Record your PLC results on the schoolwide CAP form and have individual teams record their own data on the co-teaching team's PLATE in the appropriate columns and spaces, as shown in Figure 5.6. The first time you collect family surveys is F1, the second time is F2; the same goes for student surveys (S1 and S2). For self-surveys, the data are entered in the appropriate "SS" (self-survey) column, depending on whether it is the first collection (SS1) or the second collection (SS2). Remember, the CAP and PLATE are the exact same forms, but the information on each is used differently. Co-teaching teams are looking solely at their own data on their PLATE, whereas co-teaching leadership PLCs are looking at summarized data of all teams in the school on their CAP.

As you can see in Figure 5.6, the co-teaching team enters on its PLATE the average ratings from surveys collected from its own students' families, whereas the PLC puts the entire school's summarized results on the CAP.

Determining Your Focus

Early on in this process, your co-teaching leadership team or PLC established the schoolwide vision for co-teaching. As part of that process, you should have identified the school's overall focus core competencies. All you have to do now is refer to the Focus Core Competencies Worksheet (see the sample in Figure 3.6) and put an "X" on the CAP form in the column on the far left marked "Focus" for those competencies you selected. Remember that the first time you start this process, you will be using anecdotal information to determine where you currently stand related to the competencies. Your first focus competencies will be based on that discussion (see Figure 5.7). After your first foray into data collection using the Co-Teaching Core Competencies Observation Checklist, however, much of your leadership team's discussions should revolve around where your school is with its scores on the focus competencies (i.e., your present level of performance). This helps you ensure that meetings are purposeful and that all members are working toward the same outcomes. Limiting your focus to a few competencies is doable. You don't want already busy and overworked educators to be any more overwhelmed than they already are. Trying too much all at once goes against the CTIME protocol.

Both the CAP and the PLATE provide a space for four boxes on the left column that may be marked with an "X" (see Figure 5.8). This essentially allows your teams, at both the schoolwide and individual co-teaching team levels, to identify which competencies will be the focus for each marking period. If results are showing that teams overall are scoring well on a competency that was a focus of your last collection cycle, then you may determine that it doesn't need to continue to be a focus. That would allow you to select alternative competencies to focus on in the next collection cycle. Always moving forward—that's no-fail co-teaching!

Determining focus competencies is not always as cut-and-dried as we might like. If your whole PLC is quick to agree on what you want to focus on, excellent! If not, you had the Bone Diagram to help align your vision with your focus competencies in the beginning, and you can choose to use

FIGURE 5.4

PLC and Team Responsibilities: Entering Data on the CAP and PLATE Forms

Co-Teaching Leadership PLC: CAP	Individual Co-Teaching Teams: PLATE
Enter Ease Averages: Enter the average ease score for each competency. This does not have to be redone each collection period unless teams indicate they have significantly re-evaluated their ease scores.	**Enter Ease Scores:** Enter the ease score your team assigned to each competency to reflect the ease with which your team thinks this competency may be implemented at mastery level. When possible, it is best to complete ease scores prior to your first observation.
Enter the Impact Value: Refer to the Co-Teaching Core Competencies Impact Values form (see Figure 9.13 in Chapter 9), and then enter the impact value for each competency in the space provided on the CAP.	**Enter the Impact Value:** Refer to the Co-Teaching Core Competencies Impact Values form (see Figure 9.13 in Chapter 9), and then enter the impact value for each competency in the space provided on your PLATE.
Enter Observation Scores: Enter the average competency score *for all teams* onto the CAP in the designated column, depending on the collection period.	**Enter Observation Scores:** Co-teaching teams simply enter each competency rating score received from the most recent observation onto their PLATE, so no math is required here. Make sure that the observation score is entered in the correct collection period column.
Enter Survey Averages: If co-teaching teams conducted self-surveys, family surveys, or student surveys during a collection period, then enter the *total* averaged summary scores for each competency onto the CAP.	**Enter Self-Survey Data:** If you completed the self-survey during a collection period, enter the self-survey score for each competency on your PLATE, either as an average of your two individually determined scores or as an agreed-upon rating based on discussion. If co-teaching teams conducted family or student surveys during a collection period, then enter the *total* averaged summary scores for each competency on your PLATE. Ideally, these will have been provided to you by the PLC in the form of a summary report.

CAP and PLATE Forms

Focus	Team		Content Area									
	School Term		Grade					Period				
X	LOOK FORS		SS 1	SS 2	Obs 1	Obs 2	Obs 3	Obs 4	S1	S2	F1	F2
	4.5 Two or more professionals working together in the same physical space.	*0 = Only one adult; two adults not communicating at all; class always divided into two rooms.*										
		1 = Two adults in same room, but very little communication or collaborative work.	Goals:									
		2 = Two adults in same room; both engaged in class and each other (even if not perfectly).	PIE:									
		3 = Two adults collaborating together well in the same room.	Ease:		Impact:		Rank:					
	Next Steps:											

CTSS Co-Teaching Core Competencies Observation Checklist		
General Educator: ________ Special Service Provider: ________ Date: ________		
Observer: ________ Grade: ______ Content Area: ________ Period/Room: ______		
School: ________ Term: ________ Start: ______ End: ______		
	LOOK FORS	**Rating Score**
4.5 Two or more professionals working together in the same physical space	*0 = Only one adult; two adults not communicating at all; class always divided into two rooms.* *1 = Two adults in same room but very little communication or collaborative work.* *2 = Two adults in same room; both engaged in class and each other (even if not perfectly.)* *3 = Two adults collaborating together well in the same room.*	1
9.5 Class environment demonstrates parity and collaboration (both names on board, sharing materials and space).	*0 = No demonstration of parity/collaboration; room appears to belong to one teacher only.* *1 = Some attempt at parity; both adults share a few materials and general space.* *2 = Parity exists; adults share classroom materials.* *3 = Clear parity: both names on board/report card; two desks or shared space; obvious feeling from teacher that it is "our room."*	0
11.6 Both teachers begin and end class together and remain in the room the entire time.	*0 = One adult is absent or late; adults may leave room for times not related to this class.* *1 = One adult may be late or leave early or may leave for brief time.* *2 = One adult may be late or leave early, but for remaining time they work together.* *3 = Both adults begin and end together, and are with students the entire time. Note: if adults have planned to use a regrouping approach (e.g., "parallel") and one adult takes a group of students out of the room (e.g., to the library), that is perfectly acceptable.*	1

Take-Aways

Individual teams just add their individual observation scores.

Co-teaching leadership PLCs schoolwide data requires them to enter the average *of all observation scores.*

CTSS system users will use the Team Report to complete this form.

Competencies Summary By School, Grade, Content Area **Date: Monday, 29 August 2018**

School	Team Proficiency Average	Team Proficiency Rating	1.2 Co-Instruct: DI	1.6 Cannot tell spec. ed from gen ed students	1.8 Inclusive language used with all students	1.9 Peer communication	2.7 Appropriate behavior mgmt	3.7 Utilize differentiated strategies	4.5 Two professionals, same space	5.7 Variety of instructional approaches	5.9 Positive communication
Middle School	1.28	21.19	0.50	2.00	0.82	1.35	1.90	0.37	1.52	0.60	1.29

School	6.1 Co-Assess	7.2 Co-Plan	8.1 Co-Instruct: Grouping	8.5 Co-Instruct: Parity	8.6 Both teachers assist	8.8 Universally designed environment	8.13 Learning enhanced with technology	8.16 Questions asked at a varieyt of levels	9.5 Parity in classroom	9.6 Evidence of co-planning	9.10 "We" language	11.3 Cannot tell gen ed from specialist	11.6 Both teachers working together
Middle School	1.00	0.25	1.00	1.00	2.11	0.40	0.82	1.05	1.29	1.50	1.19	0.86	2.57

FIGURE 5.5

Look Fors Totals

11.3 It is difficult to tell the specialist from the general educator.	0 = Observer could easily determine who was the general/specialist by their language/roles/lack of parity. 1 = Teacher kept traditional roles in the classroom, but shared or switched roles once or twice. 2 = Teachers worked at having parity in the class and shared most roles and responsibilities. 3 = Adults shared the roles and responsibilities in the classroom and observer would not be able to tell who was the general educator/specialist.	1
1.6 It is difficult to tell the special education students from the general education students.	0 = Observer could easily determine who were the general education or students with specials needs by their lack of integration (e.g., students at back or separated from class). 1 = There was some inclusion of most students in most activities. 2 = There was a clear attempt at inclusion of all students for most activities. 3 = All students were included and integrated seamlessly into all activities, even when adaptations were needed.	0
	LOOK FORS TOTAL	8
Notes:		

1.6 It is difficult to tell the special education students from the general education students.	*0 = Observer could easily determine who were the general education or students with special needs by their lack of integration (e.g., students at back or separated from class).*										
	1= There was some inclusion of most students in most activities.	**Goals**									
	2 = There was a clear attempt at inclusion of all students for most activities.	**PIE:**									
	3 = All students were included and integrated seamlessly into all activities, even when adaptations were needed.	**Ease:**		**Impact:**		**Rank:**					
Next Steps:											
		SS 1	**SS 2**	**Obs 1**	**Obs 2**	**Obs 3**	**Obs 4**	**S1**	**S2**	**F1**	**F2**
	LOOK FORS (GRAND) TOTAL										

FIGURE 5.6

Recording the Results

CAP and PLATE Forms												
Focus	Team		Content Area									
	School Term		Grade					Period				
X	LOOK FORS		SS 1	SS 2	Obs 1	Obs 2	Obs 3	Obs 4	S1	S2	F1	F2
	4.5 Two or more professionals working together in the same physical space.	*0 = Only one adult; two adults not communicating at all; class always divided into two rooms.*										
		1 = Two adults in same room, but very little communication or collaborative work.	Goals:									
		2 = Two adults in same room; both engaged in class and each other (even if not perfectly).	PIE:									
		3 = Two adults collaborating together well in the same room.	Ease:		Impact:		Rank:					
	Next Steps:											

Co-Teaching Team Classroom Family Survey Summary Report	
Team: ______ Area/Grade/Period: ______ Collection Period: ______	
Average the results from surveys returned and enter score for each.	**Avg Score**
4.5 My child's classroom has two teachers.	1
9.5 I receive information about the classroom rules with signatures from both teachers.	
11.6 Both my child's teachers remain in the classroom for the entire class time.	
8.6 My child receives instruction from both teachers, as evidenced by his assignments, lecture notes, and materials	
9.6 My child's class appears to be very well organized.	
8.8 Information during the class is presented in multiple formats, as evidenced by my child's assignments. They are not always paper-pencil assignments.	

Schoolwide Family Survey Summary Report	
Team: ______ Area/Grade/Period: ______ Collection Period: ______	
Average the results from surveys returned and enter score for each.	**Avg Score**
4.5 My child's classroom has two teachers.	1.75
9.5 I receive information about the classroom rules with signatures from both teachers.	
11.6 Both my child's teachers remain in the classroom for the entire class time.	
8.6 My child received instruction from both teachers, as evidenced by his assignments, lecture notes, and materials.	
9.6 My child's class appears to be very well organized.	
8.8 Information during the class is presented in multiple formats, as evidenced by my child's assignments. They are not always paper-pencil assignments.	

that same method again if it worked for you. Another method, discussed in the next section, helps co-teaching teams rank their areas of need prior to selecting focus competencies, and your co-teaching leadership PLC can use this method as well. Remember that even though your co-teaching leadership PLC may have selected competencies for *systemic* change and focus, their attention will be on those things that they can do something about at the schoolwide level. Those actions will certainly help all teams in the school that struggle with scheduling or planning or the like, but there are still going to be specific competencies that co-teachers themselves need to focus on.

The next section walks individual co-teaching teams through the process of ranking and prioritizing their competencies, using the PIE score method. As mentioned earlier, this process is also useful for PLCs that still need clarification on a schoolwide focus, particularly if the PLC wants to update its focus after subsequent data collections.

FIGURE 5.7

PLC and Team Responsibilities: Determining Focus

Co-Teaching Leadership PLC: CAP	Individual Co-Teaching Teams: PLATE
Select Focus Competencies: Determine what will be your PLC's focus competencies. You have multiple options for doing this. The team can just discuss the situation and pick a few areas, but we'd prefer you use data. Two methods for doing so are with a Bone Diagram (see Figure 3.4) or by using the PIE method (as described in the next section).	**Select Focus Competencies:** Individual co-teaching teams will select areas in which to focus their professional learning. In the next section, we describe the PIE score method for teams to use. Ultimately, it is up to the team to determine where it wants to improve, but the PIE method gives co-teachers data to inform their decision making.

Getting Your PIE Score

Once again we find ourselves having to make decisions about priorities on competencies that have all been deemed critical! This is where PIE scores will help. As much as we wish that PIE scores related to you and your partner bonding over a slice of cherry pie, they actually refer to the use of a simple formula. Let's refer to a few of the components on your action plans that we described briefly at the beginning of this chapter. You are going to need to obtain your performance score (P), apply an impact value (I), and create an ease score (E).

Performance Score. Your performance data come from the scores you obtained when someone came to your classroom to do a co-teaching observation. The observer used the Co-Teaching Core Competencies Observation Checklist to assign a score from 0 to 3 for each competency, with 0 meaning the observer didn't see it, and 3 reflecting a level of mastery. On your PLATE, you would enter these scores under Obs 1, Obs 2, and so forth. You might be thinking "Then why don't you call it the observation score instead of the performance score?" We have two answers for you: One, the observations were conducted in order to determine your performance, and two, *OIE* simply doesn't have the same ring as *PIE,* does it? At the schoolwide level, average performance scores across all teams would be entered in the "Obs" columns on the CAP.

Impact Value. The core competencies each come with an impact score or value already assigned to the competency. We give you these in Chapter 9 (see Figure 9.13). Because the core competencies have already been identified as imperative for true co-teaching, teams should be trying to address all of them. With that said, sometimes co-teaching teams will benefit from a bit of "triage" to help them determine which competencies to address first. We have found that the competencies have a hierarchical logic behind them. Thus, each core competency has been given a value score of 0–3, with

PIE score: *a way to look at data and take into account one's current performance, the potential impact of the competency, and the ease with which co-teaching partners feel they can master the competency.*

FIGURE 5.8

CAP Form with Focus Selected

Corrective Action Plan (CAP) Form												
Focus	Team		Content Area									
	School Term		Grade					Period				
X	LOOK FORS		SS 1	SS 2	Obs 1	Obs 2	Obs 3	Obs 4	S1	S2	F1	F2
	4.5 Two or more professionals working together in the same physical space.	*0 = Only one adult; two adults not communicating at all; class always divided into two rooms.*										
		1 = Two adults in same room, but very little communication or collaborative work.	Goals:									
		2 = Two adults in same room; both engaged in class and each other (even if not perfectly).	PIE:									
		3 = Two adults collaborating together well in the same room.	Ease:		Impact:		Rank:					

3 implying they have the greatest impact on implementation of the competencies. All teams have to do is transfer the values to their own PLATEs. Although we could have created the PLATE form with these values already filled in, we think it's worth transferring them yourself because good discussions often ensue between team members about why some items have higher impact scores than others. Writing the values in yourself helps with your overall understanding and internalizing of the competencies.

Ease Score. For each competency, the co-teaching team needs to collaboratively determine how easy the competency will be to implement. Zero means it will be very easy to implement, whereas 3 means it will be extremely difficult to implement. Because teams' strengths, situations, and needs differ, these scores often differ. Some teams will feel that just being present on time is a challenge, whereas others will be ready to tackle differentiation strategies. Having to determine how easy or hard a competency will be to master ensures a good discussion between co-teachers. For each competency, the two teachers need to consider how to get to mastery level from wherever they currently are, which can be determined anecdotally or after they have the performance data from their first observation.

Co-teachers should be prepared to explain their answers if an administrator or a member of the co-teaching leadership PLC asks why they scored a particular competency as they did. In one of our schools, this led to administrators learning that all of the school's co-teachers were frustrated by the lack of apparent parity between teachers due to only one teacher's name being on the report card, on the door, and on the grading website. Teachers felt they had no power to change this and scored themselves low on this competency; they thought it would be "very hard" to master because the situation was beyond their control. However, because of their shared experiences and frustrations, the co-teaching leadership PLC learned of the situation and this became a focus competency for them. The result was a change in policies, technology, and ultimately the way names were communicated for co-taught classes. Take the time to discuss and review each competency and assign the ease score. This may be a static score that you can retain all year, or you may want to change it as you go through the CTIME process. The process is flexible, as situations change, and can be applied at both the co-teaching team and PLC levels.

Calculating Your PIE Scores. Now it's time to calculate your PIE scores (see Figure 5.9). These scores can help you determine which focus competencies to concentrate on in your efforts to improve. Think of the PIE score as a composite that takes into account performance, impact, and ease, similar to the result that could be obtained from a decision matrix that incorporates all three factors. The team's actual performance, the predetermined impact value, and the team's assigned ease score create a personalized PIE score for each competency. In essence, PIE scores let you know where you currently stand on each competency in terms of current performance, impact level, and ease of mastery. Trying to decide which competencies to focus on for microteaching? Your PIE scores can help. PIE scores can range from –3 to 6.

FIGURE 5.9

Calculating Your PIE Score

Sum the **performance** rating for that particular observation (Obs) and the **ease** score the team gave each competency. Then subtract the **impact** score provided for the competency. That gives you the PIE score. And guess what? The PIE goes on your PLATE!

Obs 1 (1) + Ease (0) – Impact (3) = PIE (–2)

CAP and PLATE Forms

Focus	**Team**	Murawski & Lochner	**Content Area**	ELA								
	School Term	2017–18		**Grade**	8			**Period**	2nd			
X		**LOCK FORS**	SS 1	SS 2	Obs 1	Obs 2	Obs 3	Obs 4	S1	S2	F1	F2
X	4.5 Two or more professionals working together in the same physical space.	*0 = Only one adult; two adults not communicating at all; class always divided into two rooms.*	2		1							
		1 = Two adults in same room, but very little communication or collaborative work.	**Goals:**									
		2 = Two adults in same room; both engaged in class and each other (even if not perfectly.)	**PIE:**		-2							
		3 = Two adults collaborating together well in the same room.	**Ease:**	0	**Impact:**	3	**Rank:**	1				
	Next Steps:											

Some of you may be looking at the Co-Teaching Core Competency Decision Matrix in Figure 5.10 and wondering, "But if I have a PIE score of –1, which –1 is it on the matrix?" Great question! It doesn't matter. The decision matrix is just a visual representation of how PIE scores are calculated.

You don't need to use it in your own decision making and ranking. All you have to do is rank your PIE scores in order, with–3 being the lowest possible score and 6 being the highest possible score. Some competencies will have the same PIE scores, but don't worry about that yet.

FIGURE 5.10

Co-Teaching Core Competency Decision Matrix

Performance Score	Less Impact → More Impact: 0	1	2	3	Easy → Difficult
0	0	-1	-2	-3	0
1	2	1	0	-1	1
2	4	3	2	1	2
3	6	5	4	3	3

What if your opinion changes over time and you want to change your ease score? What if you are noticing major changes in your performance on specific competencies? Can you recalculate your PIE scores? Yes! Even though you typically create PIE scores only at the beginning of the process, when you're selecting focus competencies, you can recalculate them any time you'd like!

When ranking the competencies, which we'll explain in the next section, you can look to see which competencies have the lowest PIE scores and consider focusing on one of them as a priority. Those are usually the ones with the most impact and greatest ease of attainment. In a nutshell, they might be a "quick win" for you to address. For example, notice how a –3 rating is attached to a high-impact, easy-to-accomplish competency for which your performance score was 0. This means that it is an important competency and it won't take you much to move from a 0 performance score to a higher one; this would be a great competency to select for your focus! At the other extreme, a 6 rating is attached to a low-impact, relatively difficult-to-achieve competency for which you've already gotten a performance score of 3. There is certainly no need to focus on that one! We recommend you work on the scores that are lower (–3, –2, –1) rather than higher, but do you and your partner disagree with the PIE scores and want to work on a different competency? You can do that! The CTIME process involves a lot of choice. We are helping you collect data and analyze it systematically. How you use that data is very individualized.

Ranking Priorities

An important aspect of the no-fail co-teaching philosophy is that you are continually moving forward. Embrace baby steps and use data to ensure that you are truly moving forward, and not sliding back or side-stepping. PIE scores will help teams determine which competencies to focus on, but you need to keep an eye on the big picture as well. You may already think you know which competencies you want to select for laser-focused attention, but don't forget that there are 22 core competencies, all of which are important. So, now is the time to create a ranking for all 22 competencies. While you are identifying the competencies of focus, you are also continuing to review all 22 core competencies and give each a ranking for future improvement.

If you've used the PIE score method, rank all competencies from lowest scoring to highest scoring (negatives are low; positives are high). Typically, the lowest-scoring competency would be ranked as your number-one priority. Continue ranking all of the competencies until each has its own ranking. In the case of a tie (e.g., you have six competencies all with the rating of 2), the co-teachers simply discuss how they feel about each competency and give it a ranking they are comfortable with based on their own rationale. Remember, this is about personalized professional learning, where teams determine their own needs. See the example in Figure 5.11.

You can also create PIE scores based on data from student and family surveys. What were your scores on the competencies from the feedback you received from students and families? This may well influence your ranking. Chapter 9 contains a blank Co-Teaching Core Competencies Ranking and Priority Worksheet that you can use to complete this process (see Figure 9.14). However, school-level and individual teams can complete this ranking right on the CAP or PLATE itself. Ultimately you will want this information on your action forms in the designated space, since you are trying to keep all the data in one easy-to-access place. Once you have ranked all of the competencies, you can look back and determine if you selected the right focus competencies, if you want to make any changes, or if you want to continue as planned and just come back to new competencies for the next round.

For instance, look at the example in Figure 5.12. Say your team selects competency 4.5 as your focus as a result of the data from Collection 1 because you received a "1" in that observation. You'll put the "X" in the first box and focus on that competency. You even rank it as number one during your prioritization exercise. Time passes.... Let's say you didn't really do that much better during Collection 2 (your second observation), so what now? You just continue to focus on 4.5 and put another "X" in the second box, signifying that you will continue to work on it. If, instead, you rocked it, then you can select another competency as your focus for Collection 2.

FIGURE 5.11

Corrective Action Plan (CAP) Form with Ranking

Corrective Action Plan (CAP) Form												
Focus	Team	Murawski & Lochner	Content Area	ELA								
	School Term	2017–18	Grade	8			Period	2nd				
X	LOOK FORS		SS 1	SS 2	Obs 1	Obs 2	Obs 3	Obs 4	S1	S2	F1	F2
X	4.5 Two or more professionals working together in the same physical space.	0 = Only one adult; two adults not communicating at all; class always divided into two rooms.	2		1							
X		1 = Two adults in same room, but very little communication or collaborative work.	Goals:									
		2 = Two adults in same room; both engaged in class and each other (even if not perfectly.)	PIE:		-2							
		3 = Two adults collaborating together well in the same room.	Ease:	0	Impact:	3	Rank:	1				
	Next Steps:											

Next Steps and Goal Setting

Before we move on, let us quickly link back to the PDSA Cycle. Step one was "Planning" and in that step you identified your vision. Step two was "Doing" and at that phase you prepared your data collection procedures. This chapter has focused on the second part of the "Doing" phase—step three: conducting observations and collecting data. In chapters 6 and 7, we will describe how to conduct step four—the "Study" phase of the PDSA cycle—in which you will be analyzing your data. Though developing action steps and celebrating successes does not come until step five—the "Act" phase of the cycle—we want to preview what those action steps would look like here. Remember, as this is a recursive cycle, there will be a lot of overlap in the process.

FIGURE 5.12

Co-Teaching Core Competencies Ranking and Priority Worksheet

	Collection 1		Collection 2		Collection 3		Collection 4	
	PIE Score	Ranking	PIE Score	Ranking	PIE Score	Ranking	PIE Score	Ranking
4.5 Two or more professionals working together in the same physical space.	-2	1						
9.5 Class environment demonstrates parity and collaboration (both names on board, sharing materials and space).	-1	2						
11.6 Both teachers begin and end class together and remain in the room the entire time.	2	17						
8.6 During instruction, both teachers assist students with and without disabilities.	1	12						
9.6 The class moves smoothly, with evidence of co-planning and communication between co-teachers.	2	18						
8.8 Class instruction and activities proactively promote multiple modes of representation, engagement, and expression (universal design for learning—UDL).	1	13						
3.7 Differentiated content and strategies, based on formative assessment, are used to meet the range of needs.	-1	3						
8.13 Technology (to include assistive technology) is used to enhance accessibility and learning.	2	19						
5.7 A variety of instructional approaches (five co-teaching approaches) are used, including regrouping students.	-1	4						
2.7 Both teachers engage in appropriate behavior management strategies as needed and are consistent in their approach to behavior management.	0	7						
11.3 It is difficult to tell the specialist from the general educator.	0	8						
1.6 It is difficult to tell the special education students from the general education students.	-1	5						
9.10 Co-Teachers use language ("we"; "our") that demonstrates true collaboration and shared responsibility.	-1	6						
5.9 Communication (both verbal and nonverbal) between co-teachers is clear and positive.	0	9						
1.8 Co-teachers phrase questions and statements so that it is obvious that all students in the class are included.	1	14						
1.9 Students' conversations evidence a sense of community, including peers with disabilities and from diverse backgrounds.	2	20						
8.16 Co-teachers ask questions at a variety of levels (basic recall to higher-order thinking) to meet all students' needs.	1	15						
7.2 Co-Planning	0	10						
8.5 Co-Instruction: Parity	2	21						
8.1 Co-Instruction: Grouping	1	16						
1.2 Co-Instruction: Differentiation	0	11						
6.1 Co-Assessment	2	22						
Circle the competencies you wish to select to mark on the CAP as a "FOCUS" competency								

Have you noticed the "Next Steps" box on the CAP and PLATE forms under each competency (see Figure 5.13)? That box gives you space to record what you and your teammates plan to do to make improvements on the specified competency. We want you to think through ways to improve in each competency, but if you are strapped for time, at the minimum do this with your focus competencies! Co-teaching teams will be working with small groups called communities of practice, and they can help you problem solve, brainstorm, and find resources (see Chapter 7). In the meantime, write down the action steps you plan to take.

FIGURE 5.13

CAP Form with Next Steps Box Highlighted

Corrective Action Plan (CAP) Form												
Focus	Team	Murawski & Lochner	Content Area		ELA							
	School Term	2017–18	Grade		8				Period	2nd		
X	LOOK FORS		SS 1	SS 2	Obs 1	Obs 2	Obs 3	Obs 4	S1	S2	F1	F2
X	4.5 Two or more professionals working together in the same physical space.	*0 = Only one adult; two adults not communicating at all; class always divided into two rooms.*	2		1	1						
X		*1 = Two adults in same room, but very little communication or collaborative work.*	Goals:									
		2 = Two adults in same room; both engaged in class and each other (even if not perfectly).	PIE:		-2	-2						
		3 = Two adults collaborating together well in the same room.	Ease:	0	Impact:	3	Rank:					
	Next Steps:											

Action steps at the PLC level may include doing a book study or bringing in an expert on master scheduling or even interviewing co-teachers to determine how they think planning time could be provided. Action steps from co-teaching teams may include obtaining resources from the school or district or watching colleagues in action who address that particular competency really well. To truly improve, you need to change what you've been doing. You can't just wing it or hope your skills improve over time. We want you to focus. Focus on one thing, but really do spend some time figuring out how to change that particular competency for the better. And use your peers, your resources, and even your administrative team to help! This collaborative problem solving not only gets you where you need to go, but it can also build a great deal of trust.

Finally, you are ready for additional goal setting. After you are committed to the action steps necessary to make the desired improvement, it's time to set some realistic goals. By the next data collection, what do you feel you can score on each competency, especially those focus ones? Remember to look at all your indicators. If you said that achieving mastery was easy, then maybe you can go from a 1 to a 3. For competencies that you rated as difficult, you might just be hoping not to backslide. For those competencies, it is acceptable to keep them where they are for the next data collection.

Celebrating Successes

We guarantee that you will see some growth and will begin hitting the goals you have set due to your hard work and effort. Please, please don't forget celebrating those hits along the way! We want you to celebrate when you hit your goals. Once you get your data from subsequent observations or surveys, circle anywhere you hit your goal for the collection (see Figure 5.14). How many hits did you have? We hope your CAP or PLATE form is a whole messload of circles!

A quick note to the co-teaching leadership PLC: Pay attention to these hits. They are a good way to positively reinforce the hard, dedicated work of all your co-teaching teams since they indicate overall improvement across teams. Consider celebrating these wins in a big way. For example, you can start a tracking incentive, such as bringing in lunch when all the teams hit 10 goals in the same collection period.

Celebrating shared wins has several benefits:

1. *It helps enhance the collaborative culture of your school.* You are doing this together.
2. *It reminds your team of the goals you set and why you set them.* It helps keep teachers motivated, especially when they remember that progress on co-teaching has a positive impact on students.
3. *It sustains team motivation* and helps keep the focus on the positive aspects of collaboration and co-teaching.
4. *It encourages the team* to learn from one another and build on one another's successes.

FIGURE 5.14

CAP Form with Goal "Hits" Circled

Corrective Action Plan (CAP) Form												
Focus	Team	Murawski & Lochner	Content Area	ELA								
	School Term	2017–18		Grade	8			Period		2nd		
X	LOOK FORS		SS 1	SS 2	Obs 1	Obs 2	Obs 3	Obs 4	S1	S2	F1	F2
X	4.5 Two or more professionals working together in the same physical space.	*0 = Only one adult; two adults not communicating at all; class always divided into two rooms.*	2		1	1	2	3				
X		*1 = Two adults in same room, but very little communication or collaborative work.*	Goals:		2	2	2	3				
		2 = Two adults in same room; both engaged in class and each other (even if not perfectly).	PIE:		-2	-2	-1	0				
		3 = Two adults collaborating together well in the same room.	Ease:	0	Impact:	3	Rank:	1				

We know that there are multiple steps and actions that you can be involved in during the CTIME process once you have your data. Figure 5.15 provides a visual overview of those various responsibilities based on whether you are looking at the role of the co-teaching leadership PLC or the individual co-teaching team. Each of the tasks and actions have been explained, but consider printing Figure 5.15 for use as an easily accessible reminder as you proceed.

A great tool to assist with task management is a Gantt chart. Check them out at www.gantt.com

Closing Thoughts

Let's recap. In this chapter, we have focused on introducing two forms to help you organize your data, as well as the different ways in which that data can be summarized. The CAP is the Corrective Action Plan form that your co-teaching leadership PLC will use to keep track of the progress and needs of the school at large. Concurrently, each individual co-teaching team will have a PLATE on which to track their own personal data. The goal in both situations is to enable teams to systematically and easily identify focus competencies, collect data on progress, make decisions related to where to spend time and effort, and plan the actions that will be taken to effect change.

FIGURE 5.15

PLC and Team Responsibilities: You've Got the Data. Now What?

Co-Teaching Leadership PLC: CAP	Individual Co-Teaching Teams: PLATE
Rank and Prioritize Competencies: Using the Co-Teaching Core Competencies Ranking and Priority Worksheet, rank the competencies. Transfer the rankings to the CAP once you have them in the order that you feel best reflects your priorities.	**Rank and Prioritize Competencies:** Using the Co-Teaching Core Competencies Ranking and Priority Worksheet, rank the competencies. Transfer the rankings to your PLATE once you have them in the order that you feel best reflects your priorities.
Determine Focus Competencies: The PLC will select one to three competencies to focus on for that cycle. These are the target areas that will help the school overall with its co-teaching program.	**Determine Focus Competencies:** Teams will select one to three competencies to work on during the cycle. Their microteaching sessions will highlight these competencies.
Brainstorm Next Steps: Collaborating with the team, list some ways to improve in or attack the focus competencies. This might include sending some of your teams to observe teams in other districts, doing a book study on Murawski and Dieker's *Leading the Co-Teaching Dance* (2013), or creating a workgroup to reconfigure the master schedule. List these action steps under "Next Steps" on the CAP.	**Brainstorm Next Steps:** Collaborating with your co-teaching partner and community of practice, list some ways you can improve in or attack the focus competencies. This might include watching other teams in action, or reading articles with strategies on co-planning, or finding resources on differentiation. Whatever it takes to get better at each focus competency, list it under "Next Steps" on your PLATE.
Goal Setting: Review each of the competencies (particularly the focus competencies) and set a goal for the next collection cycle.	**Goal Setting:** Review each of the competencies (particularly the focus competencies) and set a goal for the next collection cycle.
Celebrate: Do not forget to celebrate when goals have been met!	**Celebrate:** Do not forget to celebrate when goals have been met!

Chapter 6 describes how PLCs will use their data to action plan accordingly, and Chapter 7 does the same for individual co-teaching teams. In this chapter, however, we began to preview those action planning steps and how teams can engage in different professional learning activities around specific focus competencies. We also emphasized the need to highlight successes and build on them. The next chapters will elucidate what directives like "brainstorm next steps" and "set goals" might actually entail. For now, we just want you to hang on to your CAPs and PLATEs and continue along the journey.

Worried that you might forget a step and want a handy-dandy checklist to refer to as you work through the steps? We thought so! See Figures 5.16 and 5.17.

FIGURE 5.16

Co-Teaching Leadership PLC Process Checklist

☐ **1. Collect your data sources:**
- ○ Perform all observations and summarize results
- ○ Collect and summarize data from the Co-Teaching Core Competencies Observation Self-Survey
- ○ Collect and summarize optional student or family surveys and return to teams

☐ **2. Enter data on the CAP:**
- ○ Enter the schoolwide average ease score (E) for each competency
- ○ Write down the impact value (I) for each competency
- ○ Enter averaged performance data (P) from the observation checklist schoolwide summary
- ○ Enter averaged self-survey summary scores
- ○ Enter averaged student or family survey summary scores

☐ **3. Find your focus:**
- ○ Calculate the PIE scores (P + E) – I
- ○ Identify focus competencies from prior focus worksheets and corroborate with PIE rank and prioritization of competencies
- ○ Identify one to three focus competencies
- ○ Conduct next steps brainstorming from a systems perspective
- ○ Set goals for all the competencies for the next data collection
- ○ Celebrate progress and wins

☑

FIGURE 5.17

Individual Co-Teaching Teams Process Checklist

☐ **1. Collect your data sources:**
- ○ Have an observation completed and receive your rating scores
- ○ Complete the Co-Teaching Core Competencies Observation Self-Survey, and input the ease scores
- ○ Collect optional student or family surveys

☐ **2. Enter data on your PLATE:**
- ○ Enter the ease score (E) for each competency
- ○ Write down the impact value (I) for each competency
- ○ Enter your observed performance rating score (P) for each competency
- ○ Enter team-averaged self-survey scores
- ○ Enter student or family survey results provided from the PLC

☐ **3. Find your focus:**
- ○ Calculate the PIE scores (P + E) – I
- ○ Rank and prioritize the competencies
- ○ Identify one to three focus competencies
- ○ Conduct "next steps" brainstorming
- ○ Set goals for all the competencies for the next data collection
- ○ Celebrate progress and wins

☑

6 Data Analysis and Problem Solving for Schoolwide Improvement

Analyzing the Schoolwide Data

You have your groups, you have your competencies, and you have your data. What now? What we *don't* want you to do is file the data away somewhere and forget about them. There is nothing more frustrating for busy educators than to spend time on something only to have it sit there unused. So your co-teaching leadership PLC has a bit of work to do. Data analysis is really about looking at the data in multiple ways to help you answer your questions or, in many cases, ask new questions. Now that you are familiar with the CTIME process, it is time to review the data, reflect on the results, and consider the following questions:

- What are the patterns and trends?
- Could we have predicted these outcomes?
- How different are the data from each of our data sources (observations, co-teachers' self-surveys, family surveys, and student surveys)?
- How alike are the data from each of our data sources?

These are some of the questions that will be answered during this process. Rather than merely looking at a bunch of individual surveys or observations, we again offer a more systematic way to review your data. At this stage, you are trying to get a feel for how your school is doing overall. In Chapter 7, we will drill down to the individual teacher-team level. But don't worry about that yet. You need to wait to plan your strategies until you really know what the data show.

You'll use the CAP to analyze your data. Here are *10 different ways* you might use your data to improve your co-teaching practices:

Take-Aways

- *There are myriad ways to analyze the co-teaching data based on the questions you want to answer.*
- *Having data is meaningless unless you do something with them. Be prepared to take action steps.*
- *The schoolwide PDSA part of CTIME can be boiled down to five easy steps.*

1. Ask yourselves: *What is our overall average rating for co-teaching teams?* Are we at the "not yet co-teaching" stage, or are we at least "emerging"? Does this rating correspond to how long we've been using co-teaching in our schools? Set a goal for where you want your average rating to be at the next collection period. Then drill down on the average rating scores and ask: Why do we think some teams are stronger than others? What do we know about what they are doing in the classroom with students that might be different from those teams that do not score as well? Can we use their skills to have them teach one another?
2. *What are our teams' overall average scores on each competency?* Are some competencies typically higher or lower overall? Why do we think that is? Are these competencies that we have supported from a systems level, or did they just happen? What might we do to support those competencies that appear to be low across the board? This is where your co-teaching leadership PLC works collaboratively to problem solve and brainstorm solutions to help improve your outcomes on certain competencies.
3. *How does our information look disaggregated by grade or content area?* Do we notice that some grades or content areas seem to have embraced co-teaching over others? Do we know why? Are the differences personality based, or is there something systemic that we need to address (e.g., the math department has policies that seem to run contradictory to individualized, differentiated co-taught lessons)? Bar charts are a great way to compare different groups. Consider how you might use bar charts to start a discussion with a group that seems to struggle with co-teaching as a concept. Examples you might use are in Figures 6.2, 6.3, and 6.4.
4. *What does our trend data look like?* A good way to identify trends is to create a line chart. Not sure how to do that? We provide examples in Figures 6.5 and 6.6. Since CTIME is not about forcing change, but rather providing a way for it to happen positively and regularly, we would expect some areas to hold steady and others to improve incrementally. Thus, it is important to have a way to look at overall trends, rather than merely judging our progress based on one point in time.
5. *What were the average scores on our focus competencies?* Was there a positive or negative gain between each subsequent collection? Why do we think that was? What kinds of supports or changes have we put into place at the school level to support teams? Consider walking around and actually talking to teams about the focus competencies. See if they have noticed a change in the way things are done

or how those particular focus competencies have been addressed. You want to know that real change is happening. Lip service doesn't count.

6. *How do our scores look compared to the core competency impact values (I)?* Are we stronger in those competencies that are rated with a higher impact? Find out which competencies each team addressed in their microteaching lessons. That can also help you see from a school level which competencies are the most important to teachers themselves.
7. *If we rank the competencies from lowest performing to highest performing, what do we learn?* Are the "easiest" ones highest performing and the more difficult ones lowest performing, or do the data show something different? Discuss as a team whether you are all happy with the way the scores are distributed. Find out if there are any surprises.
8. *Is there a correlation between self-survey versus observation data?* Analyze whether or not there are any significant trends or discrepancies. This is a good way to check the reliability of observers, by the way. If you find out that one observer always gives everyone 3s or 0s, while other observers are more conscientious in their scoring, that can impact the data. You can also see if observers tend to concur with the self-analysis of one population of teachers over another. For example, do special educators have their finger on the pulse of what is happening in the co-taught classroom, or do general educators? Do veteran teachers "get it," or do new teachers who might have learned more about co-teaching in their teacher training programs? Looking for a technique for analyzing these data? Try a scatter plot to look for correlations. An example is provided in Figure 6.7.
9. Is all of this data making you think that there is just a spider web of information out there? If so, *we recommend using a radar plot!* You've got a lot of quantitative data to triangulate, and you want to put it together in a way that helps your PLC make sense of it. Sometimes a graphic depiction will help you identify what additional questions to ask. A picture is worth a thousand words, right? Check out radar plot examples in Figures 6.8 and 6.9.
10. *Be creative problem solvers!* What are some other ways to look at your data? What will help you in determining if your issues are primarily systems-level or teacher-team-based? Would a pie chart (as in Figure 6.10) help? How you use your data is up to you, but we strongly recommend that you identify at least one or two people on your team who love getting into the data and making meaning of it.

Getting stuck on questions, rather than answers? We recommend the book Tool Time for Education *(Langford, 2015). It is full of group facilitation tools that will assist in moving your team forward in its problem-solving sessions.*

Data Analysis Techniques: Charts, Charts, and More Charts

Teams can create charts using poster board and markers, Microsoft Word tables, Microsoft Excel spreadsheets, or fancy software programs. (Those of you who use the Co-Teaching Solutions System, or CTSS, should remember that you can find free data tools at www.coteachsolutions.com.) No matter how high- or low-tech you go, it is important to keep your data displayed so that all teachers can see how the entire school is moving toward your shared goals (see Figure 6.1). As the data improve, administrators may want to offer some incentives as well. There is nothing like a duty-free day to work on co-planning and catching up to reward teachers for a great job working on the competencies.

FIGURE 6.1

Use Whatever Means You Have to Analyze Your Data

Grade	Obs 1	Obs 2	Obs 3	Obs 4
6th	17	36	32	57
7th	23	28	29	55
8th	18	29	41	47

Now let's look at some of the sample analysis techniques we mentioned in the list of 10 ways to use the data. Data analysis can be very complex. Charts enable you to present data in a visually pleasing way. The main challenge is determining the best charts to use. We are here to help you select the most effective chart to use in your co-teaching schoolwide data analysis. The charts described here are basic charts that can easily be made in Microsoft Excel. If you are using the Excel forms provided at www.coteachsolutions.com, these will already be programmed to work with your CAP data. The CTSS offers these same reports, as well as part of the observation system reporting module.

Bar Charts

Horizontal or vertical bar charts are best for comparing average means or percentages between different types of groups. Figures 6.2–6.4 illustrate how you can compare overall scores. In Figure 6.2, it is easy to see how teams are doing at the different grade levels and subject areas. This quick view might encourage you to ask your 8th grade social studies co-teachers to do some mentoring of your 7th grade social studies teachers.

FIGURE 6.2

Bar Chart by Grade and Content Area

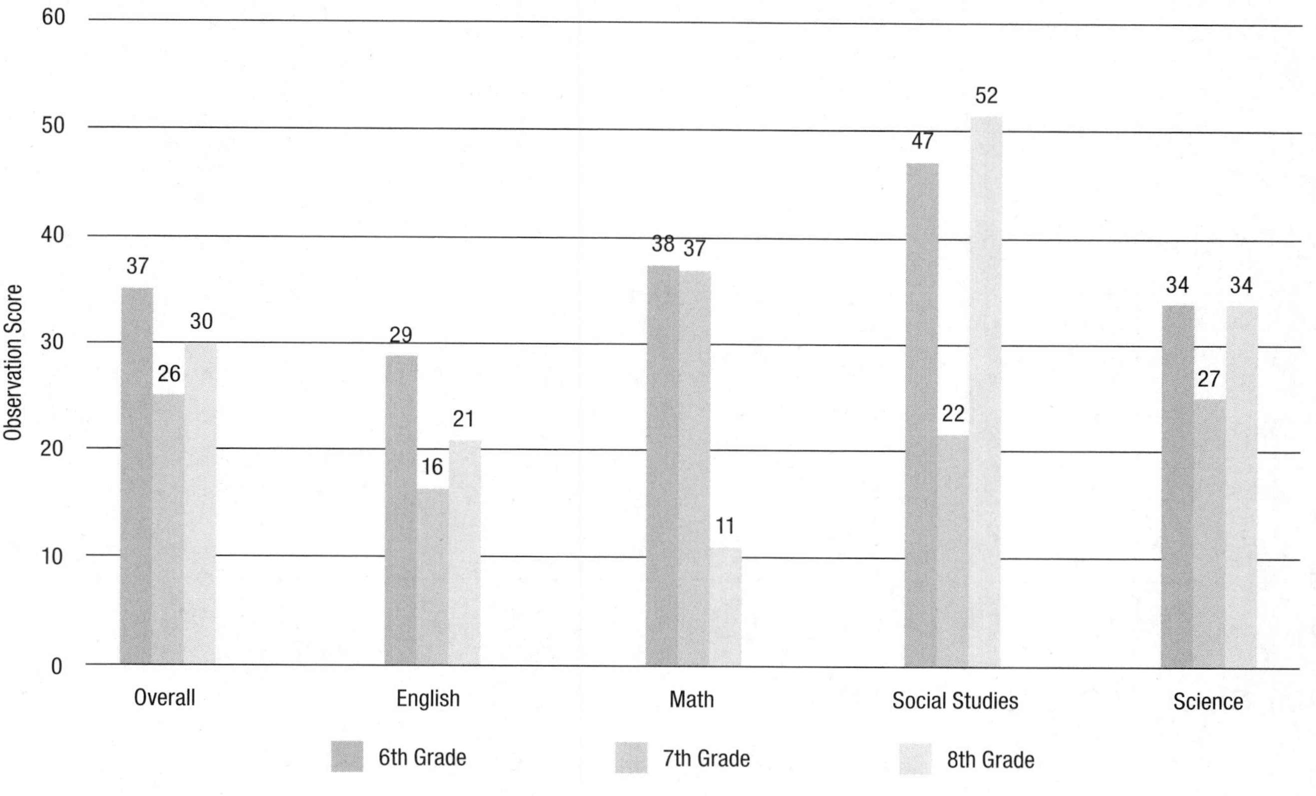

Figure 6.3 analyzes the categories of Look Fors, Listen Fors, and Ask Fors at the school level. These graphs give you a clear picture of how you are doing. In this analysis, you can quickly determine that you need to collect more permanent product data (Ask Fors) to show that teachers are co-teaching with fidelity to the process.

You can even take it to the next level. Let's compare these categories across the different sets: self-surveys, observations, student surveys, and family surveys. Now what do the data show (see Figure 6.4).

FIGURE 6.3

Bar Chart by Category

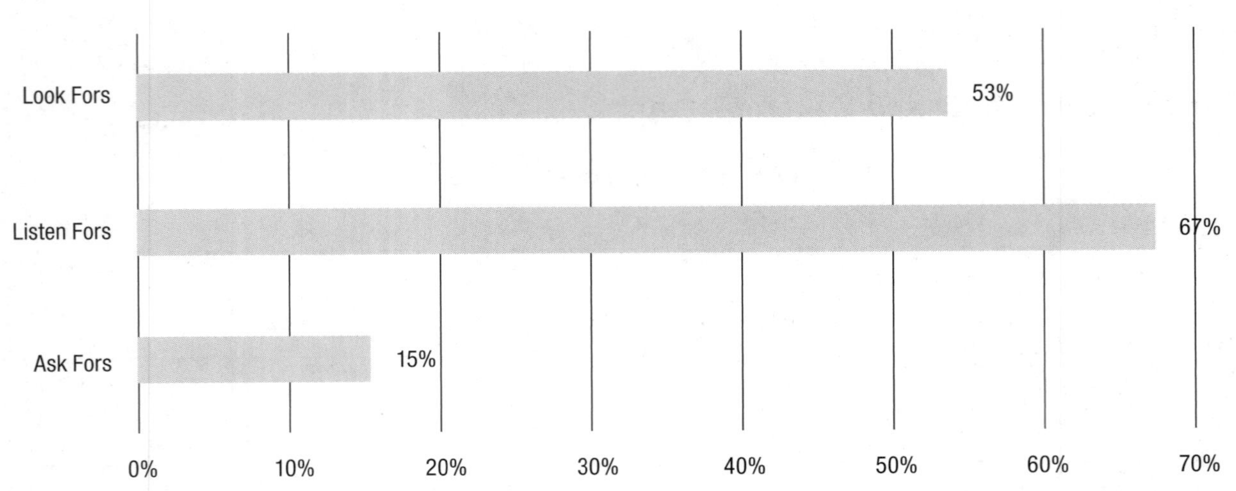

FIGURE 6.4

Bar Chart by Data Set

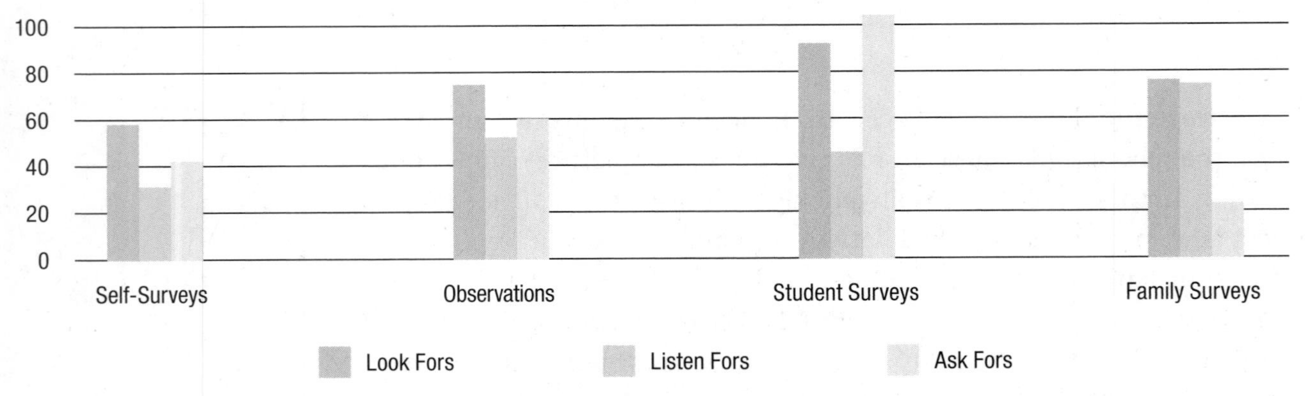

Line Charts

Line charts are used to illustrate trends or some type of progression over time (see Figure 6.5). You can compare one data set or two at the same time. An example would be if you wanted to see trends in your focus competencies on the CAP. What type of progress was made throughout the school year?

FIGURE 6.5

Line Chart of a Competencies Trend

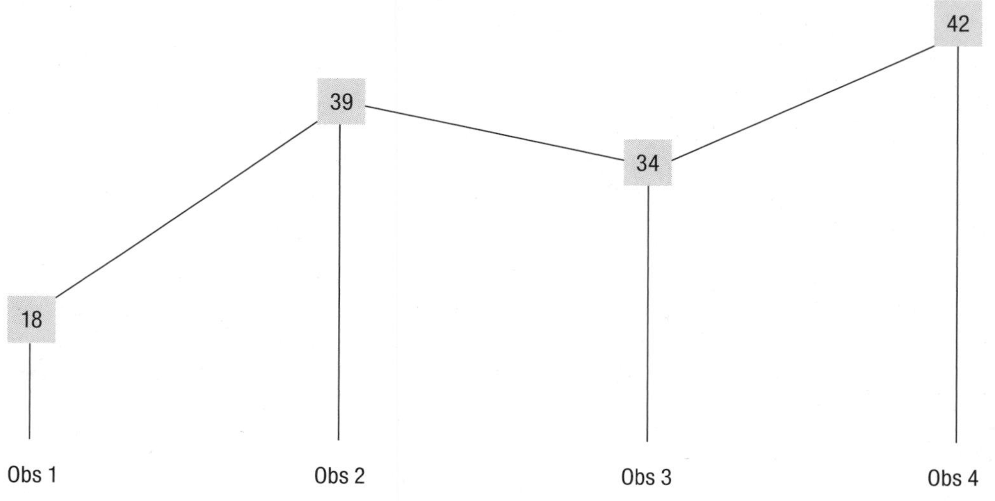

You can even compare two sets of data. What if you wanted to see your focus competencies compared to all of the core competencies to see if they were both on the same trajectory? After all, we are hypothesizing that, as co-teachers work on specific core competencies, there will be a spillover effect onto all of their co-teaching practices. Use a line chart to see if that is happening (see Figure 6.6).

Scatter Charts

Scatter charts, also called scatter plots, are used to depict the correlation between two variables. The example in Figure 6.7 could be used to see if a correlation exists between the number of microteaching sessions teams participated in this school year and the overall observation scores.

From the chart, you can see that as the number of microteaching sessions increased throughout the school year, the overall observation scores improved as well. Therefore, you can conclude that a positive correlation exists between the increase in microteaching sessions and the rise in observation scores.

FIGURE 6.6

Line Chart Comparing Focus Competencies to All Core Competencies

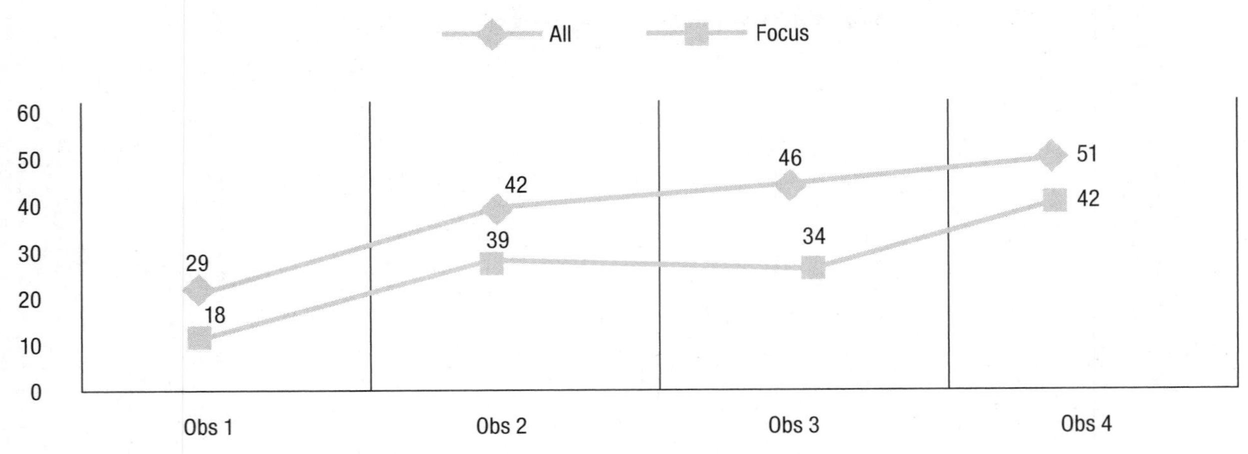

FIGURE 6.7

Scatter Chart of Microteaching Sessions Versus Observation Scores

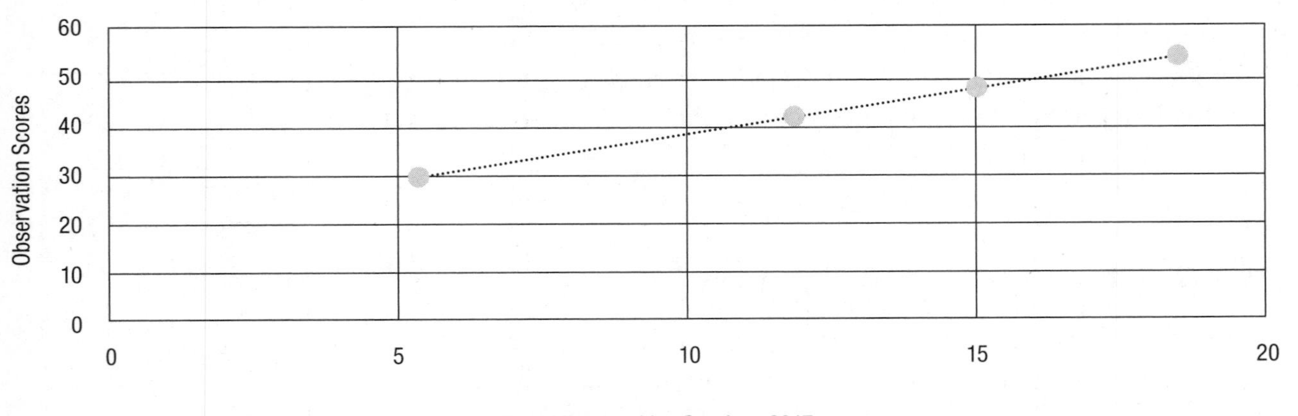

Radar Plots

Radar plots (also known as radar charts or spider charts) look quite daunting, but they are really a great way to look at multiple variables, particularly when examining several factors related to one item. So let's say you want to look at five focus competencies and their performance, impact, and ease scores—voila! A radar plot lets you do that (see Figure 6.8).

FIGURE 6.8

Spider Chart of Focus Competencies and PIE Scores

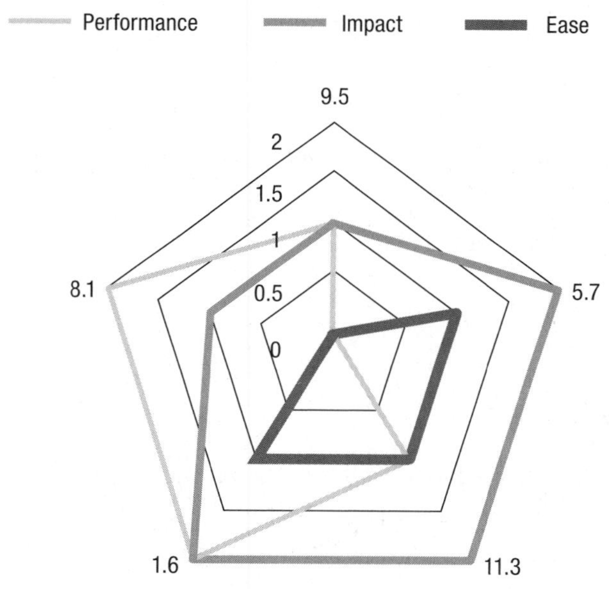

Or what if you want to look at all of your data sets (observations, self-surveys, family surveys, and student surveys) concurrently? With a quick look at the radar plot in Figure 6.9, you can see that self-surveys scored much higher than actual observations, and that family and student surveys all scored very low. Eek! What that tells us is that our co-teachers think themselves far more skilled and successful than their performance data indicate *and* than their students and students' families believe to be the case.

FIGURE 6.9

Radar Plot of All Data Sets

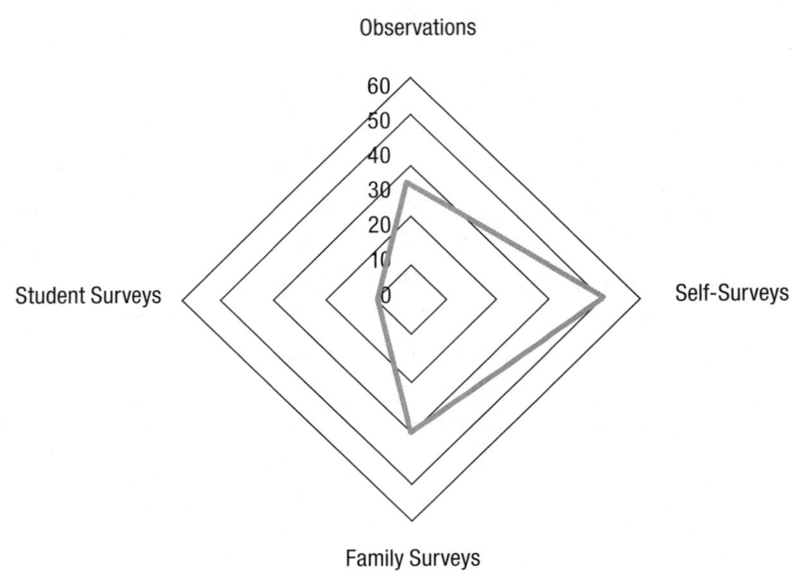

Pie Charts

Pie charts help you to see what makes up a whole. Suppose you want to see how the Look Fors, Listen Fors, and Ask Fors make up your overall school observation score. The overall school average is 39, with the Look Fors averaging 22, the Listen Fors averaging a 10, and the Ask Fors averaging a measly 6. So what does that really tell you about the makeup of your score? With a pie chart, you can easily see that Listen Fors are the strongest category (see Figure 6.10). That would not necessarily have been extrapolated easily by just looking at the raw numbers.

Though there are many more complex forms of charts for displaying data results, the ones discussed here are the most common and well known. Sometimes more complex chart types just result in confusion, so we suggest you keep it simple. You want to see progress and not get bogged down in making charts. All of these charts are part of Excel, and you can Google any of the types for a step-by-step video on how to create them in Excel.

FIGURE 6.10

Pie Chart of Look Fors, Listen Fors, and Ask Fors

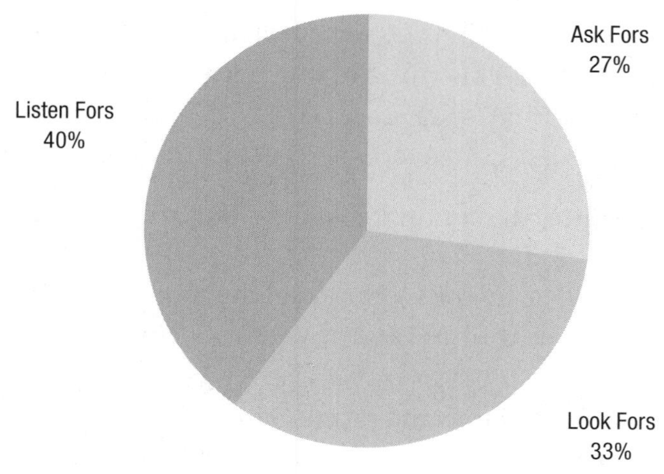

Tracking and Monitoring Progress

Although we have spent some time discussing how to set up and use the tools for data analysis, the more important issue is that you use them *continuously*. Remember, this is a *continuous* improvement model. Your schoolwide Corrective Action Plan (CAP) will easily allow your co-teaching leadership PLC to track and monitor progress on the core competencies, especially those on which the school will be focusing. With all of the data at your disposal and a variety of methods for analyzing the data, PLC team members can discuss the overall results of their data. Even those who don't love data and for whom numbers are scary can be involved in these discussions. Overarching questions might include the following:

- Are we where we thought we would be as a school?
- Did we do well where we thought we would? If not, why not?
- What is the trend after each collection? Are we getting better or worse? Why?

Spruce up collaborative meetings with animated charts. To create captivating charts that can be used with faculty, staff, and students, try these resources: Rich Chart Live, AmiChart, and LiveGap.

Let's consider one last way to look at your data. Remember, early on in Chapter 2, we talked about the *Co-Teaching Competency Framework*. Domains, strands, and competencies are all part of this framework. We've really focused so far on the *core* competencies because those are the most salient and "doable." But now you might be ready to analyze where you stand as a school on the overall framework. Use the Strand Analysis Worksheet in Chapter 9 (see Figure 9.15) to see how you are doing on the various strands. Use the data you've collected, scored, and summarized to complete the worksheet. This will give you a clear snapshot of where your school is, strand by strand (see Figure 6.11).

Here is a step-by-step way to determine your school's strand rating:

1. Enter the summarized data for the appropriate tool and collection period.
2. Add up all the scores to get the competency total.
3. Divide the total score by the total possible.

You now have the strand rating. Smile! That was easy.

In addition to the Strand Analysis Worksheet, we have also provided you with the Domain and Strand Prioritizing and Ranking Form in Chapter 9 (see Figure 9.16). So many forms, so little time! Remember, all of these are here for you if and when you are ready for them. Don't get overwhelmed. The Domain and Strand Prioritizing and Ranking Form is used if your PLC would like to enter the overall scores for each strand and then quickly rank the strands from low scoring to high scoring (see the abbreviated example in Figure 6.12). This allows the team to view the overall implementation of co-teaching. It answers the questions: Where are most of our issues? Are we consistently weak in learner differences or assessment? Is planning really a stumbling block? Essentially, by ranking your outcomes, you will be able to determine if your school excels at particular domains or strands, or if there are domains or strands that you seem to struggle with across the board. This information can lead to more personalized, focused, and meaningful professional learning. Just track and monitor how your school does throughout the year on the various domains and strands and make changes accordingly. That sounds suspiciously like data-driven decision making to us!

Key Terms

Root cause analysis: *a method of problem solving designed to get at the root or primary cause of the problem.*

Problem-Solving Tools: Conducting a Root Cause Analysis

You've got your data. You've analyzed it, and you know where your school is strong and—well, where it's not so strong. But do you know *why?* Now is a

FIGURE 6.11

Strand Analysis Worksheet

Strand Analysis										
Team:							Content Area			
School Term:							Grade		Period	
Strand 1: Learner Differences	Self-Survey		Observation				Student		Family	
	Coll 1	Coll 2	Coll 1	Coll 2	Coll 3	Coll 4	Coll 1	Coll 2	Coll 1	Coll 2
1.2 Co-Instruction: Evidence of differentiation.										
1.6 It is difficult to tell the special education students from the general education students.										
1.8 Co-Teachers phrase questions and statements so that it is obvious that all students in the class are included.										
1.9 Students' conversations evidence a sense of community, including peers with disabilities and from diverse backgrounds.										
(12 Pts possible) Competency Total:										
Strand Rating:										
Strand 2: Classroom Environment	Self-Survey		Observation				Student		Family	
	Coll 1	Coll 2	Coll 1	Coll 2	Coll 3	Coll 4	Coll 1	Coll 2	Coll 1	Coll 2
2.7 Both teachers engage in appropriate behavior management strategies as needed and are consistent in their approach to behavior management										
(3 Pts possible) Competency Total:										
Strand Rating:										
Strand 3: Content Knowledge	Self-Survey		Observation				Student		Family	
	Coll 1	Coll 2	Coll 1	Coll 2	Coll 3	Coll 4	Coll 1	Coll 2	Coll 1	Coll 2
3.7 Differentiated content and strategies, based on formative assessments, are used to meet the range of learning needs.										
(3 Pts possible) Competency Total:										
Strand Rating:										

great time for you to do a root cause analysis. Merely selecting focus competencies to work on won't result in sustainable change if you don't get at the root of the problem. At the least, you want to find out whether the issue is a school-level problem or a team-level problem. It would be even better, though, if you were able to ask the kinds of questions that would get you to the heart of why this issue exists at all! You want to eradicate the problem, not just cover it up for a semester or two. That's where the Five Whys and the Fishbone approaches to root cause analysis come in.

FIGURE 6.12

Domain and Strand Prioritizing and Ranking Form

Domain and Strand Prioritizing and Ranking Form								
Strand/ Focus	Description	Begin Rank	Observation Baseline	Collection 1	Collection 2	Collection 3	Collection 4	End Rank
1	Learner Differences							
2	Classroom Environment							
3	Content Knowledge							
4	Compliance Issues							
5	Co-Teaching Construct							
6	Assessment							
7	Planning							
8	Instruction							
9	Communication, Collaboration, and Problem Solving							
10	Families and Community							
11	Professional Practices and Ethics							

Domain Yearly Progress	**Domain 1** The Learner and Learning Strands 1–2	**Domain 2** The Task at Hand Strands 3–5	**Domain 3** Instructional Practices Strands 6–8	**Domain 4** Professional Responsibilities Strands 9–11
Beginning of Year (Baseline or Collection 1)				
End of Year (Last Observation Collection)				
Notes:				

The Five Whys Approach

The Five Whys approach (Serrat, 2010) will help your PLC in determining the root cause(s) of each low-performing competency. By asking "Why?" five times, a team can peel away the layers and identify the symptoms that may lead to the root cause of the problem. Teams may find that they will need to ask "Why?" fewer or more than five times, but five tends to be a good rule of thumb. The example in Figure 6.13 illustrates how just asking "Why?" can help.

FIGURE 6.13

Five Whys for Problem Solving—in Action

1. Why did our school score low on Competency 9.10—Professional Responsibilities?

   We never use "we" language in the classroom.

2. Why don't we use "we" language in the classroom?

   Both co-teachers are often not in the classroom at the same time.

3. Why aren't both teachers in the classroom during instructional time?

   Because one is often out running copies or doing other tasks.

4. Why is one teacher often running copies or completing other tasks?

   Because the lesson was not fully co-planned, and there was not enough time to pull together all materials for the lesson.

5. Why didn't we have the lesson fully co-planned?

   We struggle with getting through our lesson planning and how to use our planning time most effectively to co-plan.

Using the Five Whys approach can quickly help the administration or co-teaching leadership team to better understand the issues as the root causes are exposed. As you write down your answers, take some time to look at and reflect on the responses. You are trying to ascertain the following:

- To which causes are a lack of competency attainment attributed? Are you starting to notice some trends? Do you all keep blaming the same person or system?
- Are the attributions based on opinion or fact? Keep in mind that both are valid. Even if your team may disagree with *why* someone says he or she has done or not done something, the very fact that the person feels that way makes it worth addressing. Look at the example in Figure 6.13. One of the responses was that "there was not enough time to pull together all materials for the lesson." You might be thinking, "There was plenty of time if you used your time more efficiently" or even "I heard you talking about sports with your co-teacher; you

What if your co-teaching leadership PLC disagrees with the results of the data? What if you think perceptions don't match reality? Then consider that *as a problem to deal with as well! Use the Five Whys to find out why discrepancies exist among your team members' perceptions.*

should have been pulling together materials then instead!" Regardless, it is important to get the perspective of the person engaged (or in some cases, disengaged) in the process.

- Are the causes a systemic issue, or are they teacher-team-based? A bit of both might be going on, but this is an important distinction, as it determines the next steps in the process. Your PLC will likely take on system-level problems, whereas co-teaching teams can tackle the team-based problems.

The Fishbone or Ishikawa Diagram

Another problem-solving tool that can facilitate team discussions and assist you in ascertaining the root causes of low-performing competencies is the Fishbone or Ishikawa Diagram (Andersen & Fagerhaug, 2006). Both this process and the Five Whys approach can help teams understand the complexities of the competencies selected (Doggett, 2005).

The Fishbone Diagram (see Figure 6.14) is used to help identify possible causes of an effect, especially when those causes need to be visually identified and categorized for easier interpretation. This will help a team avoid jumping to a conclusion that may not be the best solution. Further, all team members can contribute their viewpoints during this process. Using the Fishbone Diagram involves the following steps:

1. Write the effect in the backbone of the fish.
2. As a team, brainstorm the causes of the effect or the major factors involved.
3. List any minor causes or factors on the lines under the identified causes or factors.
4. Determine a solution when all of the factors are exposed.
5. Complete the resolution box to the right by stating the identified issue, listing the research that will be done to assist in a resolution, and detailing the action step(s) needed for the resolution.

If you used the Bone Diagram in Chapter 3 (see Figures 3.4 and 3.5) or tried the Five Whys approach to root cause analysis, you may already be thinking of some apparent solutions to issues. Following up by using the Fishbone Diagram may add to or validate your suspicions. Excellent! If you've used these methods to find possible solutions, then go ahead and implement your quick fix. Monitor progress to determine if the fix creates the results you anticipated. In many cases, that's all it will take. However,

FIGURE 6.14

Fishbone Process for Problem Solving

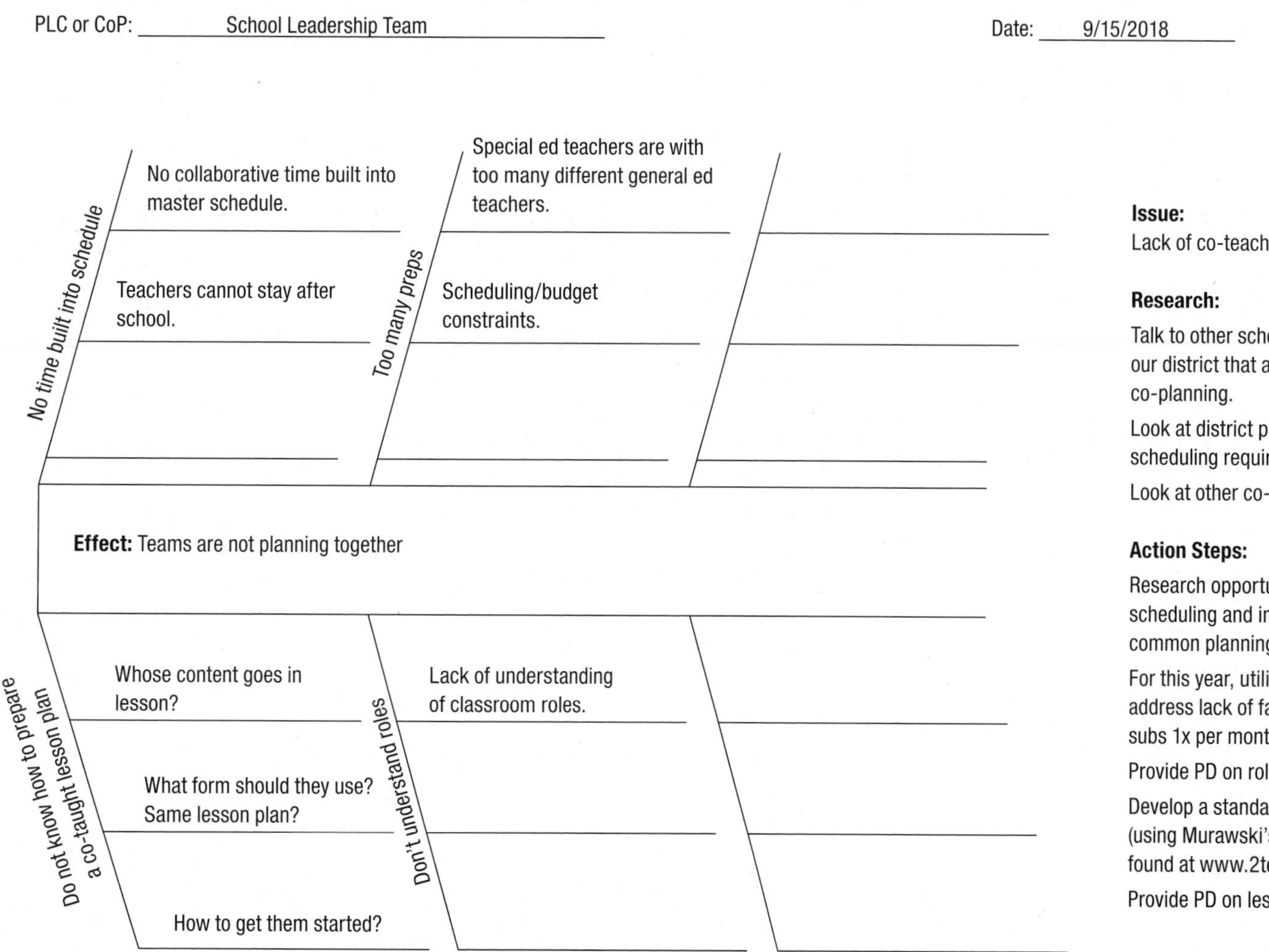

we are going to go out on a limb and assume that not all problems can be solved with a quick fix. For these problems, it is important to proceed to the next analysis step.

Using Results of a Root Cause Analysis

Let's consider a situation in which the root cause analysis indicates that administrative logistics appear to be constraining progress on a co-teaching proficiency. Don't be surprised if this happens. Common concerns include master scheduling issues, insufficient or nonexistent co-planning time for teams, inadequate use of paraprofessionals, lack of professional development, unclear or inconsistent administrative support, and the like (Murawski & Dieker, 2013; Scruggs, Mastropieri & McDuffie, 2007). No matter what the results of your root cause analysis, own them! Your co-teaching leadership PLC should provide co-teaching teams with the collected data for them to review. Try to avoid making excuses or hiding the results if you disagree with them. As we said earlier, even if *you* think teams have sufficient time or resources, the fact that *they* think they do not is an issue to address. So, own the data and meet with co-teaching teams to discuss your schoolwide results. The fact that administrators and leadership teams are willing to look at and discuss data that might reflect poorly on them makes it that much easier later when you ask teachers to do the same at the classroom level.

Not all results will point to administrative and logistical concerns, however. Some of the results for less-than-optimal co-teaching outcomes will be specific to the co-teaching team. When identified competencies and areas of concern can be pinpointed for co-teachers, they will be able to engage in the microteaching aspect of the CTIME process. During microteaching sessions, co-teachers will plan, teach, reflect, and receive feedback to enhance specific subskills from the core competencies identified as needing work. In Chapter 7, we will focus more on applying the CTIME process to individual classroom co-teachers. For now, let's keep the focus on the schoolwide level.

You've looked at the data and you've determined whether issues are systemic or team-based. You've handed off your data to the appropriate individuals—perhaps the co-teaching leadership PLC or your principal or the co-teaching teams themselves. As you prepare for the next and final step of this process, your leadership team needs to be ready to provide any necessary support and assistance in removing barriers. Your goal is to help change occur so that there can be continuous improvement. Don't forget—this is a process. And the entire process begins again as you complete the subsequent observations and surveys throughout the school year. Keep referring to the focus competencies you selected to address your vision. Were those goals met, and were they sustained throughout the school year? As data continue to come in, your team should be meeting regularly and asking:

- What do the data affirm?
- Has there been improvement? If not, why not?
- Were our goals met? If not, why not?
- What are the trends indicating? Are we moving closer to our vision?

Developing Action Steps and Strategies

You've planned a vision and determined focus competencies. You've collected data through observations and surveys. You've analyzed those results to see if any problems are systemic or team-based, and you have determined some root causes. Whew! You've been busy. Well done. Unfortunately, you can't rest on those laurels. Now you have to do something about your results. We know, we know. Life's rough. But you've got this.

This is all about a continuous improvement *cycle*. That means that the first time you do this, you'll be writing down your original goals and how you are going to address them. But you'll come back around to this stage again! At that point, your co-teaching leadership PLC, or whatever committee or team is leading the charge on co-teaching improvement at your school, continues the cycle by reviewing and acknowledging what improvements provided the most impact. Your team will discuss how the improvement efforts have been generalized into and displayed in the co-taught classrooms (or not). This is a time to reflect on the strategies used for improvement and a time to determine if there is a way to potentially prevent deficiencies, barriers, or problems in the future. This is a process of improvement; please do not expect everything to be perfect right away.

Is the school where it should be on each of the focus and core competencies? If so, that's fantastic! It's time to move to the next cycle by establishing the next round of goals. If all of the focus competencies were met during the first round of the PDSA process, well—first of all, you rock—but second, continue on. It is time to progress to the remaining co-teaching competencies. With this laser-like focus on a few co-teaching core competencies at a time, your skills in co-teaching will be acquired very rapidly, your outcomes will improve, and your school will revel in its culture of collaboration. We may be getting a bit dramatic here, but seriously, you will be proud of your progress.

Much of the literature on PLCs suggests that the most productive teams set attainable goals (DuFour, DuFour, Eaker, & Many, 2010). Not crazy, pie-in-the-sky goals, though. "We strongly recommend that goals established by collaborative teams should be attainable. Teams should feel reasonably confident they have the capacity to achieve their goals" (DuFour, DuFour, Eaker, & Many, 2006, p. 137). Were your goals attainable? Have you attained them? If so, as we mentioned in Chapter 5, start celebrating those hits! The co-teaching leadership team must celebrate when the school hits its goals. Once you've received data, identify any hits where you reached your goal for the collection. How many hits were there? Let co-teaching teams and the broader community know about those successes so that there is positive reinforcement for whatever changes or behaviors were in place to move the scores forward (see Figure 6.15).

Want to show teacher parity on the report card? Consider hyphenating the two names as if they are one. That way, you can still demonstrate that there is a highly qualified content teacher as the teacher of record, but both names are now on the students' report cards.

It would be lovely to say that you are done now. But this is where the *continuous* part of continuous improvement comes in: There is always something you can do to get better. Look back at your data. What is needed? Is there a particular competency with which teachers are struggling? Can you identify a systematic root cause? For example, all teams report that they cannot show true parity on report cards because the administration hasn't figured out a way to put two names on the report card. Or perhaps you've noted a lack of specially designed instruction (King-Sears & Bowman-Kruhm, 2011), universal design for learning (UDL) strategies (Ashton, 2015), or strong Tier 1 instruction (Murawski & Hughes, 2009) from teams overall, and you know that all of the teachers at your school might struggle in that regard. Perhaps this is an area where you will want to seek outside resources or support from the central office to bring in individuals who can work with teachers on their UDL and differentiation techniques. This can be beneficial to all teachers in your school, but it was derived from your co-teaching data analysis. What will you do as a team to make improvements on the specified competency? Figure 6.16 illustrates what problems and solutions might look like at the schoolwide level.

As you work on developing strategies for the schoolwide Corrective Action Plan, it is helpful to keep your school leadership perspective. This unique frame of reference is different from when your co-teaching teams work on identifying their goals and strategies, because they will be approaching the task from a personal or classroom level. You need to approach this process from a macro, big picture, and schoolwide level. You are considering overall school resources, needs, time frames, barriers, and strengths. Because the schoolwide co-teaching leadership PLC comprises various stakeholders with different frames of reference and resources, all of these views will have a voice in creating goals and strategies for improvement.

FIGURE 6.15

Corrective Action Plan (CAP) Form—Moving Scores Forward

Corrective Action Plan (CAP) Form												
Focus	Team	Murawski & Lochner	Content Area		Science							
	School Term	2018–19	Grade		8			Period		2nd		
X	LOOK FORS		SS 1	SS 2	Obs 1	Obs 2	Obs 3	Obs 4	S1	S2	F1	F2
X	4.5 Two or more professionals working together in the same physical space.	*0 = Only one adult; two adults not communicating at all; class always divided into two rooms.*			1	1						
X		*1 = Two adults in same room, but very little communication or collaborative work.*	Goals:			(1)						
		2 = Two adults in same room; both engaged in class and each other (even if not perfectly).	PIE:									
		3 = Two adults collaborating together well in the same room.	Ease:	0	Impact:	3	Rank:					
	Next Steps:											
X	9.5 Class environment demonstrates parity and collaboration (both names on board, sharing materials and space).	*0 = No demonstration of parity/collaboration; room appears to belong to one teacher only.*			0	0						
X		*1 = Some attempt at parity; both adults share a few materials and general space.*	Goals:			1						
		2 = Parity exists; adults share classroom materials.	PIE:									
		3 = Clear parity; both names on board/report card; two desks or shared space; obvious feeling from teacher that it is "our room."	Ease:	0	Impact:	3	Rank:					
	Next Steps:											
X	11.6 Both teachers begin and end class together and remain in the room the entire time.	*0 = One adult is absent or late; adults may leave room for times not related to this class.*			1	3						
X		*1 = One adult may be late or leave early or may leave for brief time.*	Goals:			(2)						
		2 = One adult may be late or leave early, but for remaining time they work together.	PIE:									
		3 = Both adults begin and end together, and are with students the entire time.	Ease:	1	Impact:	3	Rank:					
		Note: if adults have planned to use a regrouping approach (e.g., "parallel") and one adult takes a group of students out of the room (e.g., to the library), that is perfectly acceptable.										

FIGURE 6.16

Examples of Problems and Solutions at the Schoolwide Level

- **Problem**: ***Teachers aren't co-planning. There is no built-in planning time.***
  School-level solutions: Rework master schedule for next semester to build in common planning times. Hire substitute teachers once a month for this semester to help teachers get through. Help teachers gain access to electronic planning forms (e.g., www.2TeachLLC.com, Google Docs) so that they can plan when they are not together.
- **Problem: *Major schoolwide discussion and disagreement about assessments and grading, especially for students who receive accommodations and modifications.***
  School-level solutions: Do book study of *Fair Isn't Always Equal: Assessing and Grading in the Differentiated Classroom* (Wormeli, 2006) with the whole school. Have special educators do quick presentations at faculty meetings regarding the difference between accommodation and modification. Get together representatives to discuss grading issues at the school.

Closing Thoughts

Having a schoolwide co-teaching leadership team or PLC looking at the data and trends will ensure that there is a group in the school dedicated to spearheading efforts to improve co-teaching schoolwide. This is the launching point for terrific co-teaching. Because this group starts by ensuring a vision and identifying key co-teaching competencies, it can help make the CTIME process become an inclusive one. This is not about identifying which individual teams are doing well; it is about creating a more systemic approach to using co-teaching as a viable service delivery option. It is about building capacity and institutionalizing a process for improvement, rather than being surprised by differing outcomes each year. This team will help determine if necessary changes are related to school or team needs. Schoolwide goals and change will be accomplished through this PDSA process. As a recap, use Figure 6.17 to remind yourselves of the steps your co-teaching leadership PLC will take when using CTIME at the schoolwide level. You saw this figure in Chapter 3 (as Figure 3.3). We think that this time it will make a lot more sense to you!

FIGURE 6.17

The CTIME Process: Schoolwide Application in Five Easy Steps

PLAN	
Step 1	Craft your vision for co-teaching and determine focus competencies.
DO	
Step 2	Prepare the data collection schedule and PIE—Performance, Impact, and Ease— scores.
Step 3	Conduct observations and collect data on the corrective action plan.
STUDY	
Step 4	Analyze the data and conduct a root cause analysis (as needed).
ACT	
Step 5	Develop action steps and strategies and celebrate successes.

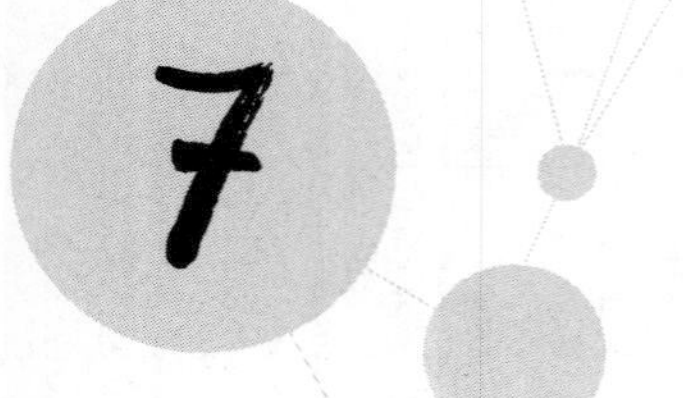

7 Team Time: Communities of Practice and Microteaching

Take-Aways

- *Communities of Practice (CoPs) are collaborative groups focused on problem solving, sharing of resources and strategies, and moving innovation forward.*
- *CoP facilitators are critical for helping CoP members share, question, research, and problem solve for improving co-teaching practices.*
- *Microteaching is a process whereby co-teachers focus on one specific competency for a 10- to 15-minute lesson and video-record the lesson for future analysis.*

Communities of Practice

Your co-teaching leadership PLC is a committed group of teachers, administrators, and others who are willing to look at your school overall and communicate about trends, strengths, needs, and next steps. Those conversations are focused at the macro level and are necessary, but they aren't the final step. You also need to look at what is happening in the classroom and at the individual teacher-team level. It can be difficult for teachers to hear feedback or be told what to change by individuals who aren't walking their walk. A principal may not know what it is like to co-teach algebra to a group of struggling learners. Even an "expert" in co-teaching hired to come in and share expertise won't know the specific culture of that school or that group of teachers. And, as we said in Chapter 3, research shows that professional development that is not internalized or that has very little buy-in does not result in meaningful change (Lumpe, 2007; Strauss, 2014). Co-teachers may be able to look at their data and make decisions about what core competencies they want to work on, but then what? Who can they go to for collegial feedback and to help problem solve when they are stuck or perhaps disagree with their partner about something? Enter the CoP! Communities of practices are the entities that ensure buy-in, problem solving, and action (Hughes, Jewson, & Unwin, 2013; Vaughn & Dornan, 2014).

The next step in the CTIME process then is to create these communities of practice (CoPs). CoPs are not the same as PLCs. These are essentially going to be your co-teaching work groups, but members of these groups will *want* to work because they are identifying and solving their own problems! Barab and Duffy (2000) recognized that learning as a part of a CoP was a powerful and useful model for teacher professional learning. Instead of the old-school methods of having professional development be a "sit and get" session of delivery of information, the CoP favors learning as knowledge constructed through collaboration, projects, and problem solving

(Dirckinck-Holmfeld, 2002). Remember that we are trying to change from being "professionally developed" by someone else to engaging in our own personalized professional *learning*! This goes back to Miller's Pyramid and our Co-Teaching Competency Pyramid (see Figures 3.9 and 3.10 for a refresher). Application and "doing" are far more powerful than just being told about something new.

Wenger (1998) provided a foundational definition of communities of practice as *"groups of people who share a concern or a passion for something they do and who interact regularly to learn how to do it better."* That certainly sounds good to us, but we've adapted Wenger's definition for the purposes of our work on co-teaching:

Co-teaching communities of practice (CoPs) are defined as groups of educators who share co-teaching as a common problem of practice (PoP). Problems of practice are key topics of conversation in schools these days. School administrators of Ohio write that:

> *"A Problem of Practice should be the focus of staff attention. Teachers will need training and continued support to address a meaningful Problem of Practice. It is something staff genuinely doesn't know how to do and is trying to learn more about and get better at. A rich problem of practice:*
>
> - *Focuses on the instructional core—what teachers and students are doing and the content being addressed.*
> - *Is directly observable.*
> - *Is actionable—is within the school's/district's control and can be improved in real time.*
> - *Connects to a broader strategy of improvement—school, feeder pattern, system.*
> - *Is high-leverage—if acted upon, it would make a significant difference for student learning.*
> - *Promotes deep learning (e.g., higher levels on Bloom's Taxonomy) for teachers and students.*
>
> *In short, the problem of practice is something that you care about that would make a difference for student learning if you improved it (www.sai-iowa.org/library/Ohio%20Identifying%20a%20POP/)."*

Clearly, co-teaching meets the criteria as a "problem of practice." Thus, a co-teaching CoP would come together to fulfill both individual or group goals through solving problems, sharing practices, providing feedback, and creating new knowledge and skills to advance the teaching and learning of all students.

We wanted to be more specific, because it is important that we clarify what CoPs are and what the expectation of a co-teaching CoP would be. Being part of a co-teaching CoP means that you will have multiple

Co-teaching communities of practice (CoPs): *share domain (interest in quality), practice (knowledge and experiences), and community (interactions and progress monitoring).*

experiences with co-teaching itself, as well as immediate access to a wide range of co-teaching expertise within your community of professionals. You will be able to share your experiences with others who are also co-teaching and who are sharing their own experiences with you. Wenger's work teaches us that three components differentiate a community of practice from any other community (e.g., a neighborhood, an organization): *domain, practice*, and *community*. When these three components come together, they are able to help a group learn, build their own skills, and begin to adopt practices that move the group forward. Figure 7.1 has been adapted from Wenger's work and applied to our efforts here.

FIGURE 7.1

The Components of a Community of Practice

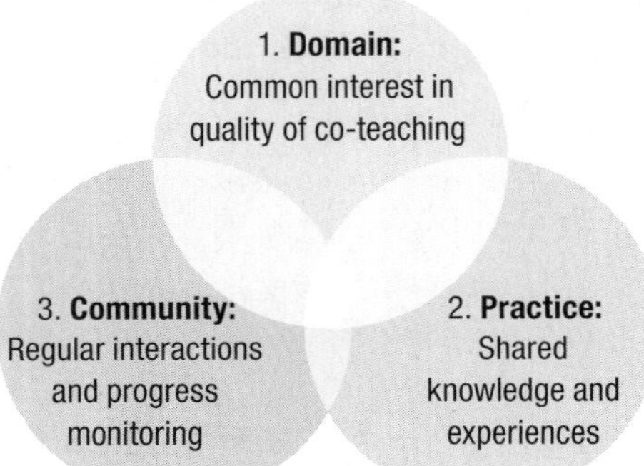

Source: Adapted with permission from Wenger, E. (2006). *Communities of Practice: A Brief Introduction.* http://www.ewenger.com/theory/communities_of_practice_intro.htm.

Component One: Domain

The first component is termed the *domain.* In this case, we have a group with a common interest in the quality of their teaching (specifically, co-teaching). By being part of this CoP, members demonstrate a commitment to improving their quality of co-teaching; thereby, this shared commitment distinguishes them from other individuals.

Technology can help create a community. Create a safe site for members to upload lessons, blog experiences, and ask questions. We recommend Google+ and Office 365. Padlets are fun, too!

Component Two: Practice

The second component focuses on *practice.* Note that this is different from the co-teaching leadership PLC, in which not all members need to be co-teachers. The co-teaching PLC is tasked with obtaining a macro view of co-teaching, so having administrators, coaches, and parents on that team makes sense. In the case of a CoP, everyone is co-teaching and all CoP members have shared knowledge, experiences, and practices. Because they are all "living" co-teaching, they will also be developing a shared repertoire of resources. These resources might include their personal experiences and anecdotes, strategies, and tools for working within inclusive settings, techniques for addressing situations and particular students, and the like. In short, this is a shared practice. It takes time and sustained interaction. CoP members will learn to trust one another and subsequently be more willing to share these experiences, resources, and ideas.

Component Three: Community

The third component centers on *community*. This group will meet frequently and interact regularly. They will share experiences, analyze data together, problem solve, create action plans, microteach, observe one another's classes, provide feedback, and monitor progress. Because of their commitment to improving their own co-teaching skills, members are more willing to engage in discussion, share information, and help one another within their CoP. Consider natural communities within your school. If there are only three co-teaching teams in the whole school, that will be your co-teaching CoP. If there are many teams, however, you might have an early elementary CoP and an upper elementary CoP, or you might have a math CoP, an English CoP, a science CoP, and a social studies CoP. This shared commitment, development of trust, willingness to support one another with strategies and ideas, and ongoing communication results in relationships that allow CoP members to learn from one another and build skills. These three components not only describe a CoP, but they also clearly demonstrate why such groups engender buy-in and result in positive outcomes.

Don't have enough co-teaching teams for a community of practice? Reach out! Schools in the Los Angeles Unified School District created CoPs around co-teaching within their focus schools and teams shared across the district.

Whereas the co-teaching leadership PLC looks at macro-level data and makes decisions that will influence the culture of co-teaching schoolwide, the co-teaching CoPs might be engaging in a variety of activities that will move the needle forward on their classroom co-teaching effectiveness. Figure 7.2 offers some examples of activities for a successful co-teaching CoP; they were adapted from the work of WestEd (2012).

Your co-teaching CoPs are not intended as a group of people who come together just to vent or share their most recent classroom experiences. CoPs must have a common and clear purpose, which is driven by data. In this case, our purpose is to identify problems that teams are having implementing co-teaching best practices. Essentially, what's not happening that should be happening in the co-taught classroom, and why? This is more than just anecdotal sharing; it is data-driven. As part of the CTIME protocol, CoP members will learn to analyze their individual and CoP data to isolate areas of concern and areas of strength. Bring your PLATEs to the meeting! By using the co-teaching core competencies, all community members will know and understand the expectations for true co-teaching. This common goal drives a clear action plan that is important to the success of a CoP.

FIGURE 7.2

Potential Activities for a Co-Teaching Community of Practice

Action	Examples
Requesting information	*Where can I find examples of how to embed effective formative assessment strategies during station teaching? What if we have a huge range of diversity in terms of ability in our class?*
Seeking experience	*Has anyone started writing their co-taught unit plans for language arts yet? What suggestions can you share with those of us just starting? How might they differ from solo-taught unit plans?*
Coordinating efforts	*Let's share responsibility for the development of our success criteria for our co-taught geometry unit. Our team can come up with criteria for students with disabilities if your team will come up with ones for students who are high-achieving or gifted.*
Analyzing data	*What trends are apparent across our students' work? Are there commonalities that might mean we need to include more differentiation strategies or adaptations for special learners?*
Solving problems	*Can we generate some ideas for how to use a regrouping approach (like parallel, station, or alternative teaching) for this science unit? We're stuck. (Don't forget that we've provided some problem-solving tools in Chapter 6.)*
Discussing developments	*What are we learning from our use of parallel teaching so far? Has it been helpful? What do you think? How might we improve?*
Documenting efforts	*Let's record these assessment adaptations so that we can all refer to them when we design our units next week. We don't want to reinvent the wheel.*
Planning visits	*Could our team observe how your team uses alternative teaching in your lessons? It sounds like you are able to use it for re-teaching as well as enrichment. What would be a useful way to discuss what we saw after we visit?*
Building agreement for action	*What microteaching lessons shall we each commit to trying in our classrooms before we meet next?*
Identifying and addressing gaps	*We need to understand how to improve our outcomes with our English-language learners. We have used a bunch of strategies, but they are still not as effective as we'd like. Who might we consult about this?*
Reflecting on group processes	*How can we improve our meetings? How can we improve our follow-through on our Corrective Action Plan commitments?*
Sharing resources	*We just read this great book on co-teaching and found a helpful, short webinar. Anyone interested in the link?*

Source: Wenger, E., (2006). *Communities of Practice: A Brief Introduction.* Retrieved from http://www.ewenger.com/theory/communities_of_practice_intro.htm; and WestEd. (2012). *Becoming a successful community of practice facilitator: Linking learning and assessment in Rhode Island schools.* Retrieved from http://www.ride.ri.gov/Portals/0/Uploads/Documents/Instruction-and-Assessment-World-Class-Standards/Assessment/Formative-Assessment-PD-Online-Modules/Becoming_a_Successful_CoP_Facilitator.pdf.

Benefits of a Community of Practice

Communities of practice provide co-teachers with various benefits. Think about how different co-teaching really is. Teachers who have for years taught only by themselves are now being asked to share the classroom, to share the "business of teaching" with someone else. That can be scary! We recognize that not everyone who is co-teaching is quite on board with this concept. Others might like the idea but are still struggling with how to do it most effectively and least painfully. Participants in the CTIME process often find they can manage this change of teaching when it is dealt with in a CoP and when they are working with others through the nuances. Going through the process with a community helps co-teachers develop trust among themselves and with all the other educators who are experiencing this way of teaching that is new for so many of them (Guillemin et al., 2016). This group ensures that teachers have access to new knowledge and a forum for venting, questioning, and sharing in a safe and trusting community. Research has shown that this type of professional learning network for job support and community ultimately increases job satisfaction, reduces burnout, and helps retain teachers who might otherwise be struggling alone with the implementation of co-teaching (Trust, Krutka, & Carpenter, 2016). In a study on reducing teacher burnout, Pietarinen, Pyhältö, Soini, and Salmela-Aro (2013) write that "Our results indicate that teachers can learn strategies that allow them to reduce burnout and construct a better working environment fit, which may further promote their well-being at work. This implies that a good fit cannot be achieved by merely adapting to the working environment, but rather by actively modifying the environment together with others" (p. 69).

There are myriad benefits to being in a CoP focused on a topic that affects you daily. We know it can feel overwhelming to add another collaborative activity to your regular agenda, but meeting a few times a semester with a group focused on supporting you and sharing ideas will be worth it! Additional benefits include the following:

- Learning from colleagues, rather than merely being told what to do by outside "experts."
- Being with others from your school who think like you do. They share your experiences, your context, and often your students.
- Spending time focused on collaborating to achieve outcomes you and your team have determined are important, rather than spending time listening to someone else talk.
- Building your own teaching toolbox as you get feedback and ideas from your colleagues.

- Feeling validated by your peers as you share your own experiences, ideas, and skills.
- Using your time efficiently and productively on a topic that has a daily effect on you.
- Focusing your attention on improving one particular area, rather than continuing to be spread so thin. Research has found that focused application accelerates learning, which means you'll do more in less time.
- Focusing your attention on how to improve co-teaching at your school, which will result in innovation and improvement that can only benefit you, your colleagues, and your students.

Let's tie these benefits back to your PLATE. Having a community of like-minded colleagues who are struggling with, and benefiting from, co-teaching in the same way you are provides you and your partner with a forum for problem solving. As a result of conversations within your CoP, you will be able to identify what you and your partner want to do next to improve your co-teaching practices. There is a place on your PLATE for you to write these next steps (see Figure 7.3). Members of your CoP may suggest additional resources, strategies, and actions for you to take. These too have a place to be documented on your PLATE. Our goal is for your PLATE to help you organize all of this information in one place: It includes not just the data you have on your progress, but also your plan of action detailing how you will use the data to improve. Your CoP is the place for sharing best practices, ideas, and strategies; everyone benefits from this type of collaboration! As we discuss the CoP life cycle in the next section, keep in mind that your partner and your CoP are there to help you navigate those times when you feel stressed, overwhelmed, or frustrated. They are the colleagues who will understand, because they are living the same experience as you. Use one another as a support system and use the CTIME process as a way to reinforce baby steps, balance, and continual forward progress!

Community of Practice Life Cycle

Wenger, McDermott, and Snyder (2002) found that most CoPs move through definitive stages. These are often referred to as the *CoP life cycle*. Interestingly, Bolam and colleagues (2005) also found that PLCs have a similar life cycle. Figure 7.4 shows how these life-cycle stages can be adapted to a co-teaching CoP.

As mentioned earlier, the CTIME protocol is about providing an opportunity for personalized professional learning. Therefore, we don't prescribe what each CoP will work on, when, or for how long. CoPs determine themselves what needs to be worked on, and they develop their own action plans. CoPs monitor their own progress and report back to the co-teaching leadership PLC regarding how they are meeting their goals (or not, as the case may be). Teachers are encouraged to stay in their specific CoP until their community members are successful and practices are sustainable. When that happens and professional development is no longer needed in a given area, then it will be time for the CoP to disband. Before then, however, we reflect on how Murawski and Dieker (2013) stated unequivocally in their book *Leading the Co-Teaching Dance* that if administrators have a good co-teaching team, they should "leave them alone!" We feel the same about co-teaching CoPs. We caution administrators to leave them alone and let them build rapport, share ideas, problem solve around the data, and not be broken up before the work is done and teams are successful. This may take time, but if you allow for that time, you will certainly have *no-fail co-teaching*!

FIGURE 7.3

Next Steps on Your PLATE

Focus	Team	Murawski & Lochner	Content Area		Social Studies							
	School Term	2018–19	Grade		8			Period		2nd		
X	**LOOK FORS**		SS 1	SS 2	Obs 1	Obs 2	Obs 3	Obs 4	S1	S2	F1	F2
X	4.5 Two or more professionals working together in the same physical space.	*0 = Only one adult; two adults not communicating at all; class always divided into two rooms.*	2		1							
		1 = Two adults in same room, but very little communication or collaborative work.	**Goals:**			2						
		2 = Two adults in same room; both engaged in class and each other (even if not perfectly).	**PIE:**		-2							
		3 = Two adults collaborating together well in the same room.	**Ease:**	0	**Impact:**		**Rank:**					

Next Steps: *General education teacher will provide lessons ahead of time so that special education teacher will have some background information until that time when we can plan together. Special education teacher will make adaptations to lesson plans where needed and communicate those back to the general education teacher prior to class time. We will utilize this process from our CoP colleague team White & Hilton and look at how they use their lesson plan as a communication tool to assist during class time.*

FIGURE 7.4

Life Cycle of a Community of Practice

COMMITTING	STARTING UP	OPERATING	SLOWING DOWN	TERMINATING
Data analysis determines CoPs are necessary	Co-teaching teams are identified and put into CoPs	Co-teaching teams participate in microteaching sessions	Co-teaching teams participate in fewer microteaching sessions as they master competencies	Co-teaching practices become pervasive and sustainable

CoPs are rooted in the collegial support found so critical in professional development research. Remember that from Chapter 3? They facilitate the ability to grow knowledge and practices internally rather than looking externally for professional learning. They are a great way to answer the question: How do we move an entire school forward in their expertise in co-teaching? Naturally, this improvement is most effective when the community institutionalizes the changes experienced as being part of the community. We don't want educators to feel that they spent hours of their time problem solving around co-teaching, with no outcomes to show for it. A major goal of the problem solving that CoPs do is not merely to determine short-term solutions, but also to identify long-term solutions that can be implemented and sustained (Saint Onge & Wallace, 2012). CoP members can share their insights with the schoolwide PLC if they come up with ideas that might need to be implemented at the schoolwide level, rather than just in individual teacher's classrooms. All of the time spent analyzing data, finding resources, reviewing and trying strategies, and sharing outcomes needs to result in change for the better. We want change that helps create capacity building and sustained practices.

The Role of the Collaborative Group Facilitator

We hope that by now you are sold on the idea of a co-teaching leadership PLC and on smaller co-teaching CoPs around particular areas (e.g., a co-teaching math CoP or a co-teaching 5th grade CoP). Although a major component of each of these committees is the communication and collaboration that are their hallmark, we know that these things do not happen in a vacuum. It is critical for collaborative teams to develop norms; discuss guidelines for participation and sharing; and establish shared accountability, resources, and expectations (Friend & Cook, 2016; Murawski & Spencer, 2011). We have also found that most of our successful schools identified an individual to be the facilitator of said groups (Wenger et al., 2002; WestEd, 2012). In some cases, the schools had designated a co-teaching coordinator; in other schools, the facilitator was merely someone who had strong organizational and communication skills and who did not mind filling that role. In any case, such a facilitator must have specific skills and take certain actions to maximize the effectiveness and comfort level of participants on a collaborative team.

Wenger and colleagues' work on CoP facilitation is excellent, as is the adaptation and synthesis of their work that WestEd did. We have adapted their suggested roles and responsibilities for co-teaching facilitators of collaborative groups (see Figure 7.5). Consider these tasks when identifying possible educators to fill the role of co-teaching coordinator or CoP

No one willing to step up as the co-teaching facilitator? Share the fun! As long as all members understand the roles and expectations, tasks can be shared. Ask members to keep one another accountable for their individual pieces of the puzzle.

FIGURE 7.5

Collaborative Group Facilitator Roles and Responsibilities

Role	Responsibilities
Organizer	• Arrange meeting space and times • Communicate meeting times and agendas to teammates • Prepare materials and activities for each CoP session
Guide	• Customize session plans to meet CoP's learning needs • Reinforce guiding principles and effective norms of collaboration • Facilitate dialogue that enables teachers to link their learning with their instructional practice and the school's context on co-teaching • Foster reflection on results from the Co-Teaching Core Competencies Observation Checklist and microteaching lessons
Supporter	• Encourage risk-taking, learning from mistakes, and group trust • Support individual co-teaching teams' learning needs • Provide extended learning opportunities (e.g., teams observe each other, book studies on co-teaching, teams visit other schools)
Documenter	• Record the group's understandings, experiments, and learning • Document how CoP meetings and feedback affect co-teacher observation scores and microteaching scores over time
Historian	• Remind participants of their previous learning • Link each new session with the learning from previous sessions • Follow up on the group's identified action steps

Source: Adapted from WestEd. (2012). *Becoming a Successful Community of Practice Facilitator: Linking Learning and Assessment in Rhode Island Schools.* Retrieved from http://www.ride.ri.gov/Portals/0/Uploads/Documents/Instruction-and-Assessment-World-Class-Standards/Assessment/Formative-Assessment-PD-Online-Modules/Becoming_a_Successful_CoP_Facilitator.pdf.

facilitator. Is the person you have in mind organized? Does he or she communicate well? Is he or she well respected by his or her peers? If a conversation begins to become heated or go off on a tangent, does this person have the skills to mediate, interrupt without offending, and get the group back on track? The goal is to find someone who truly wants co-teaching to be successful and is able to stay relentlessly positive, while still allowing participants to share experiences, frustrations, needs, and questions in a safe environment.

Let's say you've identified an individual to act as your co-teaching facilitator. That person is willing to take on the roles of organizer, guide, supporter, documenter, and historian. Or that person is willing and able to delegate said roles as needed. Well done! (Was it you? It was, wasn't it?) Regardless, agreeing to have these responsibilities covered is just the first step. Groups need someone who is also adept at techniques geared to engage group members. Luckily, we are educators and most of these strategies should come relatively naturally to us.

Needs of Group Members

Group members need opportunities to reflect, explore, and consider the different ideas that come up during PLC or CoP collaborative meetings. Every participant needs to feel safe and trust that the group is focused on supporting one another in co-teaching improvement. You will be looking at data; some participants might feel evaluated or start to become defensive about their scores. It can be helpful if the facilitator creates opportunities for individual and partner sharing during CoP meetings. Things don't need to be too formal, but having some structures in place to encourage everyone to share will reduce the possibility that one person feels singled out, or that one person over-participates, or that one person avoids participating at all. If your group is small, you might think that having structured activities for sharing will feel forced or unnecessary. However, even in small collaborative groups, activities like "think-pair-shares," journaling, and paired dialogue have been found to be meaningful and result in better outcomes (WestEd, 2012). Figure 7.6 suggests some ways your facilitator can engage the collaborative group members. This figure was adapted from the work of WestEd and applied to our CTIME protocol. See? We are all about collaborating and learning from others! We are very willing to "stand on the shoulders of giants" (Newton, 1676) in order to move forward. The entire CTIME process has been crafted by combining great research, articles, and data on evidence-based best practices in collaboration and instruction; we merely pulled it all together in a systematic and practical process.

FIGURE 7.6

Activities for Collaborative Meetings

Goal	Description
Provide Time to Get Focused on Learning	Educators are busy! It can be difficult to settle into a meeting if you are concurrently thinking about today's classes, all the work you have to grade, and what you are making for dinner. Facilitators can ask colleagues to reflect on recent efforts to improve co-teaching by looking at their goal sheets, microteaching reflections, or recent core competency observation forms. This reflection also helps the facilitator figure out how to further engage participants during the meeting.
Provide Personal "Think Time"	We have already emphasized reflection, and we will continue to do so. "In order for people to think deeply about cognitively complex material or situations, such as co-teaching, there must be time for reflection. Cognitive science literature from the 1970s referred to this as the '10-2' rule. For every 10 minutes of presentation time, there should be 2 minutes of personal reflection. Individual reflection can be structured as a simple pause in the dialogue, a written reflection, or a 'think-pair-share' activity" (WestEd, 2012, p. 9).
Create Frequent Opportunities for Paired Dialogue	No one will want to share in a hostile or judgmental environment. Facilitators need to ensure the group feels safe, and paired dialogue can do that. "Paired dialogue creates a cognitive safety zone, where a person can try things out, hear what something sounds like, or get confirmation about an idea before bringing it to the entire group" (WestEd, 2012, p. 9). Because co-teachers are partners, this makes a lot of sense. Have them share their own reflections before asking them to share them out with the CoP.
Provide Structured Small-Group Dialogue	The whole purpose of a collaborative group meeting, such as the PLC or CoP, is to give and receive feedback around a shared topic, such as co-teaching. Small-group dialogue helps accomplish this. "Small groups of three to five allow everyone to participate, provide some diversity of opinion, and allow teams to get feedback on the approaches or strategies they are trying" in their inclusive, co-taught class (WestEd, 2012, p. 9).

Source: Adapted from WestEd. (2012). *Becoming a Successful Community of Practice Facilitator: Linking Learning and Assessment in Rhode Island schools.* Retrieved from http://www.ride.ri.gov/Portals/0/Uploads/Documents/Instruction-and-Assessment-World-Class-Standards/Assessment/Formative-Assessment-PD-Online-Modules/Becoming_a_Successful_CoP_Facilitator.pdf.

Needs of Facilitators

Facilitators of collaborative work groups need, by default, to be prepared to address problematic group dynamics. If you can have pairs and small groups talk about issues themselves, before discussing a problem with the larger group, this will help reduce tensions and surprises. These smaller groups or teams, even within the relatively small PLC or CoP meeting, also help keep all group members engaged, focused, and participating. Thus, facilitators don't have to worry as much about group members who want to use the meeting to vent about a personal issue, those who would rather use the time to catch up on grading, or those who have a hard time staying on task or staying focused. As a colleague, which most facilitators are, it can be hard to address these issues in a larger group setting; it is much easier to do so with an individual teacher or a pair of co-teachers. Strong facilitators are proactive in creating agendas, having structures, managing conversations, watching time, and building in small-group work from the very beginning so that it becomes the norm, rather than an uncomfortable added activity. It is important to let participants know how meetings will be run. According to WestEd (2012), "Small-group work can significantly change the dynamic and make the entire meeting more productive" (p. 9).

It's time to move on. You've developed your CoP and you have your facilitator. You are ready for team sharing and discussions. What now? A major task of the CoP is to provide a forum whereby co-teaching team members can share their lessons and practices and get honest and helpful feedback for improvement. In order to do so, each co-teaching team will engage in what is called the microteaching process. We hope you are intrigued, considering that we've been alluding to this whole microteaching thing since we introduced CTIME!

Microteaching

Microteaching is a nonevaluative technique used for practice, personal reflection, and skill development. Microteaching has been around quite a while. Dwight Allen designed the concept back in the 1960s as a professor at Stanford University. Allen's model required educators to plan for a lesson, videotape themselves teaching the lesson, and then reflect on the lesson as they watched the videotape with other educators. Those other educators would then provide constructive criticism and thoughts after the teachers shared their own reflections and analysis (Otsupius, 2014; Zimpher & Howie, 2013). You can already see how this fits nicely in with the CTIME model, can't you? We hope so.

Microteaching: *a method by which educators plan, video-record, and reflect on a minilesson in order to focus on improving a particular skill.*

Many teacher training institutions continue to use this microteaching process with new teachers, student teachers, and interns. In fact, the National Board for Professional Teaching Standards uses a very similar process, in which national board candidates have to plan a lesson, video-record themselves, and then send in their lessons with their reflections. Interestingly, though, not only don't many schools use microteaching as part of their professional development practices, but many teachers also shy away from video-recording themselves altogether! This becomes even more "interesting" (notice how we use the word *interesting* as a euphemism when what we really mean is "sad") when you look at the research data on microteaching outcomes.

We've mentioned Hattie's popular text on *Visible Learning*. In it, Hattie (2012) provided an effect size for various educational interventions for which meta-analyses on research have been conducted. The first outcome within the "teacher" domain (with an effect size of .88), and the fourth by overall ranking, is . . . wait for it . . . microteaching! After reviewing various research articles that included microteaching, Hattie says, "[T]he conclusion was that all components should be included: theory, demonstration and practice, as well as feedback and coaching, preferably in a distributed rather than condensed manner across many sessions" (p. 112). Hmm. This sounds suspiciously like what we have been promoting all along!

Typically, microteaching is a very individualized training technique; however, it is adapted here for use with two teachers who are co-teaching. Thus, each teacher will need to commit to working collaboratively and using the best practices necessary to make co-teaching successful. This will indeed take collaboration, but you knew that, didn't you? The real key to microteaching is the opportunity to work on one or a few identified isolated skills, which allows for the reflection and conceptualization process to occur. The typical class day requires teachers to do it all, remember it all, and apply it all; there is no time or opportunity to isolate one or two areas for improvement. This process changes that. The microteaching technique encourages teachers to experiment, reflect, receive safe feedback, and, if necessary, try again.

There are four distinct stages in a microteaching session (Kilic, 2010; Otsupius, 2014). These four stages blend nicely with the four aspects of the PDSA (Plan-Do-Study-Act) model. Proponents of microteaching call for

1. A planning stage;
2. A teaching stage;
3. A reflection stage; and
4. A feedback stage.

Programs that might augment your microteaching process can be found at www.simcity.com, www.mursion.com, and www.edthena.com

We told you they fit well together! During the planning stage, skills that need improvement are identified. In the teaching stage, teachers teach a microlesson (typically only about 10–15 minutes), which may be live in front of colleagues, streamed or recorded, or even done with student avatars (Regalla, Nutta, Ashtari, & Verkler, 2014; Spencer, 2016). We know you are used to teaching longer lessons, but the microlesson is just one part or aspect of a lesson that is specifically geared to whatever skill is being practiced (e.g., modeling, question-asking, teacher feedback, classroom management, "we" language, giving of directions, differentiating instruction). Longer lesson observations tend to incorporate too many additional variables, and teachers are not as able to focus and hone in on the skill at issue. Spencer (2016) writes, "[T]his iterative process of review and practice has been shown to be effective in many other disciplines, including aviation, medicine, and the military" (p. 1). Though Spencer was specifically referring to the use of microteaching in a simulation setting, the same holds true for the classroom. In typical teaching settings, “It is not unlikely that the candidate, looking back on the stressful situation of the unsuccessful lesson, will barely remember what he or she did, much less have the wherewithal to correct it” (Spencer, 2016, p. 1). The purpose in this application is for co-teachers to simply be hyper aware of the co-teaching core competency they are working on during that 10- to 15-minute microteaching lesson, and to video-record it so that they can reflect more objectively on what occurred during the lesson at a later time with their partner and CoP.

Planning and Teaching

The planning and teaching stages in the microteaching process align completely with the definition of co-teaching. Co-teachers are required to “co-plan, co-instruct, and co-assess” (Murawski, 2003, p. 10). In this situation, as co-teachers plan collaboratively for a co-taught lesson, they also take some time to consider their focus competencies and how they can better meet them. They determine what they are going to do and when during their longer lesson they will do this microtaught portion so that they know what part to video-record. Some teachers choose to video-record their whole lesson and then simply edit down to the microteaching part. That’s up to you!

Issues with videotaping? If it’s a technology issue, consider having a student use a smartphone. If it’s a comfort issue, consider starting by just reflecting on the lesson without recording it. Once you see how others remember and are able to reflect more fully when they can see their lessons in real time, you will realize how powerful video can be!

Reflection

During the reflection stage of microteaching, all CoP members watch the video-recorded lesson, if they weren’t able to see it live. The team that did the lesson is expected to discuss how the session went and if, in their opinion, the identified skill was improved. This approach is powerful in two different ways. First, in traditional teaching, teachers often do not have time to reflect on their own teaching, so errors may be repeated and successes are not validated (Spencer, 2016). However, the reflection stage forces teachers to look back on their own teaching to ascertain what worked and what did not (Amobi & Irwin, 2012). They are empowered to take the time to individually consider their own strengths and areas for improvement and whether or not they were able to demonstrate the targeted skill. In fact, reflection in teaching has been found to result in increased skill attainment (Amobi & Irwin, 2012; Larrivee, 2010). Second, for those who are co-teaching, reflection enables the two teachers to collaboratively dialogue about what they did as a team. Dieker (2016), in her *Co-Teaching Lesson Plan Book*, provides ongoing reflection questions for teachers. She emphasizes the need for co-teachers to regularly reflect and converse about how their interactions are going. This process not only removes potential emotion, since it is merely the next step in the process, but it also requires co-teachers to communicate about a particular skill in which they are both vested in improving. The reflection stage of the microteaching process is just between the two teachers who co-taught the lesson; however, this review and conversation will typically occur in front of colleagues who form their CoP. The CTIME process really emphasizes the benefits of such a community as a support group.

Feedback

The feedback stage of the microteaching process allows for discussion with other participants as they provide feedback about the observed microlesson. This is where the CoP comes in. Since these individuals are typically other co-teaching teams, they too have planned, implemented, video-recorded, and reflected on their own microlessons. Because administrators are often the ones in classes conducting observations and providing regular feedback, they can be invited to participate in these feedback sessions, but that is up to the CoP members to decide. Administrative feedback can help validate or focus those reflections discussed by co-teachers, but sometimes observational feedback from administrators is not received in the same way that it is from colleagues at one's level (Khachatryan, 2015). If the microlesson has been recorded, short clips or elements of it can be shared with colleagues or experts for even more specific targeted feedback. Additional mentors, coaches, supervisors, consultants, or co-teaching coordinators might join in the session, as appropriate, to share their own feedback on the skill in question, but again, the intent is really to be with one's peers.

Not sure about getting feedback from peers? Maybe we'll change your mind when we mention that Hattie's *Visible Learning* meta-analyses ranked feedback as number 10 in its overall ranking of the 138 educational interventions he reviewed, and it was the fourth on the list in the "teaching" domain (Hattie, 2012). Feedback is crucially important in improving our skills, and we just do not get enough of it when we teach in our closed-door classroom silos.

When you are done with this microteaching feedback loop, you are done. Right? Wrong. Once this cycle is completed, the process is repeated so that your co-teaching team will have the opportunity to reteach the microlesson, applying any points raised during your own reflections and implementing pertinent feedback from the observers. After your team has retaught while focused on the same core co-teaching competency, has received additional feedback, and is finally satisfied that you have mastered the skill, you can then replicate those actions any time. You've got it down! You're ready to move on to another skill. If by some chance your team loses the skill, or isn't able to generalize it, the great part of job-embedded personalized professional learning is that you can simply choose that competency again and keep working it. These competencies relate to the way you are interacting with one another and the students within the co-taught classroom, so they can be applied to any content lesson at any time.

Putting It All Together

The process of microteaching, or even the PDSA cycle overall, may seem daunting, but it needn't be. Each teacher has an intrinsic ability to internalize the practices necessary to make co-teaching successful. Experimenting with teaching, receiving feedback and learning from the feedback, and having the ability to try again are paramount to the success of microteaching and teacher skill acquisition. It is rewarding to see improvement, and it can even be fun to give and receive feedback from your colleagues!

Consider the Co-Teaching Competencies Pyramid that we shared in Chapter 3 (see Figure 3.10). Whatever the situation, the first stage of learning a skill is *basic knowledge acquisition.* For our co-teaching application, this may take place through formal training on co-teaching, a book study, an online webinar, or a university course. Once you have that basic knowledge, it's time to build your skills in co-teaching. Figure 7.7 shows that microteaching comes in as the second step in the process—*skills acquisition.*

FIGURE 7.7

Co-Teaching Competencies: From Knowledge to Transfer

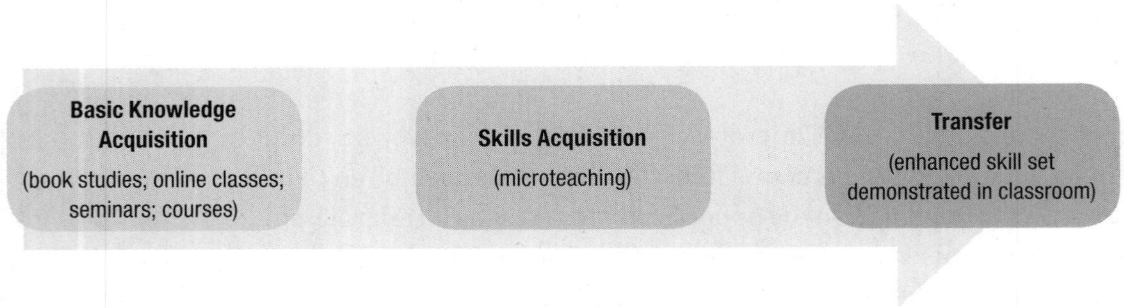

Basic Knowledge Acquisition
(book studies; online classes; seminars; courses)

Skills Acquisition
(microteaching)

Transfer
(enhanced skill set demonstrated in classroom)

You have to interpret what you've learned about co-teaching, apply it to a real co-teaching situation, and demonstrate your mastery of the co-teaching competencies through your microlesson. Once you've been able to integrate that practice into your regular daily performance, you will know that you've *transferred* that skill into your co-teaching repertoire. Well done!

Figure 7.8 outlines the four distinct stages in the microteaching improvement cycle. During the planning stage, skills that need improvement are identified. Within the teaching stage, co-teachers teach, and ideally video-record, the microlesson. The reflection stage allows the co-teachers to discuss with their CoP peer group how they felt the session went and whether the identified skill was improved. The feedback stage gives other participants the opportunity to provide feedback about the microlesson. Once the cycle is completed, the process is started again, and the co-teaching team reteaches a microlesson on that same competency as needed, applying the points raised during their own reflections and in feedback from their CoP.

FIGURE 7.8

The Microteaching Improvement Cycle

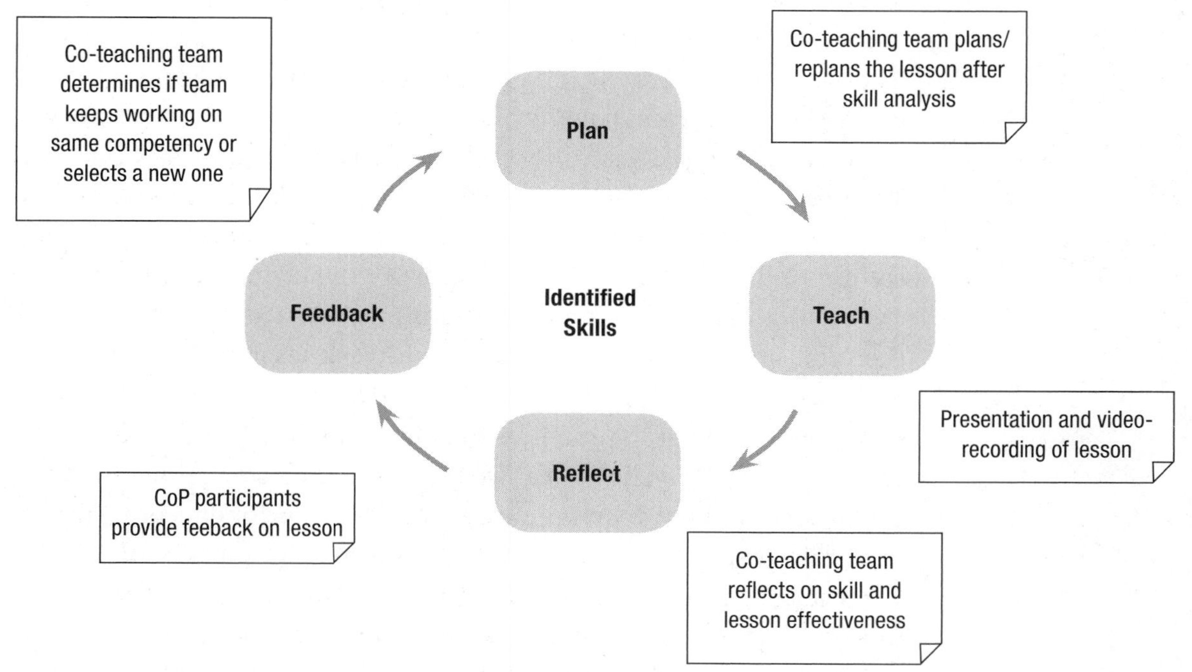

Problem Solving

Worried that you can't support two CoP meetings each quarter? Remember to take baby steps! If you need to have one meeting a semester in the first year, just to get used to the idea, then do it. Build to one meeting a quarter, and so on. This process is about building on successes systematically, not about overwhelming a system or an individual.

A Suggested Schedule for Microteaching

When does all this microteaching happen? Every day, of course! Just kidding. As much as we would love teams to really focus on their co-teaching skills on a regular basis, we also know that you are busy. Some days you are just trying to stay one day (hour?) ahead of your students, the new curriculum, the changing bell schedule, and the next fire drill. But we also know that without a consistent schedule to guide you and require a level of reflection and emphasis on skill improvement, it is simply too easy to slide back into complacency. That's why we see so many good teachers being wasted in roles that appear more like classroom aides than real teachers. It's why we see veteran teachers who used to be engaged with their students and energized start to become disengaged and lose their enthusiasm.

In our ideal world, observations of co-teachers would occur every nine weeks. These might be by administrators, coaches, coordinators, peers, and so on. Regardless of who does the observations, co-teachers would receive data every nine weeks. Once those observations are conducted, teams have their performance data to put on their PLATEs. Ideally, the following week, co-teachers would meet with their partners to analyze their data and determine their focus competency or competencies for upcoming microteaching sessions. Those sessions do not have to happen immediately; we want teams to have time to plan, prepare, and really consider how they can best improve. We find that three weeks is the maximum amount of time teams usually need to prepare for their microteaching session. Thus, their microteaching session should typically be conducted about three weeks after the data analysis. After that session, the CoP meets to review the lessons, share feedback, and then break off for individual teams to reflect and set goals. Following this format usually allows for two "rounds" of microteaching and CoP meetings every nine weeks, depending on the school calendar. The process repeats each nine weeks. This schedule allows for eight microteaching sessions and small-group CoP meetings per school year. Six to eight rounds of microteaching will ensure the fastest results. However, if two rounds of nine-week microteaching sessions are too overwhelming, then commit the first year to a one nine-week session. The process will get easier as you work through it and you will have no problem getting in the eight sessions for subsequent years. Figure 7.9 illustrates what a nine-week schedule might look like with two rounds of microteaching sessions.

In a subsequent year, teams could use their prior end-of-year data to start microteaching sessions in the first nine weeks of school. Naturally, observations can also occur more than once in nine weeks. We have seen this occur with schools that have formal observations by administrators, as well as additional observations by co-teaching coordinators, instructional coaches, and even peer mentors. In one high school using CTIME, Granada Hills Charter High School in California, a co-teacher who was part of the math CoP said right from the beginning that he would prefer to do observations in person when possible, rather than just observe his peers via a video-recording. His administrators agreed that they would make that happen. In such a case, teams have clear administrative support to learn from one another. The result at Granada Hills is that, while the math co-teacher is learning from observing his peers in action, they too will benefit from his real-time observational data. (We'd also like to congratulate Granada Hills Charter for receiving the coveted Gold Ribbon Award for their co-teaching program from the State of California!)

FIGURE 7.9

Sample Nine-Week Schedule

Date	Activity
Week of Jan 16th	Full observations
Week of Jan 23rd	Data analysis from observations and set new goals
Week of Feb 30th	Select focus competencies for upcoming session(s) and research best practices around the focus areas
Week of Feb 6th	Prep time for microteaching sessions; develop microlesson
Week of Feb 13th	Conduct microteaching session; video-recording of co-teaching
Week of Feb 20th	CoP meeting; microteaching sessions review and feedback
Week of Feb 27th	Self-reflection by co-teachers; determination of new focus competencies/goals or more work on same competencies
Week of Mar 6th	Conduct microteaching session; video-recording of co-teaching
Week of Mar 13th	CoP meeting; microteaching sessions review and feedback; self-reflection by co-teachers

Closing Thoughts

We've thrown a lot at you here. If we were standing in front of you, which we'd certainly prefer to be doing, we would likely use team teaching to role-play what all of this would look like. That isn't an option currently (though feel free to contact us and have us come work with you directly), so instead we offer, as a recap, Figure 7.10, and a vignette—which provides a brief glimpse of what this process might look like in action for a team of co-teachers.

FIGURE 7.10

The CTIME Process: Team Application in Five Easy Steps

PLAN	
Step 1	Using PIE scores, determine team focus competencies for microteaching sessions and document these on your PLATE.
Step 2	Review resources, develop strategies, and plan for microteaching sessions.
DO	
Step 3	Teams conduct live or video-recorded microteaching sessions on their focus competency.
STUDY	
Step 4	During CoP meetings, teams reflect on their microteaching sessions. CoP members also provide teams with feedback, suggestions, and strategies.
ACT	
Step 5	Determine if additional microteaching sessions are needed for the focus competency or if a new competency will be selected for focus. Repeat the cycle.

Microteaching in Action: A Vignette

Shanti Kiernan and Kou Anderson are co-teachers. This is their first year. Although they really get along and like one another's company, they are still a bit wary of sharing space and students. They've agreed to select a competency on which to microteach, just to see if it will help.

It's Wednesday after school, and Shanti and Kou meet for their weekly planning session. Using a list of the co-teaching core competencies and a self-survey they've each completed individually, they begin to see where they think they can improve. Shanti really wants to work on differentiating more for students, as well as regrouping and having more opportunities to share the lead in the class. Kou recognizes that they need to differentiate, but he also is concerned by the lack of different levels of questions they ask students and by the fact that there appear to be a few students who aren't as included in the class as they could be. They discuss their responses for a bit, looking at the PIE scores they calculated the previous week, and decide to choose "8.16 Co-teachers ask questions at a variety of levels (basic recall to higher-order thinking)." Their shared rationale is that asking different levels of questions is (1) doable for their first microlesson, (2) generalizable to later lessons, (3) related to the need to differentiate for different learners, and (4) will be a way to include all students.

Having selected their competency and objectives, Kou and Shanti spend some time that week talking about how they will address the skill and what questions they might ask. They decide to teach their microlesson the following Tuesday. On Monday, they secure a video camera and ask a paraprofessional to come in and video-record that section of the lesson. Tuesday comes and, for the first part of their lesson, Kou and Shanti really focus on asking a variety of different levels of questions to all of their students as part of their unit review. Fifteen minutes later, the camera is turned off, the paraprofessional leaves, and class continues. Kou and Shanti still try to vary their questioning throughout the remainder of the class lesson.

Wednesday comes, and Kou and Shanti are ready to watch their lesson and reflect on how it went. They haven't spent any time debriefing yet. As part of the process, their CoP team members, the co-teaching coordinator, and the instructional coach have all been invited to attend and review the video. Thankfully, the co-teaching coordinator brought everyone chocolate!

Ten minutes later, Kou and Shanti look up from the video, smile nervously, and begin to reflect. Both share the skills they thought they demonstrated well, the responses of the students, and areas in which they might improve. Following their self-reflection, which took about 10 minutes, their colleagues also shared their insights. Shanti and Kou felt comfortable asking questions, taking notes, and seeking resources and strategies. This feedback helped Kou and Shanti identify some resources to write on their PLATE to help with their next microlesson. Twenty minutes later, after their colleagues left, Kou and Shanti spent an additional 15 minutes finalizing their plan, determining next steps to write on their PLATE, and deciding when they would incorporate their next co-teaching core competency microlesson. As they left, both reflected upon how the hour was very well spent!

8 Emphasizing Facilitation, Reflection, and Feedback

Take-Aways

- *Applying the PDSA process to individual co-teaching teams means that they need to plan, teach, reflect on, and seek feedback on those outcomes.*
- *CoP meetings require a facilitator, a schedule, and a group willing to support one another.*
- *Reflection is key as teams and individuals strive for continuous improvement.*
- *The CTIME process can be applied to interventions beyond co-teaching.*

In Chapter 6, we discussed the importance of school-level analysis of co-teaching data and Chapter 7 described in detail the major components required for successful co-teaching improvement at the classroom level. We have endeavored to walk you through the continuous improvement process at both levels. We are now at the stage of the process that shows why the collegial support inherent in communities of practice is so critical to great co-teaching. This is the part of the process that brings it all together, moving from knowledge to application into true sustained practice. Remember the Co-Teaching Competencies Pyramid (see Figure 3.10)? You are at the pinnacle! All the work you have done so far leads to this moment. Figure 8.1 reviews where you have been.

We have shared information on personalized professional learning, the PDSA cycle, the observation checklist and selection of focus competencies, the PLATE for data tracking, communities of practice, and microteaching. This chapter is designed to show how all those components fit together. To start, we focus on the importance of group facilitation and peer feedback within the CoP meetings, two areas that we have not yet discussed in detail but are critical to the CTIME process. We also emphasize the need for critical reflection on the process and commitment to improvement. Finally, we conclude by highlighting the importance of institutionalization of the process as you strive for sustained practice and generalizability.

From PLATE to Microlesson

In Chapter 7, we clarified how microteaching follows the PDSA cycle with its four stages of planning, teaching, reflection, and feedback (Kilic, 2010; Otsupius, 2014). We described the role of data in helping you and your partner select your focus competencies and the role of the CoPs in providing support and suggestions as you prepare to move forward. Perhaps the action steps you identified to move forward included gathering resources, reading an article, watching a peer team, or asking someone questions about a strategy. All of this information is collected on your PLATE. Whatever steps you wanted to take, let's say you have successfully completed them, and now you and your partner are ready to conduct your first microlesson (see Figure 8.2). What's next?

FIGURE 8.1

Co-Teaching Pyramid for Individual Teams

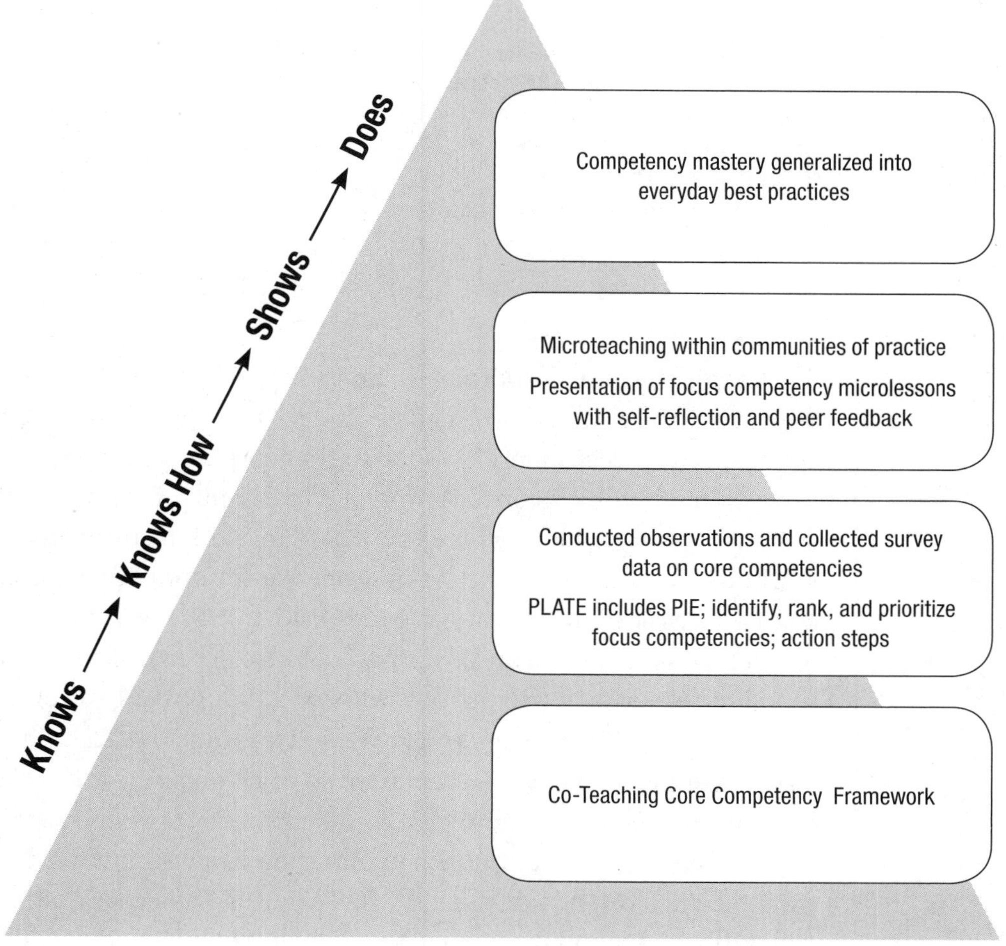

FIGURE 8.2

Review of the Microteaching Process

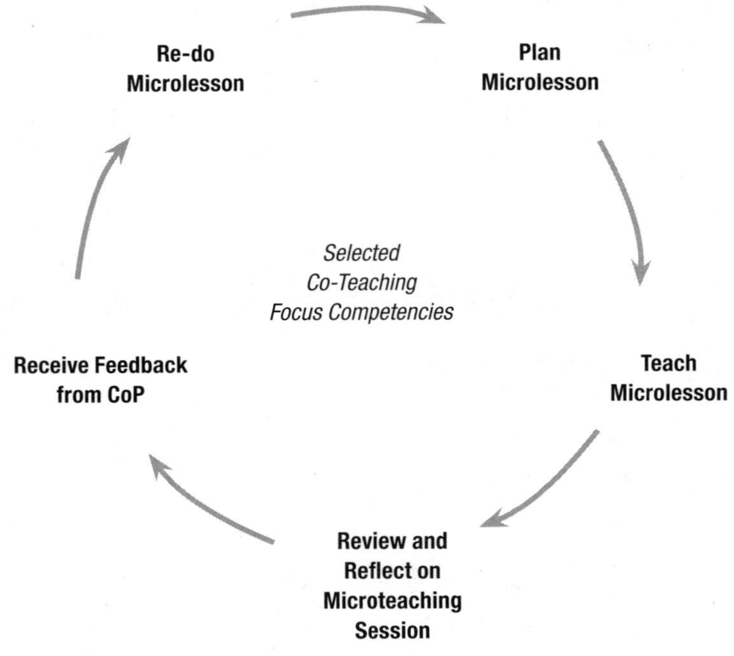

Next is the actual microlesson planning. We know (or at least desperately hope) that you and your co-teacher plan regularly for your co-taught classes. This piece is merely added to that co-planning session. Co-planning should involve a conversation in which you and your partner determine *what* you will teach, *how* you will teach it using universally designed methods, and *who* in your class may need additional differentiation strategies to access that information (Murawski, 2012). For your microteaching, we merely ask that you and your partner also determine which aspect of that dynamic lesson will purposefully and thoughtfully integrate the focus competency and strategies you identified on your PLATE. What part of that lesson would you like video-recorded so that you and your CoP colleagues can view it, reflect on it, and give feedback on your progress? If you'd like to see a typical co-teaching lesson plan, you can visit www.2TeachLLC.com and click on the tab labeled "Co-Teaching Lessons Database." There you will find a template for a co-teaching lesson plan, as well as examples of elementary and secondary co-taught lessons. In Figure 8.3, we also offer a lesson plan template for a microteaching session. Regardless of how you create your lesson plan, you should have it available to your CoP peers during the meeting at which you view your lesson in action. Either you and your partner should make copies, or the CoP facilitator can do so. Best practice dictates that your CoP group members have a visual to refer to when watching your lesson so that they can see what you were intending to accomplish during that microteaching session.

FIGURE 8.3

Microteaching Lesson Plan Template

Co-Teachers: ____________ Grade: ______ Content Area: ____________ Pd/Rm: ______ Date: ______

Competency/Competencies: ______________________________

____

____

MT Session Desc.:	Learning Objective:

Co-Teaching Approach   One Teach, One Support   Parallel Teaching   Station Teaching   Alternative Teaching   Team Teaching

Other: ______________________________

Time	General Educator/ Special Educator	Assessment(s)	Grouping By	Differentiation	Student Considerations

Did any of you pause just now when we mentioned a CoP facilitator? Did you wonder if you missed something? We have mentioned many tasks and steps in regard to the CoP process, and none of this happens in a vacuum. If you recall, we suggested that someone be identified as the CoP facilitator, or that team members share the load. Though all members of the team have parity, it will be helpful for one member to be tasked with ensuring that certain protocols are in place. In the next section, we describe the role of the CoP facilitator and the tasks that should occur before, during, and after CoP meetings. Pay close attention—this might be you!

Community of Practice Microteaching Facilitation

Should a member of the school administrative or leadership PLC team facilitate the CoP meetings? Or, instead, should a member of one of the co-teaching teams step up as CoP facilitator in order to keep this group "in the trenches"? There are pros and cons to both approaches. In the case of administrators or PLC members, they usually have an overview of how the school is doing in general related to co-teaching, they have internalized the vision and future goals for where the school or district will be in its inclusive practices, and they may have the flexibility to attend CoP meetings and meet with co-teaching teams. They also tend to be more driven by data collection and documentation. However, CoP team members may be more comfortable viewing their videos, debriefing, and strategizing when an administrator is not present. They may prefer to work with another teacher who knows what they are going through. We have worked with a few school districts that have identified a current co-teaching teacher as the co-teaching coordinator and, in that role, released the teacher for anywhere from a class period to half the day. In alignment with our policy to respect your culture and give you choice, we defer to your preferences and what will work best with your teachers. Whatever you choose, however, you will need to identify at least one person who will help you stay on top of this process—at least until it becomes systematized.

So what does this coordinator/facilitator/coach/mentor do? (From now on, we'll just call him or her the CoP facilitator, but you can change this title to co-teaching coordinator or guru, as you see fit.) This is the person who helps collect paperwork, reminds teachers to do their microteaching lessons prior to CoP meetings, helps schedule CoP meetings and ensure that teachers will be free during the meeting times, provides support in obtaining resources, liaises with administrators and the leadership PLC, and otherwise stays relentlessly positive about the whole process. In the following sections, we've broken down the CoP facilitator's role by stage: *pre-session, during a session*, and *post-session*. Each section also includes a checklist that summarizes the important tasks that need to be completed at that stage.

CoP Facilitator Role: Pre-Session

1. Prior to the CoP meeting, the facilitator should provide the co-teaching teams with the microteaching lesson plan template (see Figure 8.3). Teams should complete their lesson plans before they conduct their lessons and then return the completed forms to the facilitator. Team members should be specific in the description of what they are trying to accomplish so that when their observation peers get a copy and then watch the microteaching session, they will know exactly what they are looking for. Figure 8.4 is an example of a completed lesson plan form.

FIGURE 8.4

Completed Microteaching Lesson Plan Form

Co-Teachers: *Murawski & Lochner* Grade: *8* Content Area: *ELA* Pd/Rm: *2nd* Date: *4/15/18*

Competency/Competencies: *1.6 Cannot tell special ed students from general ed students*
3.7 Ability to differentiate

MT Session Desc.	Learning Objective:
Introduce RAFT Strategy	*Students will be able to write a paragraph*

Co-Teaching Approach: One Teach, One Support · Parallel Teaching · Station Teaching · Alternative Teaching · (Team Teaching — circled)

Other: ______

Time	General Educator/ Special Educator	Assessment(s)	Grouping By	Differentiation	Student Considerations
8:45–8:55 *8:56–9:05*	*Role play and introduce the RAFT Strategy* *Both teachers support all students as they begin their writing*	*Monitor progress when circulating; collect formative assessment data*	*Students were heterogenously seated when we passed out different requirements*	*Different levels of note-taking support* *Product - Amount of writing was adjusted and type of writing was adapted to meet student levels*	*Grace/Cameron use of tech for speech to text*

2. In collaboration with team members, the CoP facilitator schedules the microteaching lessons and provides the CoP teams with the schedule. If using the CTSS, the CoP facilitator will enter microteaching sessions in the CTSS system, which will automatically send team members reminders of the scheduled sessions. Otherwise, these sessions need to be put on a calendar so that teams can be held accountable for conducting their microteaching lessons and neither co-teacher is pulled away from the class on that day and time. Microteaching lessons can be done live if other teachers can be freed up to come and watch, or streamed online, but most often these sessions are video-recorded.
3. The CoP facilitator will also schedule the CoP debrief meetings for once every nine weeks or so. These should occur preferably within a week after each team has had the opportunity to conduct their microteaching session and when they will be ready to watch the video-recorded lessons and debrief on them with their CoP peer group. The CoP facilitator will also want to make sure the meeting takes place in a venue that enables all participants to see and hear the video easily. If time, venue, or logistics do not permit CoP members to watch the videos together, then team members can also watch the videos before coming to the meeting to reflect and give feedback.
4. Just prior to the CoP meeting, it will be helpful if the CoP facilitator makes copies of the *Microteaching Sessions 2+2 Feedback Form* and a copy of each team's microlesson plans. We will describe the 2+2 method of feedback later in this chapter. These forms may be given out at the first CoP session, or they may be sent electronically to team members, especially if you are using the CTSS. Team members generally like to see the forms they will be using and discussing in advance of the first meeting.
5. The CoP facilitator prepares the *Team Session Documentation Form* (see Figure 8.5) with the information from the microteaching lesson plan forms for each team. The purpose of this form is to help the facilitator document the competencies that co-teaching teams have focused on for microteaching sessions, as well as the scores their peers gave them when watching the video-recorded sessions and noting if additional sessions are recommended. For those of you who might be thinking about pursuing grant funding down the road, this is the type of documentation that you will need! By being able to show the ongoing feedback, scoring, and improvement of your teams, you'll be able to demonstrate that your progress is truly data-driven.

Edthena (www.EdThena.com) is an excellent resource for adding notes and feedback into videos.

FIGURE 8.5

Team Session Documentation Form

Session Date: ______________________ Co-Teachers: ______________________

Community of Practice (CoP): ______________________

Session 1:

Focus Competency	**Description**	**Rating**
		0 1 2 3
		0 1 2 3
		0 1 2 3
		0 1 2 3

Requires another session: **Yes** **No** Next Session Date: ____________

Session 2:

Focus Competency	**Description**	**Rating**
		0 1 2 3
		0 1 2 3
		0 1 2 3
		0 1 2 3

Requires another session: **Yes** **No** Next Session Date: ____________

NOTES:

MT Session(s) Close Date: ____________

Figure 8.6 provides a checklist that reviews the pre-session tasks.

FIGURE 8.6

Pre-Session Checklist

- ☐ Check that CoP members are conducting microlessons.
- ☐ Schedule CoP sessions to share microlessons and give feedback.
- ☐ Provide microlesson plan templates to teams.
- ☐ Collect all microlesson plans from teams after they complete their microteaching.
- ☐ Copy and distribute copies of lesson plans and feedback forms among CoP members.

CoP Microteaching Facilitator Role: During a Session

1. It's time for the big meeting! Even though the other members of the CoP are probably your friends and colleagues, we still recommend that the CoP facilitator go over the ground rules for providing and receiving peer feedback, as well as the process itself. This is critical for the initial meeting, but it is also recommended that the team members remind one another of the rules briefly each time they come together. It just makes everything go more smoothly!
2. Prior to watching a video of a microteaching lesson, CoP team members should have received a copy of the team-in-question's microteaching lesson plan. This will allow them to see what the co-teachers were hoping to accomplish during the lesson. Though it is suggested that team members bring a backup copy of their lesson plan, the CoP facilitator should also make copies in advance of the meeting. The CoP facilitator should also provide each CoP participant with a copy of the 2+2 Feedback Form for notes.
3. During the session, each co-teaching team will present its lesson while CoP members are making notes about the lesson and determining the rating and feedback they will give the presenting team. At the conclusion of the video-recorded or streamed microteaching lesson, the team will use self-reflective discussion with each other in front of their peers. Co-teachers will address how the session went, what they liked and did not like, and what they might have done differently as their CoP peers merely listen to their reflection.
4. CoP members typically provide their feedback to the co-teaching team in a round-robin fashion, sharing the acknowledgments and suggestions they wrote on their 2+2 Feedback Form. The CoP facilitator helps ensure that all CoP members participate, interact positively and appropriately, and share ideas and resources. He or she may also collect the 2+2 Feedback Forms to make copies for the co-teaching teams and to keep on file. Co-teachers will use these forms when they co-plan together next, reflecting on their feedback and considering what to do or change for their next microteaching session. Worried about major time constraints? Teams seem to get the most out of watching the videos together and debriefing right after, but it is possible to have teams watch the videos, score the observations, and take notes for the 2+2 prior to the session. Then CoP members can bring these notes to the session for discussion and sharing. The CoP facilitator can help teams problem solve and determine what format will work best for them.

Worried that you have no time to watch multiple 10- to 20-minute co-taught videos and then debrief all together? Other options include the following:

- *Watch the videos in advance by putting them on Dropbox or a similar file-sharing site.*
- *Have team members watch lessons "live" and take notes.*
- *Have lessons streamed and recorded so that team members can watch them from other sites in real time or asynchronously.*

Figure 8.7 provides a checklist that reviews the during-session tasks.

FIGURE 8.7

During-Session Checklist

- ☐ Review the process and ground rules.
- ☐ Initiate team's self-reflective discussion about the session.
- ☐ Facilitate 2+2 feedback session.
- ☐ Collect feedback forms.

CoP Microteaching Facilitator Role: Post-Session

1. The meeting is over and team members are feeling great! Unfortunately, the CoP facilitator's job is not yet done. It is time to calculate the overall average rating for each team, which merely entails calculating an average of the ratings for each competency from all the submitted feedback forms. The CoP facilitator documents these averages on the *Overall Rating Score Sheet* (see Figure 8.8).
2. The CoP facilitator can work with the co-teaching teams to determine if an extra microteaching session is needed on that same competency. The averages can help with that decision, though of course teams have input and discretion. Typically, if the overall rating is a 0 or 1 (meaning that pretty much everyone on the CoP thought that the lesson they observed did not indicate that the co-teachers had mastered that competency), the team would want to conduct another session on the same competency. That core competency clearly has not yet been mastered. By contrast, an overall rating of 2 or 3 may not require an additional session, unless requested by the co-teaching team. We recommend that additional microteaching sessions on the same competency occur within one to two weeks of the previous session. We want teams to stay "fresh" and "focused" on their competency. This will be indicated on the Overall Rating Score Sheet that is given to them after the discussion. The CoP facilitator can also schedule the next session date and put this on the form as well.
3. Because this process is a cyclical and continuous one, it helps if the CoP facilitator keeps track of the team's scores on the *Progress*

FIGURE 8.8

CoP Microteaching Session Overall Rating Score Sheet

Session Date: ______________________ Co-Teachers: ______________________

MT Session Desc.: ______________________

Session 1:

Focus Competency	Description	Rating
		0 1 2 3
		0 1 2 3
		0 1 2 3
		0 1 2 3

Requires another session: **Yes** **No** Next Session Date: ____________

Session 2:

Focus Competency	Description	Rating
		0 1 2 3
		0 1 2 3
		0 1 2 3
		0 1 2 3

Tracking Form (Figure 8.9). These tracking forms are managed by the facilitator throughout the process and are periodically copied and given to the teams or used when teams want to review their progress. It is just another helpful tool that may be used during the data analysis/problem-solving stage of the CTIME process.

Figure 8.10 provides a checklist that reviews the post-session tasks.

Giving and Receiving Feedback

Much of the CTIME process involves collaboration and communication with others. For some of you, this will be a strength of the process and one with which you are completely comfortable. For others, however, the giving

FIGURE 8.9

CoP Microteaching Sessions Progress Tracking Form

CoP: ______________ Team: ______________ Dates: ______________

Focus Competency	Description	Session 1 Date: ______ Overall Rating	Session 2 Date: ______ Overall Rating
		0 1 2 3	0 1 2 3
		0 1 2 3	0 1 2 3
		0 1 2 3	0 1 2 3
		0 1 2 3	0 1 2 3
		0 1 2 3	0 1 2 3
Focus Competency	**Description**	**Session 1 Date: ______ Overall Rating**	**Session 2 Date: ______ Overall Rating**
		0 1 2 3	0 1 2 3
		0 1 2 3	0 1 2 3
		0 1 2 3	0 1 2 3
		0 1 2 3	0 1 2 3
		0 1 2 3	0 1 2 3
Focus Competency	**Description**	**Session 1 Date: ______ Overall Rating**	**Session 2 Date: ______ Overall Rating**
		0 1 2 3	0 1 2 3
		0 1 2 3	0 1 2 3
		0 1 2 3	0 1 2 3
		0 1 2 3	0 1 2 3
		0 1 2 3	0 1 2 3

FIGURE 8.10

Post-Session Checklist

- ☐ Calculate all the session ratings for each team and enter them on the Team Session Documentation Form.
- ☐ Review scores with teams and determine if an additional session on the same competency is necessary.
- ☐ Schedule additional sessions, if needed.

and receiving of feedback in the PLC, CoP, or co-teaching team situation may not be second nature. We recognize that this may cause some angst for teachers as they begin this new peer-based reflective practice. We think it will be well worth it if your group takes some time in the early meetings to review how to give and receive peer feedback.

The teaching profession is one that has isolated its professionals from one another without doing so intentionally. The result is that teachers rarely have the opportunity to learn from one another. The CTIME process allows for that necessary collaborative exchange of ideas to take place at the school, in small groups or teams, while the microteaching aspect specifically supports colleagues in enhancing their co-teaching skills in a safe, supportive environment.

When giving feedback to one another, CTIME participants must remember to keep the feedback, both positive and negative, *descriptive* in nature as opposed to *evaluative* (Friend & Cook, 2016; Murawski, Carter, Sileo, & Prater, 2012). Keeping things descriptive may seem awkward at first, but (1) you'll get used to it, and (2) it will greatly reduce the likelihood that someone will get defensive or feel like they are receiving a personal attack. Figure 8.11 contains a few examples.

Even though teachers are used to providing students with feedback, they are often hesitant to give feedback to their colleagues. It can feel uncomfortable to offer teaching suggestions to a friend or to someone who has taught for longer than you have. The nice thing about this process is that you are all in it together; everyone wants to improve their co-teaching outcomes, and everyone knows the importance of peer feedback. Sometimes the stumbling block in offering feedback to colleagues is merely a matter of how to phrase your suggestions. If you tend to be timid about offering ideas, consider starting your feedback in team or CoP meetings with these phrases:

- "You may have already thought of this, but. . . ."
- "You might also consider. . . ."
- "Sometimes I find it very useful to. . . ."
- "An idea that came to me as I watched you both co-teach was. . . ."
- "I wonder if it would be helpful to. . . ."
- "Have you considered trying. . . ."

And for PLC teams:

- "What if we tried. . . ."
- "I'd love it if we were able to. . . ."
- "This may seem outside the box, but what if we. . . ."

FIGURE 8.11

Feedback Examples

Example #1

Evaluative: "The formative assessment was nice because all students could use the responders to answer the bell ringer. I liked that students didn't have to share their names. Even Bobby seemed to like it, and he rarely likes any activity in a math class!"

Descriptive: "The formative assessment allowed all students to participate by using the responders to answer the bell ringer. Because it was anonymous, students did not appear worried that others would laugh at them if their answer was incorrect. Using this strategy, students with and without disabilities were able to participate in your activity."

Example #2

Evaluative: "Brenda, you completely dominated the class today. It seemed like Jacque was your assistant, not your co-teacher. You should really try to use 'we' language, instead of always saying 'I want you to . . .' to your kids."

Descriptive: "In today's lesson, Brenda spoke for 95% of the time. Jacque spent the class period walking around and using proximity control. Two students waited to have Brenda help them, saying they would wait for the 'real teacher.' I also noticed that Brenda frequently told students what she wanted them to do, using 'I' language rather than 'we' language."

When giving feedback at any level, comments must be written down. This allows participants to feel that their input is valued and to piggyback on one another's ideas (Friend & Cook, 2016; Murawski & Spencer, 2011). At the schoolwide level, the co-teaching leadership PLC will want to be able to review suggestions and determine what changes need to be made at the systems level. They will want to have documentation of ideas for future implementation. At the CoP level, having all ideas written down and given to the co-teaching team allows the team to use that information when co-planning their next session. Even co-teaching teams that are merely debriefing together after a lesson or after engaging in a CoP meeting will find themselves giving and receiving feedback. That's the beauty of co-teaching! We learn from one another. Co-teachers should get in the habit of writing down feedback they give to and receive from one another. A great resource for planning and writing down comments for future reference is Dieker's *Co-Teaching Lesson Plan Book* (Dieker, 2016). More suggestions for giving and receiving feedback are shared in Figure 8.12.

The 2+2 Feedback Method

For CoP meetings, we recommend a very specific method for giving feedback: the *2+2 feedback method* (Allan & LeBlanc, 2005). Once all members have viewed the video-recorded co-taught lesson, and the co-teachers have had a chance to self-reflect aloud in front of their colleagues, it is time for the other CoP members to share their observations. Rather than having this become a free-for-all, in which some teams may be lambasted by one or two of their colleagues, or a dead-silent zone, in which no one says anything at all, we require all participants to share using the same methodology. This makes sharing not only safe, but also required. No one gets off the hook in this collaborative activity!

FIGURE 8.12

Giving and Receiving Feedback in the Microteaching Process

As a participant in the microteaching process, it is your role to provide attention, feedback, and encouragement to your co-teaching colleagues. All comments should be made with these three principles in mind. Change does not come by feedback alone, but rather with feedback that is solicited, descriptive, and within someone's ability to change (Friend & Cook, 2016). Co-teaching teams need to feel safe enough to try new things, to fail, and to try again until they are successful. Feedback from others provides the necessary strategies, resources, techniques, perspectives, and ideas to co-teaching teams to improve their daily practice.

When providing feedback to peers:	***When receiving feedback from peers:***
✔ **Observe the skill** the co-teachers are working on. Describe what you see and hear. Remember to provide only information on the skill to be addressed, not on the person.	✔ **Be open** to the feedback you are receiving. Take recommendations as a way to improve your co-teaching skills, not as a personal attack.
✔ **Be specific** in your observation of the skill and how it affected the lesson.	✔ **Acknowledge the observations** and remain neutral when listening to how the lesson affected the observers.
✔ **Use the 2+2 method**. Encourage co-teachers by providing feedback. Give two positives first and then two suggestions for improvement.	✔ **Confirm the positive comments** and let them reinforce your skills. The negative comments, or suggestions for improvement, should provide a start for self-reflection. Discuss these with your co-teacher and determine how you will use this feedback productively.
✔ **Offer suggestions**. No matter your role—peer, coach, or administrator—the goal of this collaborative session is to provide co-teachers with ideas and alternatives that might help improve their practices. Don't hold back just because it is not usually done or you don't do it yourself. Put your ideas out there for the group to discuss and consider.	✔ **Consider the strategies offered** and discuss how they may be integrated into future lessons. You may even consider how they can be applied to other situations you teach; the other CoP members may also be considering how to apply these strategies to their own situations.

Leave your ego at the door. This is not about you. This is about the professional collaborative process of developing and sharing what might improve your co-teaching practices and skills. Remember that the ultimate beneficiaries of this process are your students!

Source: Adapted from Friend & Cook (2016), Murawski et al. (2012), and Murawski & Spencer (2011).

The 2+2 method uses three principles that support the quickest change: *attention, feedback,* and *encouragement*. Because you know you will need to participate and share your observations, you will clearly be more apt to pay close attention to your colleague's 10- to 15-minute microlesson. You will take notes and be prepared to share your brilliant feedback on the 2+2

Feedback Form (see Figure 8.13). The balanced method of providing *two positive points and two suggested improvements* is the cornerstone of this collaborative process. Everyone knows the expectations and, thus, no one is thrown for a loop. Even the most veteran and dynamic of co-teaching teams will receive suggestions for ongoing improvement (we all have areas to improve, don't we?), while the novice and perhaps less successful teams won't be overwhelmed by too much constructive criticism. This feedback and encouragement will ensure that each CoP team walks away with concrete suggestions for continuous improvement, as well as praise for tasks well done.

FIGURE 8.13

Microteaching Session 2+2 Feedback Form

Session Date: ______________________ Co-Teachers: ______________________

Grade/Period: ______________________ Content Area: ______________________

Community of Practice (CoP): ______________________

Focus Competency	Description	Circle Rating
		0 1 2 3
		0 1 2 3
		0 1 2 3
		0 1 2 3
		0 1 2 3
		0 1 2 3

2 Acknowledgments:

2 Suggestions:

Feedback respectfully given by: ______________________

The Role of Self-Reflection in CTIME

Reflection. The very word makes some people smile and others cringe. Action-oriented teachers may think that they just want to work to improve practices, whereas others may want the time to really think and process their current actions, goals, and objectives. Luckily for both types

Reflection: *"To be reflective means to mentally wander through where we have been and make some sense out of it" (Costa & Kallick, 2008).*

of teachers, CTIME is a powerful self-reflective process that is geared toward actions that lead to improvement. We know that research shows that reflecting on and evaluating one's teaching skills after a lesson is both insightful and impactful (Costa & Kallick, 2008). Some reflection is best done alone, while at other times we are empowered by pondering with others. Costa and Kallick (2008) remind us that for reflection to be powerful, we must act upon and process our information, while synthesizing and evaluating the data available to us. So where does reflection fit into the CTIME process? Pretty much everywhere.

Reflection on data and feedback is the crux of CTIME. Rather than just flying by the seat of your pants, or changing behaviors because you are not sure what else to do to improve, you will be making changes after having a chance to think about (i.e., reflect upon) what has been working well and what has not. You'll be able to consider (i.e., reflect upon) feedback and suggestions from your peers. You'll be able to deliberate, contemplate, ponder, study, cogitate, ruminate, and mull over (we know you get the point) the co-teaching core competencies that you have mastered and those that are still causing you difficulties. In this context, *you* applies to the larger PLC group, the smaller CoP group, the co-teaching team, and individual co-teachers. Reflection on the data at all stages is key.

Are you trying to do this process with just two people? Concerned that you do not have enough people at your school to create a community of practice or professional learning community? Don't worry! We can differentiate for you as well. You will still engage in most of these steps, but self-reflection is going to become so much more important for you.

We have already highlighted the value of the PLC working collaboratively to create a vision and review data to determine overall focus competencies, and we've discussed strategies for giving and receiving feedback within the CoP. Let's take a moment to focus on the co-teaching team itself. As teams watch their own microteaching lessons with their CoP peers, or even at home on their own, they should be reflecting on what they think went well and what they might do individually and as a team to improve. Using our *Co-Teaching Team Self-Reflection Form* (see Figure 8.14), co-teachers give themselves a self-rating. They do this together, discussing how they believe they did on their focus competency and where it falls on the rubric (with scores ranging from 0 to 3). This discussion and scoring ideally happens in front of their CoP members right after everyone watches the video. This way, the rest of the CoP gets to hear the co-teachers think aloud about what they saw in their own video. Remember that CoP members are also scoring the team themselves on their 2+2 Feedback Form (Figure 8.13).

Once teams dialogue about what they saw and determine aloud what score they give themselves, the rest of the CoP shares their scores and 2+2 feedback. The process repeats with another team sharing their video, reflecting aloud about their own progress, and receiving 2+2 feedback from the community. The end of that CoP meeting does not connote the end of the reflection on that video, however.

FIGURE 8.14

Co-Teaching Team Self-Reflection Form

Co-Teachers: ______	MT Session Date: ______
Competency	**Self-Rating Score (0–3)**

What We Did	Our Results Were	Next Time We Will Try
• ______	• ______	• ______
• ______	• ______	• ______
• ______	• ______	• ______
• ______	• ______	• ______

What did we learn most?

______

______

______

______

How will our technique change as a result of this session?

______

______

______

______

Co-teaching teams now plan to spend some time reflecting on the reflections. Work with us on this. What we mean is that they now need to get together as a co-teaching team of two—at a special co-planning session or just as a part of their typical co-planning meetings—to talk about what their peers shared with them during the CoP. There are a few reasons that this occurs outside of the CoP meeting and between just the co-teachers themselves. First, few teachers have the time to watch videos, debrief individually, share observations, *and* react to those observations *and* plan for the future. We need to keep CoP meetings to a reasonable amount of time. Second, there is a tendency for teachers to get defensive about their own teaching; not reacting immediately to suggestions or feedback gives teachers an opportunity to process and allows others to feel more comfortable sharing their thoughts on a lesson. Finally, being able to review notes, consider suggestions provided on the 2+2 forms, and think about what peers said following their observation of the microteaching lesson allows partners to talk together about what aspects to disregard and what ones need to be taken to heart.

Using the *Co-Teaching Team Self-Reflection Form* (Figure 8.14), teams first document the date and the competency or competencies on which they were focusing. In the far left column, they record (as bullet points) what they did to address that competency. These are the actions they took during the microteaching lesson they just video-recorded and observed. In the middle column, the team will record the results (again, as bullet points). What happened as a result of their focused attention on that particular competency? Did anything change? Did work with students improve? Did teachers feel more comfortable? Did the environment feel more inclusive or differentiated or organized or well-managed or fun? Finally, in the far right column, co-teachers reflect on what they plan to try next time. "Next time" might mean when they do another microteaching lesson on the same competency, or it might simply mean the next time they are co-teaching, if this is a competency they feel they have mastered but that now needs to be incorporated into their daily repertoire.

We like the simple bulleted format because it respects busy teachers' time and still gets the gist of what was done, why, and what the end result was. After these quick bullets, though, we provide a space for co-teachers to record what they learned from this experience and how their co-teaching techniques will (or won't, as the case may be) change as a result of their microteaching. Having to record this information encourages teachers to spend a few minutes talking about their teaching and the changes they will want to sustain in the future.

Monitoring Results and Sustainability

Woo-hoo! You have now "completed" the CTIME continuous improvement cycle. That wasn't so bad, was it? Note that we put the word *completed* in quotation marks. That is because we hope that you see this process as a cyclical and sustainable one. The CTIME process is about perpetual learning for co-teachers, but consider how it is also supporting the meaning-making of data on a systemic level as well. We want the CTIME process to inspire innovation and experimentation, to be viewed not as just one more thing to do, but rather as a way to continually work to improve ourselves as educators. The CTIME continuous improvement model encourages teachers and teams to examine their strengths and weaknesses in a collaborative environment, where it is the responsibility of each and every team member to grow and to support one another's growth.

What if every one of your co-teachers has used the process and is now getting 3s on all the co-teaching core competencies? Are you done? Well, sure, you could be (and, by the way, wow!). But you could also dust off all 120 co-teaching competencies and see if you are at the mastery level on all of them. Or you could start to apply this same process to other aspects of teaching. Think about it. Couldn't CTIME be applied to supporting all teachers as they implement a new reading practice, or Tier 1 differentiation strategies, or a social skills intervention? Remember that CTIME stands for *Collaborative* Teaching Improvement Model of Excellence. We want to see collaboration in schools because we know that when teachers support one another, great things happen. Consider how this model can be institutionalized at your school and applied regularly to ensure data-driven improvement.

Take a look again at the CTIME process. You started with a school-level group committed to improvement in a particular area. This was your co-teaching leadership PLC, which collaborated to create a vision of where you wanted to be. Next, the school-level team collected data to determine where the discrepancies between current performance and desired performance were and did a root cause analysis to determine whether those gaps were due to systemic issues or team-based issues. The PLC then worked to address systemic issues and continued to circle back to the data to see if improvements were made based on those changes. Concurrently, small CoP groups were created, composed of individuals who were implementing the intervention (in this case, co-teaching). These small groups also used data to determine their present level of performance, given very concrete competencies to measure their progress. CoP members implemented their intervention, video-recorded themselves doing a microlesson involving the intervention, and then shared those video-recordings with their group.

With the aid of a facilitator, the group members reflected on their own practice and gave feedback to their teammates. Buy-in was increased because teachers selected the areas in which they wanted to improve and had input on how easy or difficult they thought each competency would be to attain. Finally, for both the PLC and CoP groups, teams worked collaboratively to use data to set goals and track progress.

Doesn't this sound like a process that can be institutionalized and generalized as needed? In addition, thanks to the wonders of technology, you are not even confined by issues that require a large community. Consider this scenario: You have two students at your school who are blind. This is new for you, and you don't know the best way to ensure that these students' needs are being met. You can still create a PLC to determine whether their struggles are systemic or classroom-based; you can still create a CoP to focus on how these students are taught in the classroom. However, perhaps you reach out to other schools in the district to form your PLC or CoP. Now, you have a virtual group meeting regularly and providing support to one another. You are not dependent on having focus areas that are "big enough" to warrant a large team; the CTIME process can be applied for any need. Just find individuals who share your concerns and want to improve in a given area; they might be across the country, but they are there!

Online collaboration is becoming part of the norm today. Here are two of our favorite online collaborative tools that CoPs can use:

- *SLACK (don't let the name fool you) has a plethora of collaborative options (www.slack.com).*
- *MightyMeeting provides all the tools necessary to host a virtual meeting where everyone is connected (www.mightymeeting.com).*

Closing Thoughts

CTIME provides you with a model that can be applied beyond co-teaching. When in doubt, keep coming back to the evidence-based components that make CTIME successful:

- A vision
- Collaborative groups
- Data-driven decision making
- Plan-Do-Study-Act process
- Microteaching
- Critical reflection
- Collegial feedback
- Corrective action planning and goal setting

Each of these components alone is supported by research; together they are a no-fail combination for improvement! We wish you the best as you go forth and conquer...with data on your side.

9 Resources, Forms, and Templates

Throughout the book, we shared numerous strategies, resources, and forms. We recognize that some of you may want to create your own personalized versions of our creations and we are fine with that (though, of course, we do always like to be credited for our work). However, because we know how busy most educators are, we tried to create all the forms and templates you will need as you engage in the CTIME process. This chapter provides some of the key forms required for CTIME—ones that were too lengthy or too important to be hidden away in the body of a chapter. Feel free to copy and use these forms. If you prefer to download them so that you have them electronically, you can do so (using the password "BeyondCoteaching 118007" to unlock the PDF) at http://www.ascd.org/ASCD/pdf/books/murawski2017.pdf.

Take-Aways

- *A plethora of resources are available to you to aid in data collection. Do not feel you need to re-create the wheel.*
- *The CTSS Co-Teaching Core Competencies Observation Checklist enables observers to know what to look for, listen for, and ask for. It is available in hard copy and electronically.*
- *The forms included here are available electronically at http://www.ascd.org/ASCD/pdf/books/murawski2017.pdf*

In this chapter you will find the following documents:

Figure	Title	Purpose	Chapter in which it is described
9.1	CTSS Co-Teaching Core Competencies Observation Checklist	Used for all co-teaching observations	4
9.2	S.H.A.R.E. Worksheet	Used by co-teachers to share expectations and pet peeves prior to co-teaching	4
9.3	CTSS Co-Teaching Core Competencies Observation Self-Survey	Used by co-teachers to evaluate themselves on co-teaching core competencies and input ease scores	4
9.4	Co-Teaching Core Competencies Observation Checklist: Self-Reflection Comparison	Used to compare self-reflection scores of both co-teachers with observation scores by an administrator	4
9.5	Co-Teaching Team Classroom Family Survey	Used to obtain feedback about co-teaching from families	4
9.6	Co-Teaching Team Classroom Student Survey	Used to obtain feedback about co-teaching from students	4
9.7	Schoolwide Family Survey Summary Report	Used to record average family scores from all classes to obtain schoolwide score	4
9.8	Co-Teaching Team Classroom Family Survey Summary Report	Used to record average scores from families of students in one class to obtain co-teaching team score	4
9.9	Schoolwide Student Survey Summary Report	Used to record average student scores from all classes to obtain schoolwide score	4
9.10	Co-Teaching Team Classroom Student Survey Summary Report	Used to record average scores from all students in one class to obtain co-teaching team score	4
9.11	Corrective Action Plan (CAP) Form	Used by the schoolwide co-teaching leadership PLC to collect and analyze data, rank and prioritize focus competencies, and set goals	5

Figure	Title	Purpose	Chapter in which it is described
9.12	Professional Learning Actions for Teaching Effectiveness (PLATE) Form	Used by individual co-teaching teams to collect and analyze data, rank and prioritize focus competencies, and set goals	5
9.13	CTSS Co-Teaching Core Competencies Impact Values	Used to help triage core competencies and create PIE scores	5
9.14	CTSS Co-Teaching Core Competencies Ranking and Priority Worksheet	Used to document PIE scores and help identify focus competencies by ranking them in order	5
9.15	Strand Analysis Worksheet	Used to collect data from various sources to determine how the school or teams are doing on all strands	6
9.16	Domain and Strand Prioritizing and Ranking Form	Used to rank how well the school or teams are doing on domains and strands in order to rank and prioritize for future improvement	6

FIGURE 9.1

CTSS Co-Teaching Core Competencies Observation Checklist

General Educator: ____________ Special Service Provider: ____________ Date: ____________

Observer: ____________ Grade: ________ Content Area: ________ Period/Room: ____________

School: ____________ Term: ____________ Start: ____________ End: ____________

	LOOK FORS	Rating Score
4.5 Two or more professionals working together in the same physical space.	*0 = Only one adult; two adults not communicating at all; class always divided into two rooms.* *1 = Two adults in same room, but very little communication or collaborative work.* *2 = Two adults in same room; both engaged in class and each other (even if not perfectly).* *3 = Two adults collaborating together well in the same room.*	
9.5 Classroom environment demonstrates parity and collaboration (both names on board, sharing materials and space).	*0 = No demonstration of parity/collaboration; room appears to belong to one teacher only.* *1 = Some attempt at parity; both adults share a few materials and general space.* *2 = Parity exists; adults share classroom materials.* *3 = Clear parity; both names on the board/report card; two desks or shared space; obvious feeling from teachers that it is "our room."*	
11.6 Both teachers begin and end class together and remain in the room the entire time.	*0 = One adult is absent or late; adults may leave room for times not related to this class.* *1 = One adult may be late or leave early or may leave for brief time.* *2 = One adult may be late or leave early, but for remaining time they work together.* *3 = Both adults begin and end together, and are with students the entire time.* *Note: If adults have planned to use a regrouping approach (e.g., "parallel") and one adult takes a group of students out of the room (e.g., to the library), that is perfectly acceptable.*	
8.6 During instruction, both teachers assist students with and without disabilities.	*0 = Adults are not helping students or are only helping "their own" students.* *1 = There is some helping of various students, but at least one adult primarily stays with a few of "their own."* *2 = Both adults are willing to help all students, but students seem to have one adult they prefer to work with.* *3 = It is clear that both adults are willing to help all students and that students are used to this.*	
9.6 The class moves smoothly, with evidence of co-planning and communication between co-teachers.	*0 = Little to no prior planning is evident.* *1 = All planning appears to have been done by one adult.* *2 = Minimal planning is evident; most appears to have been done by one adult.* *3 = It is clear that both adults are comfortable with the lesson and know what is supposed to happen.*	
8.8 Class instruction and activities proactively promote multiple modes of representation, engagement, and expression (universal design for learning—UDL).	*0 = There is no evidence of universal design; all students are expected to do the same thing.* *1 = There is minimal evidence of universal design; limited opportunities for choice in how students learn, engage, and show what they've learned.* *2 = There is some evidence of universal design; some opportunities for choice in how students learn, engage, and show what they've learned.* *3 = The class was universally designed; opportunities for choice in how students learn, engage, and show what they've learned were well selected.*	
3.7 Differentiated content and strategies, based on formative assessment, are used to meet the range of learning needs.	*0 = There is no evidence of differentiation of instruction in the classroom.* *1 = There is minimal differentiation; most differentiation appears to be focused on groups rather than individuals.* *2 = Some differentiation is evident for individuals or groups.* *3 = It is clear that adults consider individual students' needs and regular use of differentiation is evident.*	

LOOK FORS		Rating Score
8.13 Technology (to include assistive technology) is used to enhance accessibility and learning.	*0 = There is no evidence of technology use.* *1 = There is limited use of technology.* *2 = Technology provides students with access and is used intermittently or sporadically.* *3 = Multiple technologies are utilized to make materials and content accessible and are used regularly.*	
5.7 A variety of instructional approaches (five co-teaching approaches) are used, including regrouping students.	*0 = Students remain in large class setting and adults use one teach, one support with one adult primarily in lead.* *1 = Adults rely solely on one teach, one support or team teaching.* *2 = Adults regroup students (using alternative, parallel, or station) at least once.* *3 = Adults use more than one of the five approaches (Friend & Cook's one teach, one support; team, parallel, station and alternative); at least one of the approaches involves regrouping students.* *Note: If teachers have been observed using other approaches in the past, and only one approach is observed today (e.g., station), it is acceptable to recall previous observations and give a 2 for using a variety of approaches as adults have demonstrated competency.*	
2.7 Both teachers engage in appropriate behavior management strategies as needed and are consistent in their approach to behavior management.	*0 = There is no obvious plan for behavior management, nor do adults appear to communicate about how they are approaching class management; possibly inappropriate class management.* *1 = Very little classroom management; mainly conducted by one teacher.* *2 = Behavior management strategies are utilized, but there is very little clear evidence of how adults have communicated about their use.* *3 = It is evident that adults have discussed how they will approach classroom/behavior management and adults are consistent in their approach.*	
11.3 It is difficult to tell the specialist from the general educator.	*0 = Observer could easily determine who was the general educator/specialist by their language/roles/lack of parity.* *1 = Teachers kept traditional roles in the classroom, but shared or switched roles once or twice.* *2 = Teachers worked at having parity in the class and shared most roles and responsibilities.* *3 = Adults shared the roles and responsibilities in the classroom and observer would not be able to tell who was the general educator/specialist.*	
1.6 It is difficult to tell the special education students from the general education students.	*0 = Observer could easily determine who were the general education or students with special needs by their lack of integration (e.g., students at back or separated from class).* *1 = There was some inclusion of most students in most activities.* *2 = There was a clear attempt at inclusion of all students for most activities.* *3 = All students were included and integrated seamlessly into all activities, even when adaptations were needed.*	
	LOOK FORS TOTAL	

Notes:

Continued on next page

LISTEN FORS		Rating Score
9.10 Co-teachers use language ("we"; "our") that demonstrates true collaboration and shared responsibility.	*0 = Adults do not communicate with each other.* *1 = Adults use "I" language frequently (e.g., "I want you to . . ." or "In my class . . ."), lacking parity.* *2 = Adults attempt to use "we" language and include each other, but it is clear that one adult is more used to "ruling" the class.* *3 = Adults clearly use "we" language (e.g., "We would like you to . . ."), showing that they both share the responsibility and students know they are equally in charge.*	
5.9 Communication (both verbal and nonverbal) between co-teachers is clear and positive.	*0 = Little to no communication is evident.* *1 = Communication is minimal, directive, or negative.* *2 = Limited communication, but it is positive in nature.* *3 = Both adults communicate regularly as class progresses and are respectful and positive.*	
1.8 Co-teachers phrase questions and statements so that it is obvious that all students in the class are included.	*0 = Class is very teacher-directed, with little involvement by students.* *1 = Questions/statements are general and not inclusive of all students.* *2 = Most statements/questions are phrased to encourage participation from a variety of students.* *3 = A clear attempt is made by both adults to engage all students through the use of a variety of types of questions and statements.*	
1.9 Students' conversations evidence a sense of community, including peers with disabilities and from diverse backgrounds.	*0 = Students do not talk to one another during class.* *1 = Specific students appear to be excluded from the majority of student interactions.* *2 = Most students appear to be included in the majority of student interactions.* *3 = It is evident from the students' actions and words that all students are considered an equal part of the class and are included in all student interactions.*	
8.16 Co-teachers ask questions at a variety of levels (basic recall to higher-order thinking) to meet all students' needs.	*0 = Adults do not use questions and most instruction is directive.* *1 = Questions are almost all geared just to one level (to the middle or "watered down").* *2 = Teachers use closed and open questions at a variety of levels in a general manner.* *3 = Closed and open questions are asked at a variety of levels in a way that demonstrates they are able to differentiate for specific students in order to ensure maximum (appropriate) levels of challenge.*	
	LISTEN FORS TOTAL	

Notes:

	ASK FORS*	Rating Score	Circle Evidence
7.2 Co-Planning	*0 = There is no evidence that this team co-plans. Most planning, if done at all, is done by one teacher.* *1 = This team rarely co-plans and communicates primarily on the fly.* *2 = This team co-plans at irregular times, but does try to integrate both teachers' perspectives when possible.* *3 = This team co-plans its lessons and integrates both teachers' areas of expertise to the maximum extent possible.*		**Lesson Plans** **Modified Materials** **Letters Home/Syllabi** **S.H.A.R.E. Worksheets** **Problem-Solving Worksheets** **Other:**
8.5 Co-Instruction: Parity	*0 = There is no evidence that this team co-instructs. One teacher is clearly responsible, as evidenced in documentation/plans, etc.* *1 = One teacher is clearly "lead"; however, the other does have intermittent areas of responsibility.* *2 = Both teachers are provided turns in co-instruction.* *3 = Teachers are comfortable in any role and roles are interchanging and fluid throughout the lesson plan.*		**Lesson Plans** **Behavior Documentation** **Tiered Lessons** **Class Notes** **Other:**
8.1 Co-Instruction: Grouping	*0 = There is no evidence that this team regroups during instruction. Whole group instruction is the norm.* *1 = At irregular times and for very specific activities, this class is regrouped into smaller groups.* *2 = Cooperative learning is used in class regularly and small groups are used at least once a week.* *3 = Whole group and regrouping approaches are used to match learning needs. Teachers clearly use regrouping regularly and are comfortable with a variety of the co-instructional approaches.*		**Lesson Plans** **Behavior Documentation** **Tiered Lessons** **Class Notes** **Other:**
1.2 Co-Instruction: Differentiation	*0 = There is no evidence that this team differentiates for the class. All lessons appear created so that students are expected to do the same things.* *1 = Minimal evidence demonstrates differentiation. What is available appears to focus on one or two specific students for limited activities or events (e.g., read test to Johnny).* *2 = Teachers appear to integrate differentiated instruction, content, and assessments into some lessons.* *3 = Teachers regularly include differentiated instruction, content, and assessments into their lessons. They clearly consider the needs of all students.*		**Lesson Plans** **Behavior Documentation** **Tiered Lessons** **Class Notes** **Other:**
6.1 Co-Assessment	*0 = There is no evidence that this team co-assesses. One teacher is in charge of the grades and gradebook.* *1 = Teachers talk about assessments at times, but each teacher is primarily in charge of his or her "own" students.* *2 = Teachers use differentiated assessments occasionally and are willing to share responsibility for grading.* *3 = Teachers share responsibility for creating assessments, grading, and for students' overall success. Differentiated assessments are created when needed, and both teachers are comfortable with adaptations.*		**Grade Book** **Modified Assignments** **Individual Grading Reports** **Other:**
Notes:		**ASK FORS TOTAL**	
		GRAND TOTAL	
0–29 **Not Yet Co-Teaching** 30–45 **Emerging Co-Teaching** 46–52 **Developing Co-Teaching** 53–59 **Proficient Co-Teaching** 60–66 **Master Co-Teaching**			

*See adapted growth ranges (Figure 4.4) if Ask Fors were not included in analysis.

Murawski, W.W., & Lochner, W.W. (2015). Co-Teaching Solutions Systems (CTSS) Observation Checklist. 2 TEACH LLC: Winnetka, CA.

FIGURE 9.2

S.H.A.R.E. Worksheet

S.H.A.R.E.
Sharing Hopes, Attitudes, Responsibilities, and Expectations

Directions: Take a few minutes to individually complete this worksheet. Be honest in your responses. After completing it individually, share the responses with your co-teaching partner by taking turns reading the responses. Do not use this time to comment on your partner's responses—merely read. After reading through the responses, take a moment or two to jot down any thoughts you have regarding what your partner has said. Then, come back together and begin to share reactions to the responses. Your goal is to either (a) Agree, (b) Compromise, or (c) Agree to Disagree.

1. Right now, my main **hope** regarding this co-teaching situation is:

___

___

2. My **attitude**/philosophy regarding teaching students with disabilities in a general education classroom is:

___

___

3. I would like to have the following **responsibilities** in a co-taught classroom:

___

___

4. I would like my co-teacher to have the following **responsibilities**:

___

___

5. I have the following **expectations** in a classroom:

(a) regarding discipline -

____

(b) regarding classwork -

____

(c) regarding materials -

____

(d) regarding homework -

____

(e) regarding planning -

____

(f) regarding adaptations for individual students -

____

(g) regarding grading -

____

(h) regarding noise level -

____

(i) regarding cooperative learning -

____

(j) regarding giving/receiving feedback -

____

(k) other important **expectations** I have-

____

First published in: Murawski, W.W. (2003). *Co-teaching in the inclusive classroom.* Bureau of Education & Research: Bellevue, WA. Also published in Murawski, W.W., & Dieker, L.A. (2004). Tips and strategies for co-teaching at the secondary level. *Teaching Exceptional Children, 36*(5), 52–58.

FIGURE 9.3

CTSS Co-Teaching Core Competencies Observation Self-Survey

General Educator: ______ Special Service Provider: ______ Date: ______

LOOK FORS		Rating Score	Ease Score
For the competency rating score, use the provided rubrics to rate each competency. The ease score is determined by how easy (0) to difficult (3) you feel it will be to implement the competency into your daily co-teaching practices.			
4.5 Two or more professionals working together in the same physical space.	*0 = Only one adult; two adults not communicating at all; class always divided into two rooms.* *1 = Two adults in same room, but very little communication or collaborative work.* *2 = Two adults in same room; both engaged in class and each other (even if not perfectly).* *3 = Two adults collaborating together well in the same room.*		
9.5 Classroom environment demonstrates parity and collaboration (both names on board, sharing materials and space).	*0 = No demonstration of parity/collaboration; room appears to belong to one teacher only.* *1 = Some attempt at parity; both adults share a few materials and general space.* *2 = Parity exists; adults share classroom materials.* *3 = Clear parity; both names on the board/report card; two desks or shared space; obvious feeling from teachers that it is "our room."*		
11.6 Both teachers begin and end class together and remain in the room the entire time.	*0 = One adult is absent or late; adults may leave room for times not related to this class.* *1 = One adult may be late or leave early or may leave for brief time.* *2 = One adult may be late or leave early, but for remaining time they work together.* *3 = Both adults begin and end together, and are with students the entire time.* *Note: If adults have planned to use a regrouping approach (e.g., "parallel") and one adult takes a group of students out of the room (e.g., to the library), that is perfectly acceptable.*		
8.6 During instruction, both teachers assist students with and without disabilities.	*0 = Adults are not helping students or are only helping "their own" students.* *1 = There is some helping of various students, but at least one adult primarily stays with a few of "their own."* *2 = Both adults are willing to help all students, but students seem to have one adult they prefer to work with.* *3 = It is clear that both adults are willing to help all students and that students are used to this.*		
9.6 The class moves smoothly, with evidence of co-planning and communication between co-teachers.	*0 = Little to no prior planning is evident.* *1 = All planning appears to have been done by one adult.* *2 = Minimal planning is evident; most appears to have been done by one adult.* *3 = It is clear that both adults are comfortable with the lesson and know what is supposed to happen.*		
8.8 Class instruction and activities proactively promote multiple modes of representation, engagement, and expression (universal design for learning—UDL).	*0 = There is no evidence of universal design; all students are expected to do the same thing.* *1 = There is minimal evidence of universal design; limited opportunities for choice in how students learn, engage, and show what they've learned.* *2 = There is some evidence of universal design; some opportunities for choice in how students learn, engage, and show what they've learned.* *3 = The class was universally designed; opportunities for choice in how students learn, engage, and show what they've learned were well selected.*		

LOOK FORS		Rating Score	Ease Score
3.7 Differentiated content and strategies, based on formative assessment, are used to meet the range of learning needs.	*0 = There is no evidence of differentiation of instruction in the classroom.* *1 = There is minimal differentiation; most differentiation appears to be focused on groups rather than individuals.* *2 = Some differentiation is evident for individuals or groups.* *3 = It is clear that adults consider individual students' needs and regular use of differentiation is evident.*		
8.13 Technology (to include assistive technology) is used to enhance accessibility and learning.	*0 = There is no evidence of technology use.* *1 = There is limited use of technology.* *2 = Technology provides students with access and is used intermittently or sporadically.* *3 = Multiple technologies are utilized to make materials and content accessible and are used regularly.*		
5.7 A variety of instructional approaches (five co-teaching approaches) are used, including regrouping students.	*0 = Students remain in large class setting and adults use one teach, one support with one adult primarily in lead.* *1 = Adults rely solely on one teach, one support or team teaching.* *2 = Adults regroup students (using alternative, parallel, or station) at least once.* *3 = Adults use more than one of the five approaches (Friend & Cook's one teach, one support; team, parallel, station, and alternative); at least one of the approaches involves regrouping students.* *Note: If teachers have been observed using other approaches in the past, and only one approach is observed today (e.g., station), it is acceptable to recall previous observations and give a 2 for using a variety of approaches as adults have demonstrated competency.*		
2.7 Both teachers engage in appropriate behavior management strategies as needed and are consistent in their approach to behavior management.	*0 = There is no obvious plan for behavior management, nor do adults appear to communicate about how they are approaching class management; possibly inappropriate class management.* *1 = Very little classroom management; mainly conducted by one teacher.* *2 = Behavior management strategies are utilized, but there is very little clear evidence of how adults have communicated about their use.* *3 = It is evident that adults have discussed how they will approach classroom/behavior management and adults are consistent in their approach.*		
11.3 It is difficult to tell the specialist from the general educator.	*0 = Observer could easily determine who was the general educator/specialist by their language/roles/ lack of parity.* *1 = Teachers kept traditional roles in the classroom, but shared or switched roles once or twice.* *2 = Teachers worked at having parity in the class and shared most roles and responsibilities.* *3 = Adults shared the roles and responsibilities in the classroom and observer would not be able to tell who was the general educator/specialist.*		
1.6 It is difficult to tell the special education students from the general education students.	*0 = Observer could easily determine who were the general education or students with special needs by their lack of integration (e.g., students at back or separated from class).* *1 = There was some inclusion of most students in most activities.* *2 = There was a clear attempt at inclusion of all students for most activities.* *3 = All students were included and integrated seamlessly into all activities, even when adaptations were needed.*		
	LOOK FORS TOTAL		
Notes:			

Continued on next page

	LISTEN FORS	Rating Score	Ease Score
9.10 Co-teachers use language ("we"; "our") that demonstrates true collaboration and shared responsibility.	*0 = Adults do not communicate with each other.* *1 = Adults use "I" language frequently (e.g., "I want you to . . ." or "In my class . . ."), lacking parity.* *2 = Adults attempt to use "we" language and include each other, but it is clear that one adult is more used to "ruling" the class.* *3 = Adults clearly use "we" language (e.g., "We would like you to . . ."), showing that they both share the responsibility and students know they are equally in charge.*		
5.9 Communication (both verbal and nonverbal) between co-teachers is clear and positive.	*0 = Little to no communication is evident.* *1 = Communication is minimal, directive, or negative.* *2 = Limited communication, but it is positive in nature.* *3 = Both adults communicate regularly as class progresses and are respectful and positive.*		
1.8 Co-teachers phrase questions and statements so that it is obvious that all students in the class are included.	*0 = Class is very teacher-directed, with little involvement by students.* *1 = Questions/statements are general and not inclusive of all students.* *2 = Most statements/questions are phrased to encourage participation from a variety of students.* *3 = A clear attempt is made by both adults to engage all students through the use of a variety of types of questions and statements.*		
1.9 Students' conversations evidence a sense of community, including peers with disabilities and from diverse backgrounds.	*0 = Students do not talk to one another during class.* *1 = Specific students appear to be excluded from the majority of student interactions.* *2 = Most students appear to be included in the majority of student interactions.* *3 = It is evident from the students' actions and words that all students are considered an equal part of the class and are included in all student interactions.*		
8.16 Co-teachers ask questions at a variety of levels (basic recall to higher-order thinking) to meet all students' needs.	*0 = Adults do not use questions and most instruction is directive.* *1 = Questions are almost all geared just to one level (to the middle or "watered down").* *2 = Teachers use closed and open questions at a variety of levels in a general manner.* *3 = Closed and open questions are asked at a variety of levels in a way that demonstrates they are able to differentiate for specific students in order to ensure maximum (appropriate) levels of challenge.*		
	LISTEN FORS TOTAL		

Notes:

ASK FORS*		Rating Score	Ease Score	Circle Evidence
7.2 Co-Planning	*0 = There is no evidence that this team co-plans. Most planning, if done at all, is done by one teacher.* *1 = This team rarely co-plans and communicates primarily on the fly.* *2 = This team co-plans at irregular times, but does try to integrate both teachers' perspectives when possible.* *3 = This team co-plans its lessons and integrates both teachers' areas of expertise to the maximum extent possible.*			**Lesson Plans** **Modified Materials** **Letters Home/Syllabi** **S.H.A.R.E. Worksheets** **Problem-Solving Worksheets** **Other:**
8.5 Co-Instruction: Parity	*0 = There is no evidence that this team co-instructs. One teacher is clearly responsible, as evidenced in documentation/plans, etc.* *1 = One teacher is clearly "lead"; however, the other does have intermittent areas of responsibility.* *2 = Both teachers are provided turns in co-instruction.* *3 = Teachers are comfortable in any role and roles are interchanging and fluid throughout the lesson plan.*			**Lesson Plans** **Behavior Documentation** **Tiered Lessons** **Class Notes** **Other:**
8.1 Co-Instruction: Grouping	*0 = There is no evidence that this team regroups during instruction. Whole group instruction is the norm.* *1 = At irregular times and for very specific activities, this class is regrouped into smaller groups.* *2 = Cooperative learning is used in class regularly and small groups are used at least once a week.* *3 = Whole group and regrouping approaches are used to match learning needs. Teachers clearly use regrouping regularly and are comfortable with a variety of the co-instructional approaches.*			**Lesson Plans** **Behavior Documentation** **Tiered Lessons** **Class Notes** **Other:**
1.2 Co-Instruction: Differentiation	*0 = There is no evidence that this team differentiates for the class. All lessons appear created so that students are expected to do the same things.* *1 = Minimal evidence demonstrates differentiation. What is available appears to focus on one or two specific students for limited activities or events (e.g., read test to Johnny).* *2 = Teachers appear to integrate differentiated instruction, content, and assessments into some lessons.* *3 = Teachers regularly include differentiated instruction, content, and assessments into their lessons. They clearly consider the needs of all students.*			**Lesson Plans** **Behavior Documentation** **Tiered Lessons** **Class Notes** **Other:**
6.1 Co-Assessment	*0 = There is no evidence that this team co-assesses. One teacher is in charge of the grades and gradebook.* *1 = Teachers talk about assessments at times, but each teacher is primarily in charge of his or her "own" students.* *2 = Teachers use differentiated assessments occasionally and are willing to share responsibility for grading.* *3 = Teachers share responsibility for creating assessments, grading, and for students' overall success. Differentiated assessments are created when needed, and both teachers are comfortable with adaptations.*			**Grade Book** **Modified Assignments** **Individual Grading Reports** **Other:**
Notes:		**ASK FORS TOTAL**		
		GRAND TOTAL		
0–29 **Not Yet Co-Teaching** 30–45 **Emerging Co-Teaching** 46–52 **Developing Co-Teaching** 53–59 **Proficient Co-Teaching** 60–66 **Master Co-Teaching**				

*See adapted growth ranges (Figure 4.4) if Ask Fors were not included in analysis.

FIGURE 9.4

Co-Teaching Core Competencies Observation Checklist: Self-Reflection Comparison

General Educator: ______ Special Service Provider: ______ Date: ______
Observer: ______ Grade: ______ Content Area: ______ Period/Room: ______
School: ______ Term: ______ Start: ______ End: ______

	LOOK FORS	General Educator Rating	Specialist Rating	Administrator Rating
4.5 Two or more professionals working together in the same physical space.	*0 = Only one adult; two adults not communicating at all; class always divided into two rooms.* *1 = Two adults in same room, but very little communication or collaborative work.* *2 = Two adults in same room; both engaged in class and each other (even if not perfectly).* *3 = Two adults collaborating together well in the same room.*			
9.5 Class environment demonstrates parity and collaboration (both names on board, sharing materials and space).	*0 = No demonstration of parity/collaboration; room appears to belong to one teacher only.* *1 = Some attempt at parity; both adults share a few materials and general space.* *2 = Parity exists; adults share classroom materials.* *3 = Clear parity; both names on the board/report card; two desks or shared space; obvious feeling from teachers that it is "our room."*			
11.6 Both teachers begin and end class together and remain in the room the entire time.	*0 = One adult is absent or late; adults may leave room for times not related to this class.* *1 = One adult may be late or leave early or may leave for brief time.* *2 = One adult may be late or leave early, but for remaining time they work together.* *3 = Both adults begin and end together, and are with students the entire time.* *Note: If adults have planned to use a regrouping approach (e.g., "parallel") and one adult takes a group of students out of the room (e.g., to the library), that is perfectly acceptable.*			
8.6 During instruction, both teachers assist students with and without disabilities.	*0 = Adults are not helping students or are only helping "their own" students.* *1 = There is some helping of various students but at least one adult primarily stays with a few of "their own."* *2 = Both adults are willing to help all students, but students seem to have one adult they prefer to work with.* *3 = It is clear that both adults are willing to help all students and that students are used to this.*			
9.6 The class moves smoothly, with evidence of co-planning and communication between co-teachers.	*0 = Little to no prior planning is evident.* *1 = All planning appears to have been done by one adult.* *2 = Minimal planning is evident; most appears to have been done by one adult.* *3 = It is clear that both adults are comfortable with the lesson and know what is supposed to happen.*			

	LOOK FORS	General Educator Rating	Specialist Rating	Administrator Rating
8.8 Class instruction and activities proactively promote multiple modes of representation, engagement, and expression (universal design for learning—UDL)	*0 = There is no evidence of universal design; all students are expected to do the same thing.* *1 = There is minimal evidence of universal design; limited opportunities for choice in how students learn, engage, and show what they've learned.* *2 = There is some evidence of universal design; some opportunities for choice in how students learn, engage, and show what they've learned.* *3 = The class was universally designed; opportunities for choice in how students learn, engage, and show what they've learned were well selected.*			
3.7 Differentiated content and strategies, based on formative assessment, are used to meet the range of learning needs.	*0 = There is no evidence of differentiation of instruction in the classroom.* *1 = There is minimal differentiation; most differentiation appears to be focused on groups rather than individuals.* *2 = Some differentiation is evident for individuals or groups.* *3 = It is clear that adults consider individual students' needs and regular use of differentiation is evident.*			
8.13 Technology (to include assistive technology) is used to enhance accessibility and learning	*0 = There is no evidence of technology use.* *1 = There is limited use of technology.* *2 = Technology provides students with access and is used intermittently or sporadically.* *3 = Multiple technologies are utilized to make materials and content accessible and are used regularly.*			
5.7 A variety of instructional approaches (five co-teaching approaches) are used, including regrouping students.	*0 = Students remain in large class setting and adults use one teach, one support with one adult primarily in lead.* *1 = Adults rely solely on one teach, one support or team teaching.* *2 = Adults regroup students (using alternative, parallel, or station) at least once.* *3 = Adults use more than one of the five approaches (Friend & Cook's one teach, one support; team, parallel, station and alternative); at least one of the approaches involves regrouping students.* *Note: If teachers have been observed using other approaches in the past, and only one approach is observed today (e.g., station), it is acceptable to recall previous observations and give a 2 for using a variety of approaches as adults have demonstrated competency.*			
2.7 Both teachers engage in appropriate behavior management strategies as needed and are consistent in their approach to behavior management.	*0 = There is no obvious plan for behavior management, nor do adults appear to communicate about how they are approaching class management; possibly inappropriate class management.* *1 = Very little classroom management; mainly conducted by one teacher.* *2 = Behavior management strategies are utilized, but there is very little clear evidence of how adults have communicated about their use.* *3 = It is evident that adults have discussed how they will approach classroom/behavior management and adults are consistent in their approach.*			

Continued on next page

	LOOK FORS	General Educator Rating	Specialist Rating	Administrator Rating
11.3 It is difficult to tell the specialist from the general educator.	*0 = Observer could easily determine who was the general educator/ specialist by their language/roles/ lack of parity.* *1 = Teachers kept traditional roles in the classroom, but shared or switched roles once or twice.* *2 = Teachers worked at having parity in the class and shared most roles and responsibilities.* *3 = Adults shared the roles and responsibilities in the classroom and observer would not be able to tell who was the general educator/ specialist.*			
1.6 It is difficult to tell the special education students from the general education students.	*0 = Observer could easily determine who were the general education or students with special needs by their lack of integration (e.g., students at back or separated from class).* *1 = There was some inclusion of most students in most activities.* *2 = There was a clear attempt at inclusion of all students for most activities.* *3 = All students were included and integrated seamlessly into all activities, even when adaptations were needed.*			
	LOOK FORS TOTAL			

	LISTEN FORS	General Educator Rating	Specialist Rating	Administrator Rating
9.10 Co-teachers use language ("we"; "our") that demonstrates true collaboration and shared responsibility.	*0 = Adults do not communicate with each other.* *1 = Adults use "I" language frequently (e.g., "I want you to . . ." or "In my class . . ."), lacking parity.* *2 = Adults attempt to use "we" language and include each other, but it is clear that one adult is more used to "ruling" the class.* *3 = Adults clearly use "we" language (e.g., "We would like you to . . ."), showing that they both share the responsibility and students know they are equally in charge.*			
5.9 Communication (both verbal and nonverbal) between co-teachers is clear and positive.	*0 = Little to no communication is evident.* *1 = Communication is minimal, directive, or negative.* *2 = Limited communication; but it is positive in nature.* *3 = Both adults communicate regularly as class progresses and are respectful and positive.*			
1.8 Co-teachers phrase questions and statements so that it is obvious that all students in the class are included.	*0 = Class is very teacher-directed, with little involvement by students.* *1 = Questions/statements are general and not inclusive of all students.* *2 = Most statements/questions are phrased to encourage participation from a variety of students.* *3 = A clear attempt is made by both adults to engage all students through the use of a variety of types of questions and statements.*			
1.9 Students' conversations evidence a sense of community, including peers with disabilities and from diverse backgrounds.	*0 = Students do not talk to one another during class.* *1 = Specific students appear to be excluded from the majority of student interactions.* *2 = Most students appear to be included in the majority of student interactions.* *3 = It is evident from the students' actions and words that all students are considered an equal part of the class and are included in all student interactions.*			
8.16 Co-teachers ask questions at a variety of levels (basic recall to higher-order thinking) to meet all students' needs.	*0 = Adults do not use questions and most instruction is directive.* *1 = Questions are almost all geared just to one level (to the middle or "watered down").* *2 = Teachers use closed and open questions at a variety of levels in a general manner.* *3 = Closed and open questions are asked at a variety of levels in a way that demonstrates they are able to differentiate for specific students in order to ensure maximum (appropriate) levels of challenge.*			
	LISTEN FORS TOTAL			

Continued on next page

	ASK FORS*	General Educator Rating	Specialist Rating	Administrator Rating
7.2 Co-Planning	*0 = There is no evidence that this team co-plans. Most planning, if done at all, is done by one teacher.* *1 = This team rarely co-plans and communicates primarily on the fly.* *2 = This team co-plans at irregular times, but does try to integrate both teachers' perspectives when possible.* *3 = This team co-plans its lessons and integrates both teachers' areas of expertise to the maximum extent possible.* ***Examples: Lesson Plans, Modified Materials, Letters Home/Syllabi, S.H.A.R.E. Worksheets, Problem-Solving Worksheets***			
8.5 Co-Instruction: Parity	*0 = There is no evidence that this team co-instructs. One teacher is clearly responsible, as evidenced in documentation/plans, etc.* *1 = One teacher is clearly "lead"; however, the other does have intermittent areas of responsibility.* *2 = Both teachers are provided turns in co-instruction.* *3 = Teachers are comfortable in any role and roles are interchanging and fluid throughout the lesson plan.* ***Examples: Lesson Plans, Behavior Documentation, Tiered Lessons, Class Notes***			
8.1 Co-Instruction: Grouping	*0 = There is no evidence that this team regroups during instruction. Whole group instruction is the norm.* *1 = At irregular times and for very specific activities, this class is regrouped into smaller groups.* *2 = Cooperative learning is used in class regularly and small groups are used at least once a week.* *3 = Whole group and regrouping approaches are used to match learning needs. Teachers clearly use regrouping regularly and are comfortable with a variety of the co-instructional approaches.* ***Examples: Lesson Plans, Behavior Documentation, Tiered Lessons, Class Notes***			
1.2 Co-Instruction: Differentiation	*0 = There is no evidence that this team differentiates for the class. All lessons appear created so that students are expected to do the same things.* *1 = Minimal evidence demonstrates differentiation. What is available appears to focus on one or two specific students for limited activities or events (e.g., read test to Johnny).* *2 = Teachers appear to integrate differentiated instruction, content, and assessments into some lessons.* *3 = Teachers regularly include differentiated instruction, content, and assessments into their lessons. They clearly consider the needs of all students.* ***Examples: Lesson Plans, Behavior Documentation, Tiered Lessons, Class Notes***			

	ASK FORS	General Educator Rating	Specialist Rating	Administrator Rating
6.1 Co-Assessment	*0 = There is no evidence that this team co-assesses. One teacher is in charge of the grades and gradebook.* *1 = Teachers talk about assessments at times, but each teacher is primarily in charge of his or her "own" students.* *2 = Teachers use differentiated assessments occasionally and are willing to share responsibility for grading.* *3 = Teachers share responsibility for creating assessments, grading, and for students' overall success. Differentiated assessments are created when needed, and both teachers are comfortable with adaptations.* ***Examples: Grade Book, Modified Assignments, Individual Grading Reports***			
	ASK FORS TOTAL			

*See adapted growth ranges (Figure 4.4) Ask Fors were not included in analysis.

FIGURE 9.5

Co-Teaching Team Classroom Family Survey

Team: ____________ Area/Grade/Period: ____________ Date: ____________

Directions: Please rate each indicator using the following scale: ***0-Disagree; 1-Agree Somewhat; 2-Agree; 3-Agree Strongly; DNK-Do Not Know***	**Rating Score**
4.5 My child's classroom has two teachers.	
9.5 I receive information about the classroom rules with signatures from both teachers.	
11.6 Both my child's teachers remain in the classroom for the entire class time.	
8.6 My child receives instruction from both teachers, as evidenced by his assignments, lecture notes, and materials.	
9.6 My child's class appears to be very well organized.	
8.8 Information during the class is presented in multiple formats, as evidenced by my child's assignments. They are not always paper-pencil assignments.	
3.7 My child receives choices of options for activities, assignment, and homework.	
8.13 My child is provided with electronic tools, if needed, to assist with assignments or work.	
5.7 My child works in groups in his collaborative class.	
2.7 I receive letters and materials sent home that have both teachers' names or signatures on them.	
11.3 During parent-teacher conferences or communication, I cannot tell the general educator from the special educator.	
1.6 My child accepts all students in his classroom.	
9.10 I receive information from both teachers regarding my child's attendance, tardies, behavior issues, classwork, or homework.	
5.9 My child expresses that both teachers get along during class.	
1.8 The teachers include my child in all activities.	
1.9 My child feels accepted in the inclusive classroom.	
8.16 Both teachers ask questions that help my child learn his classwork.	
7.2 My child brings home assignment notifications prior to having to complete projects or assignments, demonstrating to me that the class has been very well planned.	
8.5 I feel my child receives quality instruction from BOTH teachers.	
8.1 My child gets put into more than one group during class.	
1.2 My child's tests are adapted, if needed.	
6.1 My child's work is returned with comments/grades/feedback from both teachers.	

FIGURE 9.6

Co-Teaching Team Classroom Student Survey

Team: ______ Area/Grade/Period: ______ Date: ______	
Directions: Please rate each indicator using the following scale: ***0-Disagree; 1-Agree Somewhat; 2-Agree; 3-Agree Strongly; DNK-Do Not Know***	**Rating Score**
4.5 Our classroom displays both teachers' names in the room and on materials.	
9.5 Our classroom has two teachers in the classroom.	
11.6 Both teachers begin and end class together and remain in the room the entire time.	
8.6 Both teachers work with all students in the classroom.	
9.6 It is obvious that both teachers plan lessons together and class time runs smoothly.	
8.8 Both teachers use multiple types of materials (in print, audio, or video) to present the lesson.	
3.7 Students are given a choice of options for activities, assignments, and homework.	
8.13 Classwork, tests, and homework are provided on paper, computer, tablet, phone, or other tools that work best for me.	
5.7 The co-teachers regroup students and each teacher works with all groups.	
2.7 Both teachers are consistent with the classroom rules and rewards.	
11.3 I cannot tell which teacher is the general education teacher and which is the special education teacher.	
1.6 All students in the class are accepted.	
9.10 Both teachers use language such as "we" and "our" to make the students feel like they are both our teachers and any letters or materials sent home have both teachers' names on them.	
5.9 Both teachers get along during class.	
1.8 Both teachers ask questions that all students can answer.	
1.9 Students have conversations with all students in the classroom.	
8.16 Both teachers ask questions that are both difficult and easy.	
7.2 Both teachers collect and check classwork and homework, check attendance, and address tardies or behavior issues.	
8.5 Both my teachers provide instruction during class.	
8.1 We often change groups throughout class time.	
1.2 Tests are adapted so that not everyone always takes the same test at the same time.	
6.1 Both teachers grade assignments.	

FIGURE 9.7

Schoolwide Family Survey Summary Report

Team: ______ Area/Grade/Period: ______ Collection Period: ______	
Average the results from surveys returned and enter score for each.	**Average Score**
4.5 My child's classroom has two teachers.	
9.5 I receive information about the classroom rules with signatures from both teachers.	
11.6 Both my child's teachers remain in the classroom for the entire class time.	
8.6 My child receives instruction from both teachers, as evidenced by her assignments, lecture notes, and materials.	
9.6 My child's class appears to be very well organized.	
8.8 Information during the class is presented in multiple formats, as evidenced by my child's assignments. They are not always paper-pencil assignments.	
3.7 My child receives choices of options for activities, assignment, and homework.	
8.13 My child is provided with electronic tools, if needed, to assist with assignments or work.	
5.7 My child works in groups in her collaborative class.	
2.7 I receive letters and materials sent home that have both teachers' names or signatures on them.	
11.3 During parent-teacher conferences or communication, I cannot tell the general educator from the special educator.	
1.6 My child accepts all students in her classroom.	
9.10 I receive information from both teachers regarding my child's attendance, tardies, behavior issues, classwork, or homework.	
5.9 My child expresses that both teachers get along during class.	
1.8 The teachers include my child in all activities.	
1.9 My child feels accepted in the inclusive classroom.	
8.16 Both teachers ask questions that help my child learn her classwork.	
7.2 My child brings home assignment notifications prior to having to complete projects or assignments, demonstrating to me that the class has been very well planned.	
8.5 I feel my child receives quality instruction from BOTH teachers.	
8.1 My child gets put into more than one group during class.	
1.2 My child's tests are adapted, if needed.	
6.1 My child's work is returned with comments/grades/feedback from both teachers.	

FIGURE 9.8

Co-Teaching Team Classroom Family Survey Summary Report

Team: ____________ Area/Grade/Period: ____________ Collection Period: ____________

Average the results from surveys returned and enter score for each.	**Average Score**
4.5 My child's classroom has two teachers.	
9.5 I receive information about the classroom rules with signatures from both teachers.	
11.6 Both my child's teachers remain in the classroom for the entire class time.	
8.6 My child receives instruction from both teachers, as evidenced by her assignments, lecture notes, and materials.	
9.6 My child's class appears to be very well organized.	
8.8 Information during the class is presented in multiple formats, as evidenced by my child's assignments. They are not always paper-pencil assignments.	
3.7 My child receives choices of options for activities, assignment, and homework.	
8.13 My child is provided with electronic tools, if needed, to assist with assignments or work.	
5.7 My child works in groups in her collaborative class.	
2.7 I receive letters and materials sent home that have both teachers' names or signatures on them.	
11.3 During parent-teacher conferences or communication, I cannot tell the general educator from the special educator.	
1.6 My child accepts all students in her classroom.	
9.10 I receive information from both teachers regarding my child's attendance, tardies, behavior issues, classwork, or homework.	
5.9 My child expresses that both teachers get along during class.	
1.8 The teachers include my child in all activities.	
1.9 My child feels accepted in the inclusive classroom.	
8.16 Both teachers ask questions that help my child learn her classwork.	
7.2 My child brings home assignment notifications prior to having to complete projects or assignments, demonstrating to me that the class has been very well planned.	
8.5 I feel my child receives quality instruction from BOTH teachers.	
8.1 My child gets put into more than one group during class.	
1.2 My child's tests are adapted, if needed.	
6.1 My child's work is returned with comments/grades/feedback from both teachers.	

FIGURE 9.9

Schoolwide Student Survey Summary Report

Team: ______________ Area/Grade/Period: ______________ Collection Period: ______________

Average the results from surveys returned and enter score for each.	**Average Score**
4.5 Our classroom displays both teachers' names in the room and on materials.	
9.5 Our classroom has two teachers in the classroom.	
11.6 Both teachers begin and end class together and remain in the room the entire time.	
8.6 Both teachers work with all students in the classroom.	
9.6 It is obvious that both teachers plan lessons together and class time runs smoothly.	
8.8 Both teachers use multiple types of materials (in print, audio, or video) to present the lesson.	
3.7 Students are given a choice of options for activities, assignments, and homework.	
8.13 Classwork, tests, and homework are provided on paper, computer, tablet, phone, or other tools that work best for me.	
5.7 The co-teachers regroup students and each teacher works with all groups.	
2.7 Both teachers are consistent with the classroom rules and rewards.	
11.3 I cannot tell which teacher is the general education teacher and which is the special education teacher.	
1.6 All students in the class are accepted.	
9.10 Both teachers use language such as "we" and "our" to make the students feel like they are both our teachers and any letters or materials sent home have both teachers' names on them.	
5.9 Both teachers get along during class.	
1.8 Both teachers ask questions that all students can answer.	
1.9 Students have conversations with all students in the classroom.	
8.16 Both teachers ask questions that are both difficult and easy.	
7.2 Both teachers collect and check classwork and homework, check attendance, and address tardies or behavior issues.	
8.5 Both my teachers provide instruction during class.	
8.1 We often change groups throughout class time.	
1.2 Tests are adapted so that not everyone always takes the same test at the same time.	
6.1 Both teachers grade assignments.	

FIGURE 9.10

Co-Teaching Team Classroom Student Survey Summary Report

Team: ______________ Area/Grade/Period: ______________ Collection Period: ______________

Average the results from surveys returned and enter score for each.	**Average Score**
4.5 Our classroom displays both teachers' names in the room and on materials.	
9.5 Our classroom has two teachers in the classroom.	
11.6 Both teachers begin and end class together and remain in the room the entire time.	
8.6 Both teachers work with all students in the classroom.	
9.6 It is obvious that both teachers plan lessons together and class time runs smoothly.	
8.8 Both teachers use multiple types of materials (in print, audio, or video) to present the lesson.	
3.7 Students are given a choice of options for activities, assignments, and homework.	
8.13 Classwork, tests, and homework are provided on paper, computer, tablet, phone, or other tools that work best for me.	
5.7 The co-teachers regroup students and each teacher works with all groups.	
2.7 Both teachers are consistent with the classroom rules and rewards.	
11.3 I cannot tell which teacher is the general education teacher and which is the special education teacher.	
1.6 All students in the class are accepted.	
9.10 Both teachers use language such as "we" and "our" to make the students feel like they are both our teachers and any letters or materials sent home have both teachers' names on them.	
5.9 Both teachers get along during class.	
1.8 Both teachers ask questions that all students can answer.	
1.9 Students have conversations with all students in the classroom.	
8.16 Both teachers ask questions that are both difficult and easy.	
7.2 Both teachers collect and check classwork and homework, check attendance, and address tardies or behavior issues.	
8.5 Both my teachers provide instruction during class.	
8.1 We often change groups throughout class time.	
1.2 Tests are adapted so that not everyone always takes the same test at the same time.	
6.1 Both teachers grade assignments.	

FIGURE 9.11

Corrective Action Plan (CAP) Form

Focus	Team		Content Area									
	School Term		Grade					Period				
X	LOOK FORS		SS 1	SS 2	Obs 1	Obs 2	Obs 3	Obs 4	S1	S2	F1	F2
	4.5 Two or more professionals working together in the same physical space.	*0 = Only one adult; two adults not communicating at all; class always divided into two rooms.*										
		1 = Two adults in same room, but very little communication or collaborative work.	Goals:									
		2 = Two adults in same room; both engaged in class and each other (even if not perfectly).	PIE:									
		3 = Two adults collaborating together well in the same room.	Ease:		Impact:		Rank:					
	Next Steps:											
	9.5 Class environment demonstrates parity and collaboration (both names on board, sharing materials and space).	*0 = No demonstration of parity/collaboration; room appears to belong to one teacher only.*										
		1 = Some attempt at parity; both adults share a few materials and general space.	Goals:									
		2 = Parity exists; adults share classroom materials.	PIE:									
		3 = Clear parity; both names on board/report card; two desks or shared space; obvious feeling from teacher that it is "our room."	Ease:		Impact:		Rank:					
	Next Steps:											
	11.6 Both teachers begin and end class together and remain in the room the entire time.	*0 = One adult is absent or late; adults may leave room for times not related to this class.*										
		1 = One adult may be late or leave early or may leave for brief time.	Goals:									
		2 = One adult may be late or leave early, but for remaining time they work together.	PIE:									
		3 = Both adults begin and end together, and are with students the entire time.	Ease:		Impact:		Rank:					
		Note: if adults have planned to use a regrouping approach (e.g., "parallel") and one adult takes a group of students out of the room (e.g., to the library), that is perfectly acceptable.										

Focus	Team		Content Area									
	School Term			Grade				Period				
X	LOOK FORS		SS 1	SS 2	Obs 1	Obs 2	Obs 3	Obs 4	S1	S2	F1	F2
	Next Steps:											
	8.6 During instruction, both teachers assist students with and without disabilities.	*0 = Adults are not helping students or are only helping "their own" students.*										
		1 = There is some helping of various students, but at least one adult primarily stays with a few of "their own."	**Goals:**									
		2 = Both adults are willing to help all students, but students seem to have one adult they prefer to work with.	**PIE:**									
		3 = It is clear that both adults are willing to help all students and that students are used to this.	**Ease:**		**Impact:**		**Rank:**					
	Next Steps:											
	9.6 The class moves smoothly, with evidence of co-planning and communication between co-teachers.	*0 = Little to no prior planning is evident.*										
		1 = All planning appears to have been done by one adult.	**Goals:**									
		2 = Minimal planning is evident; most appears to have been done by one adult.	**PIE:**									
		3 = It is clear that both adults are comfortable with the lesson and know what is supposed to happen.	**Ease:**		**Impact:**		**Rank:**					
	Next Steps:											
	8.8 Class instruction and activities proactively promote multiple modes of representation, engagement, and expression (universal design for learning—UDL)	*0 = There is no evidence of universal design; all students are expected to do the same thing.*										
		1 = There is minimal evidence of universal design; limited opportunities for choice in how students learn, engage, and show what they've learned.	**Goals:**									
		2 = There is some evidence of universal design; some opportunities for choice in how students learn, engage, and show what they've learned.	**PIE:**									
		3 = The class was universally designed; opportunities for choice in how students learn, engage, and show what they've learned were well selected.	**Ease:**		**Impact:**		**Rank:**					
	Next Steps:											

Continued on next page

Focus	Team		Content Area									
	School Term		Grade					Period				
X	**LOOK FORS**		SS 1	SS 2	Obs 1	Obs 2	Obs 3	Obs 4	S1	S2	F1	F2
	3.7 Differentiated content and strategies, based on formative assessment, are used to meet the range of learning needs.	*0 = There is no evidence of differentiation of instruction in the classroom.*										
		1 = There is minimal differentiation; most differentiation appears to be focused on groups rather than individuals.	Goals:									
		2 = Some differentiation is evident for individuals or groups.	PIE:									
		3 = It is clear that adults consider individual students' needs and regular use of differentiation is evident.	Ease:		Impact:		Rank:					
	Next Steps:											
	8.13 Technology (to include assistive technology) is used to enhance accessibility and learning.	*0 = There is no evidence of technology use.*										
		1 = There is limited use of technology.	Goals:									
		2 = Technology provides students with access and is used intermittently or sporadically.	PIE:									
		3 = Multiple technologies are utilized to make materials and content accessible and are used regularly.	Ease:		Impact:		Rank:					
	Next Steps:											
	5.7 A variety of instructional approaches (five co-teaching approaches) are used, including regrouping students.	*0 = Students remain in large class setting and adults use one teach, one support with one adult primarily in lead.*										
		1 = Adults rely solely on one teach, one support or team teaching.	Goals:									
		2 = Adults regroup students (using alternative, parallel, or station) at least once.	PIE:									
		3 = Adults use more than one of the five approaches (Friend & Cook's one teach, one support; team, parallel, station and alternative); at least one of the approaches involves regrouping students.	Ease:		Impact:		Rank:					
		Note: If teachers have been observed using other approaches in the past and only one approach is observed today (e.g., station), it is acceptable to recall previous observations and give a 2 for using a variety of approaches as adults have demonstrated competency.										

Focus	Team		Content Area									
	School Term		Grade					Period				
X	LOOK FORS		SS 1	SS 2	Obs 1	Obs 2	Obs 3	Obs 4	S1	S2	F1	F2
	Next Steps:											
	2.7 Both teachers engage in appropriate behavior management strategies as needed and are consistent in their approach to behavior management.	*0 = There is no obvious plan for behavior management, nor do adults appear to communicate about how they are approaching class management; possibly inappropriate class management.*										
		1 = Very little classroom management; mainly conducted by one teacher	Goals:									
		2 = Behavior management strategies are utilized, but there is very little clear evidence of how adults have communicated about their use.	PIE:									
		3 = It is evident that adults have discussed how they will approach classroom/behavior management, and adults are consistent in their approach.	Ease:		Impact:		Rank:					
	Next Steps:											
	11.3 It is difficult to tell the specialist from the general educator.	*0 = Observer could easily determine who was the general educator/specialist by their language/roles/lack of parity.*										
		1 = Teachers kept traditional roles in the classroom, but shared or switched roles once or twice.	Goals:									
		2 = Teachers worked at having parity in the class and shared most roles and responsibilities.	PIE:									
		3 = Adults shared the roles and responsibilities in the classroom and observer would not be able to tell who was the general educator/specialist.	Ease:		Impact:		Rank:					
	Next Steps:											
	1.6 It is difficult to tell the special education students from the general education students.	*0 = Observer could easily determine who were the general education or students with special needs by their lack of integration (e.g., students at back or separated from class).*										
		1 = There was some inclusion of most students in most activities.	Goals:									
		2 = There was a clear attempt at inclusion of all students for most activities.	PIE:									

Continued on next page

Focus	Team		Content Area							
	School Term		Grade				Period			
X	LOOK FORS		SS 1	SS 2	Obs 1	Obs 2	Obs 3	Obs 4	S1	S2	F1	F2
		3 = All students were included and integrated seamlessly into all activities, even when adaptations were needed.	Ease:		Impact:		Rank:					
	Next Steps:											
			SS 1	SS 2	Obs 1	Obs 2	Obs 3	Obs 4	S1	S2	F1	F2
		LOOK FORS TOTAL										

Focus	Team		Content Area									
	School Term		Grade					Period				
X	LISTEN FORS		SS 1	SS 2	Obs 1	Obs 2	Obs 3	Obs 4	S1	S2	F1	F2
	9.10 Co-teachers use language ("we"; "our") that demonstrates true collaboration and shared responsibility.	*0 = Adults do not communicate with each other.*										
		1 = Adults use "I" language frequently (e.g., "I want you to . . ." or "In my class . . ."), lacking parity.	Goals:									
		2 = Adults attempt to use "we" language and include each other, but it is clear that one adult is more used to "ruling" the class.	PIE:									
		3 = Adults clearly use "we" language (e.g., "We would like you to . . ."), showing that they both share the responsibility and students know they are equally in charge.	Ease		Impact:		Rank:					
	Next Steps:											
	5.9 Communication (both verbal and nonverbal) between co-teachers is clear and positive.	*0 = Little to no communication is evident.*										
		1 = Communication is minimal, directive, or negative.	Goals:									
		2 = Limited communication, but it is positive in nature.	PIE:									
		3 = Both adults communicate regularly as class progresses and are respectful and positive.	Ease		Impact:		Rank:					
	Next Steps:											
	1.8 Co-teachers phrase questions and statements so that it is obvious that all students in the class are included.	*0 = Class is very teacher-directed and little involvement by students.*										
		1 = Questions/statements are general and not inclusive of all students.	Goals:									
		2 = Most statements/questions are phrased to encourage participation from a variety of students.	PIE:									
		3 = A clear attempt is made by both adults to engage all students through the use of a variety of types of questions and statements.	Ease		Impact:		Rank:					
	Next Steps:											

Continued on next page

<table>
<tr><td rowspan="2">Focus</td><td>Team</td><td></td><td>Content Area</td><td colspan="8"></td></tr>
<tr><td>School Term</td><td></td><td colspan="2">Grade</td><td colspan="3"></td><td colspan="2">Period</td><td colspan="2"></td></tr>
<tr><td>X</td><td colspan="2">LISTEN FORS</td><td>SS 1</td><td>SS 2</td><td>Obs 1</td><td>Obs 2</td><td>Obs 3</td><td>Obs 4</td><td>S1</td><td>S2</td><td>F1</td><td>F2</td></tr>
<tr><td></td><td rowspan="3">1.9 Students' conversations evidence a sense of community, including peers with disabilities and from diverse backgrounds.</td><td rowspan="4">0 = Students do not talk to one another during class.
1 = Specific students appear to be excluded from the majority of student interactions.
2 = Most students appear to be included in the majority of student interactions.
3 = It is evident from the students' actions and words that all students are considered an equal part of the class and are included in all student interactions.</td><td></td><td></td><td></td><td></td><td></td><td></td><td></td><td></td><td></td><td></td></tr>
<tr><td></td><td>Goals:</td><td></td><td></td><td></td><td></td><td></td><td></td><td></td><td></td><td></td></tr>
<tr><td></td><td>PIE:</td><td></td><td></td><td></td><td></td><td></td><td></td><td></td><td></td><td></td></tr>
<tr><td></td><td></td><td>Ease:</td><td></td><td>Impact:</td><td></td><td>Rank:</td><td></td><td></td><td></td><td></td><td></td></tr>
<tr><td></td><td colspan="12">Next Steps:</td></tr>
<tr><td></td><td rowspan="3">8.16 Co-teachers ask questions at a variety of levels (basic recall to higher-order thinking) to meet all students' needs.</td><td rowspan="4">0 = Adults do not use questions and most instruction is directive.
1 = Questions are almost all geared just to one level (to the middle or "watered down").
2 = Teachers use closed and open questions at a variety of levels in a general manner.
3 = Closed and open questions are asked at a variety of levels in a way that demonstrates they are able to differentiate for specific students in order to ensure maximum (appropriate) levels of challenge.</td><td></td><td></td><td></td><td></td><td></td><td></td><td></td><td></td><td></td><td></td></tr>
<tr><td></td><td>Goals:</td><td></td><td></td><td></td><td></td><td></td><td></td><td></td><td></td><td></td></tr>
<tr><td></td><td>PIE:</td><td></td><td></td><td></td><td></td><td></td><td></td><td></td><td></td><td></td></tr>
<tr><td></td><td></td><td>Ease</td><td></td><td>Impact:</td><td></td><td>Rank:</td><td></td><td></td><td></td><td></td><td></td></tr>
<tr><td></td><td colspan="12">Next Steps:</td></tr>
<tr><td colspan="3"></td><td>SS 1</td><td>SS 2</td><td>Obs 1</td><td>Obs 2</td><td>Obs 3</td><td>Obs 4</td><td>S1</td><td>S2</td><td>F1</td><td>F2</td></tr>
<tr><td colspan="3">LISTEN FORS TOTAL</td><td></td><td></td><td></td><td></td><td></td><td></td><td></td><td></td><td></td><td></td></tr>
</table>

Focus	Team		Content Area									
	School Term		Grade					Period				
X	ASK FORS		SS 1	SS 2	Obs 1	Obs 2	Obs 3	Obs 4	S1	S2	F1	F2
	7.2 Co-Planning	*0 = There is no evidence that this team co-plans. Most planning, if done at all, is done by one teacher.*										
		1 = This team rarely co-plans and communicates primarily on the fly.	Goals:									
		2 = This team co-plans at irregular times, but does try to integrate both teachers' perspectives when possible.	PIE:									
		3 = This team co-plans its lessons and integrates both teachers' areas of expertise to the maximum extent possible.	Ease		Impact:		Rank:					
	Next Steps:											
	8.5 Co-Instruction: Parity	*0 = There is no evidence that this team co-instructs. One teacher is clearly responsible, as evidenced in documentation/plans, etc.*										
		1 = One teacher is clearly "lead"; however, the other does have intermittent areas of responsibility.	Goals:									
		2 = Both teachers are provided turns in co-instruction.	PIE:									
		3 = Teachers are comfortable in any role and roles are interchanging and fluid throughout the lesson plan.	Ease		Impact:		Rank:					
	Next Steps:											
	8.1 Co-Instruction: Grouping	*0 = There is no evidence that this team regroups during instruction. Whole group instruction is the norm.*										
		1 = At irregular times and for very specific activities, this class is regrouped into smaller groups.	Goals:									
		2 = Cooperative learning is used in class regularly, and small groups are used at least once a week.	PIE:									
		3 = Whole group and regrouping approaches are used to match learning needs. Teachers clearly use regrouping regularly and are comfortable with a variety of the co-instructional approaches.	Ease		Impact:		Rank:					
	Next Steps:											

Continued on next page

Focus												
	Team		Content Area									
	School Term		Grade					Period				
X	**ASK FORS**		SS 1	SS 2	Obs 1	Obs 2	Obs 3	Obs 4	S1	S2	F1	F2
	1.2 Co-Instruction: Differentiation	*0 = There is no evidence that this team differentiates for the class. All lessons appear created so that students are expected to do the same things.*										
		1 = Minimal evidence demonstrates differentiation. What is available appears to focus on one or two specific students for limited activities or events (e.g., read test to Johnny).	Goals:									
		2 = Teachers appear to integrate differentiated instruction, content, and assessments into some lessons.	PIE:									
		3 = Teachers regularly include differentiated instruction, content, and assessments into their lessons. They clearly consider the needs of all students.	Ease:		Impact:		Rank:					
	Next Steps:											
	6.1 Co-Assessment	*0 = There is no evidence that this team co-assesses. One teacher is in charge of the grades and gradebook.*										
		1 = Teachers talk about assessments at times, but each teacher is primarily in charge of his "own" students.	Goals:									
		2 = Teachers use differentiated assessments occasionally and are willing to share responsibility for grading.	PIE:									
		3 = Teachers share responsibility for creating assessments, grading, and for students' overall success. Differentiated assessments are created when needed and both teachers are comfortable with adaptations.	Ease		Impact:		Rank:					
	Next Steps:											
		ASK FORS TOTAL										
			SS 1	SS 2	Obs 1	Obs 2	Obs 3	Obs 4	S1	S2	F1	F2
		GRAND TOTAL										
			0–29	Not Yet Co-Teaching				Student Total Possible: 66				
			30–45	Emerging Co-Teaching								
			46–52	Developing Co-Teaching								
			53–59	Proficient Co-Teaching				Family Total Possible: 66				
			60–66	Master Co-Teaching								

FIGURE 9.12

Professional Learning Actions for Teaching Effectiveness (PLATE) Form

Focus	Team		Content Area									
	School Term		Grade					Period				
X	LOOK FORS		SS 1	SS 2	Obs 1	Obs 2	Obs 3	Obs 4	S1	S2	F1	F2
	4.5 Two or more professionals working together in the same physical space.	*0 = Only one adult; two adults not communicating at all; class always divided into two rooms.*										
		1 = Two adults in same room, but very little communication or collaborative work.	Goals:									
		2 = Two adults in same room; both engaged in class and each other (even if not perfectly).	PIE:									
		3 = Two adults collaborating together well in the same room.	Ease:		Impact:		Rank:					
	Next Steps:											
	9.5 Class environment demonstrates parity and collaboration (both names on board, sharing materials and space).	*0 = No demonstration of parity/collaboration; room appears to belong to one teacher only.*										
		1 = Some attempt at parity; both adults share a few materials and general space.	Goals:									
		2 = Parity exists; adults share classroom materials.	PIE:									
		3 = Clear parity; both names on board/report card; two desks or shared space; obvious feeling from teacher that it is "our room."	Ease:		Impact:		Rank:					
	Next Steps:											
	11.6 Both teachers begin and end class together and remain in the room the entire time.	*0 = One adult is absent or late; adults may leave room for times not related to this class.*										
		1 = One adult may be late or leave early or may leave for brief time.	Goals:									
		2 = One adult may be late or leave early, but for remaining time they work together.	PIE:									
		3 = Both adults begin and end together, and are with students the entire time.	Ease:		Impact:		Rank:					
		Note: if adults have planned to use a regrouping approach (e.g., "parallel") and one adult takes a group of students out of the room (e.g., to the library), that is perfectly acceptable.										

Continued on next page

Focus	Team		Content Area									
	School Term		Grade				Period					
X	LOOK FORS		SS 1	SS 2	Obs 1	Obs 2	Obs 3	Obs 4	S1	S2	F1	F2
	Next Steps:											
	8.6 During instruction, both teachers assist students with and without disabilities.	*0 = Adults are not helping students or are only helping "their own" students.*										
		1 = There is some helping of various students, but at least one adult primarily stays with a few of "their own."	Goals:									
		2 = Both adults are willing to help all students, but students seem to have one adult they prefer to work with.	PIE:									
		3 = It is clear that both adults are willing to help all students and that students are used to this.	Ease:		Impact:		Rank:					
	Next Steps:											
	9.6 The class moves smoothly, with evidence of co-planning and communi-cation between co-teachers.	*0 = Little to no prior planning is evident.*										
		1 = All planning appears to have been done by one adult.	Goals:									
		2 = Minimal planning is evident; most appears to have been done by one adult.	PIE:									
		3 = It is clear that both adults are com-fortable with the lesson and know what is supposed to happen.	Ease:		Impact:		Rank:					
	Next Steps:											
	8.8 Class instruction and activities proactively promote mul-tiple modes of representation, engagement, and expres-sion (universal design for learning—UDL)	*0 = There is no evidence of universal design; all students are expected to do the same thing.*										
		1 = There is minimal evidence of uni-versal design; limited opportunities for choice in how students learn, engage, and show what they've learned.	Goals:									
		2 = There is some evidence of universal design; some opportunities for choice in how students learn, engage, and show what they've learned.	PIE:									
		3 = The class was universally designed; opportunities for choice in how students learn, engage, and show what they've learned were well selected.	Ease:		Impact:		Rank:					
	Next Steps:											

Focus	Team		Content Area									
	School Term		Grade					Period				
X	LOOK FORS		SS 1	SS 2	Obs 1	Obs 2	Obs 3	Obs 4	S1	S2	F1	F2
	3.7 Differentiated content and strategies, based on formative assessment, are used to meet the range of learning needs.	*0 = There is no evidence of differentiation of instruction in the classroom.*										
		1 = There is minimal differentiation; most differentiation appears to be focused on groups rather than individuals.	Goals:									
		2 = Some differentiation is evident for individual students' or groups.	PIE:									
		3 = It is clear that adults consider individual students' needs and regular use of differentiation is evident.	Ease:		Impact:		Rank:					
	Next Steps:											
	8.13 Technology (to include assistive technology) is used to enhance accessibility and learning.	*0 = There is no evidence of technology use.*										
		1 = There is limited use of technology.	Goals:									
		2 = Technology provides students with access and is used intermittently or sporadically.	PIE:									
		3 = Multiple technologies are utilized to make materials and content accessible and are used regularly.	Ease:		Impact:		Rank:					
	Next Steps:											
	5.7 A variety of instructional approaches (five co-teaching approaches) are used, including regrouping students.	*0 = Students remain in large class setting and adults use one teach, one support with one adult primarily in lead.*										
		1 = Adults rely solely on one teach, one support or team teaching.	Goals:									
		2 = Adults regroup students (using alternative, parallel, or station) at least once.	PIE:									
		3 = Adults use more than one of the five approaches (Friend & Cook's one teach, one support; team, parallel, station, and alternative); at least one of the approaches involves regrouping students.	Ease:		Impact:		Rank:					
		Note: If teachers have been observed using other approaches in the past and only one approach is observed today (e.g., station), it is acceptable to recall previous observations and give a 2 for using a variety of approaches as adults have demonstrated competency.										

Continued on next page

Focus	Team		Content Area									
	School Term		Grade					Period				
X	**LOOK FORS**		**SS 1**	**SS 2**	**Obs 1**	**Obs 2**	**Obs 3**	**Obs 4**	**S1**	**S2**	**F1**	**F2**
	Next Steps:											
	2.7 Both teachers engage in appropriate behavior management strategies as needed and are consistent in their approach to behavior management.	*0 = There is no obvious plan for behavior management, nor do adults appear to communicate about how they are approaching class management; possibly inappropriate class management.*										
		1 = Very little classroom management; mainly conducted by one teacher.	**Goals:**									
		2 = Behavior management strategies are utilized, but there is very little clear evidence of how adults have communicated about their use.	**PIE:**									
		3 = It is evident that adults have discussed how they will approach classroom/behavior management, and adults are consistent in their approach.	**Ease:**		**Impact:**		**Rank:**					
	Next Steps:											
	11.3 It is difficult to tell the specialist from the general educator.	*0 = Observer could easily determine who was the general educator/specialist by their language/roles/lack of parity.*										
		1 = Teachers kept traditional roles in the classroom but shared or switched roles once or twice.	**Goals:**									
		2 = Teachers worked at having parity in the class and shared most roles and responsibilities.	**PIE:**									
		3 = Adults shared the roles and responsibilities in the classroom and observer would not be able to tell who was the general educator/specialist.	**Ease:**		**Impact:**		**Rank:**					
	Next Steps:											
	1.6 It is difficult to tell the special education students from the general education students.	*0 = Observer could easily determine who were the general education or students with special needs by their lack of integration (e.g., students at back or separated from class).*										
		1 = There was some inclusion of most students in most activities.	**Goals:**									
		2 = There was a clear attempt at inclusion of all students for most activities.	**PIE:**									

Focus	Team		Content Area								
	School Term		Grade				Period				
X	LOOK FORS		SS 1	SS 2	Obs 1	Obs 2	Obs 3	Obs 4	S1	S2	F1	F2
		3 = All students were included and integrated seamlessly into all activities, even when adaptations were needed.	Ease:		Impact:		Rank					
	Next Steps:											
			SS 1	SS 2	Obs 1	Obs 2	Obs 3	Obs 4	S1	S2	F1	F2
		LOOK FORS TOTAL										

Continued on next page

Focus	Team		Content Area									
	School Term		Grade				Period					
X	**LISTEN FORS**		SS 1	SS 2	Obs 1	Obs 2	Obs 3	Obs 4	S1	S2	F1	F2
	9.10 Co-teachers use language ("we"; "our") that demonstrates true collaboration and shared responsibility.	*0 = Adults do not communicate with each other.* *1 = Adults use "I" language frequently (e.g., "I want you to..." or "In my class..."), lacking parity.* *2 = Adults attempt to use "we" language and include each other, but it is clear that one adult is more used to "ruling" the class.* *3 = Adults clearly use "we" language (e.g., "We would like you to..."), showing that they both share the responsibility and students know they are equally in charge.*	Goals: PIE: Ease:		Impact:		Rank:					
	Next Steps:											
	5.9 Communication (both verbal and nonverbal) between co-teachers is clear and positive.	*0 = Little to no communication is evident.* *1 = Communication is minimal, directive, or negative.* *2 = Limited communication, but it is positive in nature.* *3 = Both adults communicate regularly as class progresses and are respectful and positive.*	Goals: PIE: Ease:		Impact:		Rank:					
	Next Steps:											
	1.8 Co-teachers phrase questions and statements so that it is obvious that all students in the class are included.	*0 = Class is very teacher-directed and little involvement by students.* *1 = Questions/statements are general and not inclusive of all students.* *2 = Most statements/questions are phrased to encourage participation from a variety of students.* *3 = A clear attempt is made by both adults to engage all students through the use of a variety of types of questions and statements.*	Goals: PIE: Ease:		Impact:		Rank:					
	Next Steps:											

Focus	Team		Content Area									
	School Term		Grade				Period					
X	LISTEN FORS		SS 1	SS 2	Obs 1	Obs 2	Obs 3	Obs 4	S1	S2	F1	F2
	1.9 Students' conversations evidence a sense of community, including peers with disabilities and from diverse backgrounds.	*0 = Students do not talk to one another during class.*										
		1 = Specific students appear to be excluded from the majority of student interactions.	Goals:									
		2 = Most students appear to be included in the majority of student interactions.	PIE:									
		3 = It is evident from the students' actions and words that all students are considered an equal part of the class and are included in all student interactions.	Ease:		Impact:		Rank:					
	Next Steps:											
	8.16 Co-teachers ask questions at a variety of levels (basic recall to higher-order thinking) to meet all students' needs.	*0 = Adults do not use questions and most instruction is directive.*										
		1 = Questions are almost all geared just to one level (to the middle or "watered down").	Goals:									
		2 = Teachers use closed and open questions at a variety of levels in a general manner.	PIE:									
		3 = Closed and open questions are asked at a variety of levels in a way that demonstrates they are able to differentiate for specific students in order to ensure maximum (appropriate) levels of challenge.	Ease:		Impact:		Rank:					
	Next Steps:											
			SS 1	SS 2	Obs 1	Obs 2	Obs 3	Obs 4	S1	S2	F1	F2
		LISTEN FORS TOTAL										

Continued on next page

Focus	Team		Content Area									
	School Term		Grade					Period				
X	**ASK FORS**		**SS 1**	**SS 2**	**Obs 1**	**Obs 2**	**Obs 3**	**Obs 4**	**S1**	**S2**	**F1**	**F2**
	7.2 Co-Planning	*0 = There is no evidence that this team co-plans. Most planning, if done at all, is done by one teacher.*										
		1 = This team rarely co-plans and communicates primarily on the fly.	Goals:									
		2 = This team co-plans at irregular times, but does try to integrate both teachers' perspectives when possible.	PIE:									
		3 = This team co-plans its lessons and integrates both teachers' areas of expertise to the maximum extent possible.	Ease:		Impact:		Rank:					
	Next Steps:											
	8.5 Co-Instruction: Parity	*0 = There is no evidence that this team co-instructs. One teacher is clearly responsible, as evidenced in documentation/plans, etc.*										
		1 = One teacher is clearly "lead"; however, the other does have intermittent areas of responsibility.	Goals:									
		2 = Both teachers are provided turns in co-instruction.	PIE:									
		3 = Teachers are comfortable in any role and roles are interchanging and fluid throughout the lesson plan.	Ease:		Impact:		Rank:					
	Next Steps:											
	8.1 Co-Instruction: Grouping	*0 = There is no evidence that this team regroups during instruction. Whole group instruction is the norm.*										
		1 = At irregular times and for very specific activities, this class is regrouped into smaller groups.	Goals:									
		2 = Cooperative learning is used in class regularly, and small groups are used at least once a week.	PIE:									
		3 = Whole group and regrouping approaches are used to match learning needs. Teachers clearly use regrouping regularly and are comfortable with a variety of the co-instructional approaches.	Ease:		Impact:		Rank:					
	Next Steps:											

Focus	Team		Content Area									
	School Term		Grade					Period				
X	ASK FORS		SS 1	SS 2	Obs 1	Obs 2	Obs 3	Obs 4	S1	S2	F1	F2
	1.2 Co-Instruction: Differentiation	*0 = There is no evidence that this team differentiates for the class. All lessons appear created so that students are expected to do the same things.*										
		1 = Minimal evidence demonstrates differentiation. What is available appears to focus on one or two specific students for limited activities or events (e.g., read test to Johnny).	Goals:									
		2 = Teachers appear to integrate differentiated instruction, content, and assessments into some lessons.	PIE:									
		3 = Teachers regularly include differentiated instruction, content, and assessments into their lessons. They clearly consider the needs of all students.	Ease:		Impact:		Rank:					
	Next Steps:											
	6.1 Co-Assessment	*0 = There is no evidence that this team co-assesses. One teacher is in charge of the grades and gradebook.*										
		1 = Teachers talk about assessments at times, but each teacher is primarily in charge of her "own" students.	Goals:									
		2 = Teachers use differentiated assessments occasionally and are willing to share responsibility for grading.	PIE:									
		3 = Teachers share responsibility for creating assessments, grading, and for students' overall success. Differentiated assessments are created when needed and both teachers are comfortable with adaptations.	Ease:		Impact:		Rank:					
	Next Steps:											
		ASK FORS TOTAL										
			SS 1	SS 2	Obs 1	Obs 2	Obs 3	Obs 4	S1	S2	F1	F2
		GRAND TOTAL										

	Range	Level	
	0–29	Not Yet Co-Teaching	Student Total Possible: 66
	30–45	Emerging Co-Teaching	
	46–52	Developing Co-Teaching	
	53–59	Proficient Co-Teaching	Family Total Possible: 66
	60–66	Master Co-Teaching	

FIGURE 9.13

CTSS Co-Teaching Core Competencies Impact Values

	Impact 0-Low Impact 1-Moderate Impact 2-Impact 3-High Impact
4.5 Two or more professionals working together in the same physical space.	3
9.5 Class environment demonstrates parity and collaboration (both names on board, sharing materials and space).	1
11.6 Both teachers begin and end class together and remain in the room the entire time.	1
8.6 During instruction, both teachers assist students with and without disabilities.	3
9.6 The class moves smoothly, with evidence of co-planning and communication between co-teachers.	2
8.8 Class instruction and activities proactively promote multiple modes of representation, engagement, and expression (universal design for learning—UDL).	2
3.7 Differentiated content and strategies, based on formative assessment, are used to meet the range of learning needs.	3
8.13 Technology (to include assistive technology) is used to enhance accessibility and learning.	1
5.7 A variety of instructional approaches (five co-teaching approaches) are used, including regrouping students.	2
2.7 Both teachers engage in appropriate behavior management strategies as needed and are consistent in their approach to behavior management.	2
11.3 It is difficult to tell the specialist from the general educator.	2
1.6 It is difficult to tell the special education students from the general education students.	2
9.10 Co-teachers use language ("we"; "our") that demonstrates true collaboration and shared responsibility.	1
5.9 Communication (both verbal and nonverbal) between co-teachers is clear and positive.	3
1.8 Co-teachers phrase questions and statements so that it is obvious that all students in the class are included.	2
1.9 Students' conversations evidence a sense of community, including peers with disabilities and from diverse backgrounds.	1
8.16 Co-teachers ask questions at a variety of levels (basic recall to higher-order thinking) to meet all students' needs.	1
7.2 Co-Planning	3
8.5 Co-Instruction: Parity	2
8.1 Co-Instruction: Grouping	2
1.2 Co-Instruction: Differentiation	2
6.1 Co-Assessment	1

FIGURE 9.14

CTSS Co-Teaching Core Competencies Ranking and Priority Worksheet

	Collection 1		Collection 2		Collection 3		Collection 4	
	PIE Score	Ranking	PIE Score	Ranking	PIE Score	Ranking	PIE Score	Ranking
4.5 Two or more professionals working together in the same physical space.								
9.5 Class environment demonstrates parity and collaboration (both names on board, sharing materials and space).								
11.6 Both teachers begin and end class together and remain in the room the entire time.								
8.6 During instruction, both teachers assist students with and without disabilities.								
9.6 The class moves smoothly, with evidence of co-planning and communication between co-teachers.								
8.8 Class instruction and activities proactively promote multiple modes of representation, engagement, and expression (universal design for learning—UDL).								
3.7 Differentiated content and strategies, based on formative assessment, are used to meet the range of learning needs.								
8.13 Technology (to include assistive technology) is used to enhance accessibility and learning.								
5.7 A variety of instructional approaches (five co-teaching approaches) are used, including regrouping students.								
2.7 Both teachers engage in appropriate behavior management strategies as needed and are consistent in their approach to behavior management.								
11.3 It is difficult to tell the specialist from the general educator.								
1.6 It is difficult to tell the special education students from the general education students.								
9.10 Co-teachers use language ("we"; "our") that demonstrates true collaboration and shared responsibility.								
5.9 Communication (both verbal and nonverbal) between co-teachers is clear and positive.								
1.8 Co-teachers phrase questions and statements so that it is obvious that all students in the class are included.								
1.9 Students' conversations evidence a sense of community, including peers with disabilities and from diverse backgrounds.								
8.16 Co-teachers ask questions at a variety of levels (basic recall to higher-order thinking) to meet all students' needs.								
7.2 Co-Planning								

Continued on next page

	Collection 1		Collection 2		Collection 3		Collection 4	
	PIE Score	Ranking	PIE Score	Ranking	PIE Score	Ranking	PIE Score	Ranking
8.5 Co-Instruction: Parity								
8.1 Co-Instruction: Grouping								
1.2 Co-Instruction: Differentiation								
6.1 Co-Assessment								
Circle the competencies you wish to select to mark on the CAP as a "FOCUS" competency.								

FIGURE 9.15

Strand Analysis Worksheet

Team: ______________________________ Content Area: ____________

School Term: ______________________________ Grade: _______ Period: _______

✔	Strand 1: Learner Differences	Self-Survey		Observation				Student		Family	
		Coll 1	Coll 2	Coll 1	Coll 2	Coll 3	Coll 4	Coll 1	Coll 2	Coll 1	Coll 2
	1.2 Co-Instruction: Evidence of differentiation.										
	1.6 It is difficult to tell the special education students from the general education students.										
	1.8 Co-teachers phrase questions and statements so that it is obvious that all students in the class are included.										
	1.9 Students' conversations evidence a sense of community, including peers with disabilities and from diverse backgrounds.										
	Competency Total:										
	Strand Rating:										

✔	Strand 2: Classroom Environment	Self-Survey		Observation				Student		Family	
		Coll 1	Coll 2	Coll 1	Coll 2	Coll 3	Coll 4	Coll 1	Coll 2	Coll 1	Coll 2
	2.7 Both teachers engage in appropriate behavior management strategies as needed and are consistent in their approach to behavior management.										
	Competency Total:										
	Strand Rating:										

✔	Strand 3: Content Knowledge	Self-Survey		Observation				Student		Family	
		Coll 1	Coll 2	Coll 1	Coll 2	Coll 3	Coll 4	Coll 1	Coll 2	Coll 1	Coll 2
	3.7 Differentiated content and strategies, based on formative assessments, are used to meet the range of learning needs.										
	Competency Total:										
	Strand Rating:										

✔	Strand 4: Compliance Issues	Self-Survey		Observation				Student		Family	
		Coll 1	Coll 2	Coll 1	Coll 2	Coll 3	Coll 4	Coll 1	Coll 2	Coll 1	Coll 2
	4.5 Two or more professionals working together in the same physical space.										
	Competency Total:										
	Strand Rating:										

Continued on next page

✔	Strand 5: Co-Teaching Construct	Self-Survey		Observation				Student		Family	
		Coll 1	Coll 2	Coll 1	Coll 2	Coll 3	Coll 4	Coll 1	Coll 2	Coll 1	Coll 2
	5.7 A variety of instructional approaches (five co-teaching approaches) are used, including regrouping students.										
	5.9 Communication (both verbal and nonverbal) between co-teachers is clear and positive.										
	Competency Total:										
	Strand Rating:										

✔	Strand 6: Assessment	Self-Survey		Observation				Student		Family	
		Coll 1	Coll 2	Coll 1	Coll 2	Coll 3	Coll 4	Coll 1	Coll 2	Coll 1	Coll 2
	6.1 Teachers share responsibility for creating assessments, grading, and for students' overall success.										
	Competency Total:										
	Strand Rating:										

✔	Strand 7: Planning	Self-Survey		Observation				Student		Family	
		Coll 1	Coll 2	Coll 1	Coll 2	Coll 3	Coll 4	Coll 1	Coll 2	Coll 1	Coll 2
	7.2 This team co-plans its lessons and integrates both teachers' areas of expertise to the maximum extent possible.										
	Competency Total:										
	Strand Rating:										

✔	Strand 8: Instruction	Self-Survey		Observation				Student		Family	
		Coll 1	Coll 2	Coll 1	Coll 2	Coll 3	Coll 4	Coll 1	Coll 2	Coll 1	Coll 2
	8.1 Co-Instruction: Grouping										
	8.5 Co-Instruction: Evidence of Parity										
	8.6 During instruction, both teachers assist students with and without disabilities.										
	8.8 Class instruction and activities proactively promote multiple modes of representation, engagement, and expression (universal design for learning—UDL).										
	8.13 Technology (to include assistive technology) is used to enhance accessibility and learning.										
	8.16 Co-teachers ask questions at a variety of levels (basic recall to higher-order thinking) to meet all students' needs.										
	Competency Total:										
	Strand Rating:										

✔	Strand 9: Communication, Collaboration, and Problem Solving	Self-Survey		Observation				Student		Family	
		Coll 1	Coll 2	Coll 1	Coll 2	Coll 3	Coll 4	Coll 1	Coll 2	Coll 1	Coll 2
	9.5 Class environment demonstrates parity and collaboration (both names on board, sharing materials and space).										
	9.6 The class moves smoothly, with evidence of co-planning between co-teachers.										
	9.10 Co-teachers use language ("we"; "our") that demonstrates true collaboration and shared responsibility.										
	Competency Total:										
	Strand Rating:										

✔	Strand 11: Professional Practices and Ethics	Self-Survey		Observation				Student		Family	
		Coll 1	Coll 2	Coll 1	Coll 2	Coll 3	Coll 4	Coll 1	Coll 2	Coll 1	Coll 2
	11.3 It is difficult to tell the specialist from the general educator.										
	11.6 Both teachers begin and end class together and remain in the room the entire time.										
	Competency Total:										
	Strand Rating:										

FIGURE 9.16

Domain and Strand Prioritizing and Ranking Form

School:									
Term:									
Strand/ Focus		**Description**	**Begin Rank**	**Observation Baseline**	**Collection 1**	**Collection 2**	**Collection 3**	**Collection 4**	**End Rank**
1		Learner Differences							
2		Classroom Environment							
3		Content Knowledge							
4		Compliance Issues							
5		Co-Teaching Construct							
6		Assessment							
7		Planning							
8		Instruction							
9		Communication, Collaboration, and Problem Solving							
10		Families and Community							
11		Professional Practices and Ethics							

Domain Yearly Progress	**Domain 1** The Learner and Learning Strands 1–2	**Domain 2** The Task at Hand Strands 3–5	**Domain 3** Instructional Practices Strands 6–8	**Domain 4** Professional Responsibilities Strands 9–11
Beginning of Year (Baseline or Collection 1)				
End of Year (Last Observation Collection)				
Notes:				

Bibliography

Aguayo, R. (1991). *Dr. Deming: The American who taught the Japanese about quality*. New York: Simon & Schuster.

Ahmadi, A., Vogel, B., & Collins, C. (2016). An initial framework for the role of leader fear in the knowing-doing gap of leadership. *Research on Emotion in Organizations, 12*, 313–340.

Aliakbari, M., & Nejad, A. M. (2013). On the effectiveness of team teaching in promoting learners' grammatical proficiency. *Canadian Journal of Education, 36*(3), 5–22.

Allan, D. W., & LeBlanc, A. C. (2005). *Collaborative peer coaching that improves instruction: The 2+ 2 performance appraisal model*. Thousand Oaks, CA: Corwin.

Allen, D. S., Perl, M., Goodson, L., & Sprouse, T. (2014). Changing traditions: Supervision, co-teaching, and lessons learned in a professional development school partnership. *Educational Considerations, 42*(1), 19–29.

Amobi, F., & Irwin, L. (2012). Implementing on-campus microteaching to elicit preservice teachers' reflection on teaching actions: Fresh perspective on an established practice. *Journal of the Scholarship of Teaching and Learning, 9*(1), 27–34.

Andersen, B., & Fagerhaug, T. (2006). *Root cause analysis: Simplified tools and techniques* (2nd ed.). Milwaukee, WI: ASQ Quality Press.

Ashton, T. (2015). Unique universal design for learning. In W. W. Murawski & K. L. Scott (Eds.), *What really works in secondary education* (pp. 170–182). Thousand Oaks, CA: Corwin.

Auerbach, S. (2015). Fantastic family collaboration. In W. W. Murawski & K. L. Scott (Eds.), *What really works in elementary education* (pp. 319–333). Thousand Oaks, CA: Corwin.

Austin, V. L. (2001). Teachers' beliefs about co-teaching. *Remedial and Special Education, 22*(4), 245–255.

Barab, S. A., & Duffy, T. (2000). From practice fields to communities of practice. *Theoretical Foundations of Learning Environments, 1*(1), 25–55.

Bateman, D., & Cline, J. L. (2016). *A teachers' guide to special education*. Alexandria, VA: Council for Exceptional Children.

Bolam, R., McMahon, A., Stoll, L., Thomas, S., Wallace, M., Greenwood, A., Smith, M. (2005). *Creating and sustaining professional learning communities: Research report 637*. London, England: Department for Education and Skills and University of Bristol.

Cinici, A. (2016). Pre-service teachers' science teaching self-efficacy beliefs: The influence of a collaborative peer microteaching program. *Mentoring and Tutoring: Partnership in Learning*. Retrieved from http://www.tandfonline.com/doi/full/10.1080/13611267.2016.1222812

Cleghorn, G. D., & Headrick, L. A. (1996). The PDSA cycle at the core of learning in health professions education. *The Joint Commission Journal on Quality Improvement, 22*(3), 206–212.

Cobb, C., & Sharma, M. (2015). I've got you covered: Adventures in social justice-informed co-teaching. *Journal of the Scholarship of Teaching and Learning, 15*(4), 41–57.

Conderman, G. (2011). Middle school co-teaching: Effective practices and student reflections. *Middle School Journal, 42*(4), 24–31.

Conderman, G., Bresnahan, V., Teacher, S. E., & Pedersen, T. (2008). *Purposeful co-teaching: Real cases and effective strategies.* Thousand Oaks, CA: Corwin.

Cornell University. (2015, June 17). Love, factually: Gerontologist finds the formula to a happy marriage. *ScienceDaily.* Retrieved from http://www.sciencedaily.com/releases/2015/06/150617134613.htm

Costa, A. L., & Kallick, B. (2008). *Learning and leading with habits of mind: 16 essential characteristics for success.* Alexandria, VA: ASCD.

Danielson, C. (2007). *Enhancing professional practice: A framework for teaching* (2nd ed.). Alexandria, VA: ASCD.

Deming, W. E. (1950). *Elementary principles of the statistical control of quality.* Tokyo, Japan: Japanese Union of Scientists and Engineers.

Deming, W. E. (1993). *The new economics for industry, government, education.* Cambridge, MA: MIT Press.

Dieker, L. A. (2016). *The co-teaching lesson plan book* (4th ed.). Whitefish Bay, WI: Knowledge by Design.

Dieker, L. A., & Murawski, W. W. (2003). Co-teaching at the secondary level: Unique issues, current trends, and suggestions for success. *The High School Journal, 86*(4), 1–13.

Dirckinck-Holmfeld, L. (2002). Problem oriented project pedagogy. In B. Fibiger & L. Dirckinck-Holmfeld (Eds.), *Learning in virtual environments.* Denmark: Samfundslitteratur.

Doggett, A. M. (2005). Root cause analysis: A framework for tool selection. *Quality Management Journal, 12*(4), 34.

DuFour, R., & DuFour, R. (2010). The role of professional learning communities in advancing 21st century skills. In J. Bellanca & R. Brandt (Eds.), *21st century skills: Rethinking how students learn* (pp. 77–95). Bloomfield, IN: Solution Tree Press.

DuFour, R., DuFour, R., Eaker, R., & Many, T. (2006). *Learning by doing: A handbook for professional learning communities at work.* Bloomfield, IN: Solution Tree Press.

DuFour, R., DuFour, R., Eaker, R., & Many, T. (2010). *Learning by doing: A handbook for professional learning communities at work* (2nd ed.). Bloomfield, IN: Solution Tree Press.

Durant, W. (1991). *The story of philosophy: The lives and opinions of the world's greatest philosophers.* New York: Pocket Books.

Embury, D. C., & Kroeger, S. D. (2012). Let's ask the kids: Consumer constructions of co-teaching. *International Journal of Special Education, 27*(2), 102–112.

Frey, L. M., & Kaff, M. S. (2014). Results of co-teaching instruction to special education teacher candidates in Tanzania. *Journal of the International Association of Special Education, 15*(1), 4–15.

Friend, M. (2008). Co-teaching: A simple solution that isn't simple after all. *Journal of Curriculum and Instruction, 2*(2), 9–19.

Friend, M., & Cook, L. (2016). *Interactions: Collaboration skills for school professionals* (8th ed.). Boston, MA: Pearson.

Friend, M., Cook, L., Hurley-Chamberlain, D., & Shamberger, C. (2010). Co-teaching: An illustration of the complexity of collaboration in special education. *Journal of Educational and Psychological Consultation, 20*(1), 9–27.

Garet, M. S., Porter, A. C., Desimone, L., Birman, B. F., & Yoon, K. S. (2001). What makes professional development effective? Results from a national sample of teachers. *American Educational Research Journal, 38*(4), 915–945.

Ghosh, S. (2016). Collaborative micro teaching: An innovative approach leading to improved real classroom teaching. *Siddhant: A Journal of Decision Making, 16*(1), 51–54.

Great Schools. (2016, March 9). The role of the school site council. Retrieved from http://www.greatschools.org/gk/articles/the-role-of-the-school-site-council/

Guillemin, M., Gillam, L., Barnard, E., Stewart, P., Walker, H., & Rosenthal, D. (2016). "Doing trust": How researchers conceptualize and enact trust in their research practice. *Journal of Empirical Research on Human Research Ethics,* 1556264616668975.

Hall, T. E., Meyer, A., & Rose, D. H. (2012). *Universal design for learning in the classroom: Practical applications*. New York: Guilford.

Hallam, P. R., Smith, H. R., Hite, J. M., Hite, S. J., & Wilcox, B. R. (2015). Trust and collaboration in PLC teams: Teacher relationships, principal support, and collaborative benefits. *NASSP Bulletin, 99*(3), 193–216.

Hang, Q., & Rabren, K. (2009). An examination of co-teaching perspectives and efficacy indicators. *Remedial and Special Education, 30*(5), 259–268.

Harris, P. P., Pollingue, A. B., Hearrington, D., & Holmes, A. (2014). Effects of training on pre-service special educators' abilities to co-teach math vocabulary in preparation for inclusion settings. *Journal of the International Association of Special Education,* 15(2), 94–99.

Harvard University. (n.d.). *Harvard University competency dictionary*. Retrieved from https://apps2.campusservices.harvard.edu/cas/empldocs/cs/harvard_competency_dictionary_complete.pdf

Hattie, J. (2012). *Visible learning for teachers: Maximizing impact on learning*. New York: Routledge.

Hopkins, G. (2006). What do principals look for as they observe and evaluate? *Education World*. Retrieved from http://www.educationworld.com/a_admin/admin/admin400_b.shtml

Huffman, J. B. (2011). Professional learning communities in the USA: Demystifying, creating, and sustaining. *International Journal of Learning, 17*(12), 321–336.

Hughes, J., Jewson, N., & Unwin, L. (Eds.). (2013). *Communities of practice: Critical perspectives*. New York: Routledge.

Hussein, A. (2009). The use of triangulation in social sciences research: Can qualitative and quantitative methods be combined? *Journal of Comparative Social Work, 4*(1), 1–12.

Joyce, B. R., & Showers, B. (2002). *Student achievement through staff development* (3rd ed.). Alexandria, VA: ASCD.

Kelly, J., & Cherkowski, S. (2015). Collaboration, collegiality, and collective reflection: A case study of professional development for teachers. *Canadian Journal of Educational Administration and Policy, 169*, 1–37.

Khachatryan, E. (2015). Feedback on teaching from observations of teaching: What do administrators say and what do teachers think about it? *NASSP Bulletin, 99*(2), 0192636515583716.

Kilic, A. (2010). Learner-centered micro teaching in teacher education. *International Journal of Instruction, 3*(1), 77–100.

King-Sears, M. E., & Bowman-Kruhm, M. (2011). Specialized reading instruction for adolescents with learning disabilities: What special education co-teachers say. *Learning Disabilities Research and Practice, 26*(3), 172–184.

King-Sears, M. E., Brawand, A. E., Jenkins, M. C., & Preston-Smith, S. (2014). Co-teaching perspectives from secondary science co-teachers and their students with disabilities. *Journal of Science Teacher Education, 25*(6), 651–680.

Kinne, L. J., Ryan, C., & Faulkner, S. A. (2016). Perceptions of co-teaching in the clinical experience: How well is it working? *The New Educator, 12*(4), 343–360.

Kramer, A., & Murawski, W. (2017). Beyond just "playing nicely": Collaboration and co-teaching. In W. W. Murawski & K. L. Scott (Eds.), *What really works with exceptional learners*. Thousand Oaks, CA: Corwin.

Langford, D. (2015). *Tool time for education: Choosing and implementing quality improvement tools*. Molt, MT: Langford International.

Larrivee, B. (2010). Transforming teacher practice: Becoming the critically reflective teacher. *Reflective Practice, 1*(3), 293–307.

Learning Forward. (2015, December 10). ESSA includes improved definition of professional development [press release]. Retrieved from https://learningforward.org/blog-landing/press-releases/2015/12/10/essa-includes-improved-definition-of-professional-development

Loertscher, D. V., & Koechlin, C. (2015). Finland, collaboration, and co-teaching. *Teacher Librarian, 42*(3), 56.

Luczak, J., Rubalcaba, C., & Frades, K. S. (2014). Classroom observations:

Measuring teachers' professional practices. Retrieved from http://education-first.com/wp-content/uploads/2015/10/01-Gates_Eval-and-Support-Strategies-for-Success_ClassObservations.pdf

Lumpe, A. T. (2007). Research-based professional development: Teachers engaged in professional learning communities. *Journal of Science Teacher Education, 18*(1), 125–128.

Magiera, K., & Zigmond, N. (2005). Co-teaching in middle school classrooms under routine conditions: Does the instructional experience differ for students with disabilities in co-taught and solo-taught classes? *Learning Disabilities Research and Practice, 20*(2), 79–85.

Martin, C., & Hauth, C. (2015). *Survival guide for new special education teachers* (2nd ed.). Alexandria, VA: Council for Exceptional Children.

Mastropieri, M. A., Scruggs, T. E., Graetz, J., Norland, J., Gardizi, W., & McDuffie, K. (2005). Case studies in co-teaching in the content areas successes, failures, and challenges. *Intervention in School and Clinic, 40*(5), 260–270.

McConnell, B. M., & Murawski, W. W. (2017). The importance of partnerships: School-to-home collaboration. In W. W. Murawski & K. L. Scott (Eds.), *What really works with exceptional learners*. Thousand Oaks, CA: Corwin.

Mensah, F. M. (2011). A case for culturally relevant teaching in science education and lessons learned for teacher education. *Journal of Negro Education, 80*(3), 296–309.

Miller, G. E. (1990). The assessment of clinical skills/competence/performance. *Academic Medicine, 65*(9), 63–67.

Mind Tools. (n.d.). Developing a competency framework. Retrieved from https://www.mindtools.com/pages/article/newISS_91.htm

Moen, R. D., & Norman, C. L. (2010). Circling back. *Quality Progress, 43*(11), 22.

Murawski, W. W. (2003). *Co-teaching in the inclusive classroom: Working together to help all your students find success* [handbook; grades 6–12]. Medina, WA: Institute for Educational Development.

Murawski, W. W. (2006). Student outcomes in co-taught secondary English classes: How can we improve? *Reading and Writing Quarterly, 22*(3), 227–247.

Murawski, W. W. (2009). *Collaborative teaching in secondary schools: Making the co-teaching marriage work!* Thousand Oaks, CA: Corwin.

Murawski, W. W. (2010). *Collaborative teaching in elementary schools: Making the co-teaching marriage work!* Thousand Oaks, CA: Corwin.

Murawski, W. W. (2012). 10 tips for using co-planning time more efficiently. *Teaching Exceptional Children, 44*(4), 8–15.

Murawski, W. W., Ashton, T. A., & Scott, K. L. (in progress). *A multi-state analysis of the fidelity to co-teaching* [Research study].

Murawski, W. W., & Bernhardt, P. (2016). An administrator's guide to co-teaching. *Educational Leadership, 73*(4), 30–34.

Murawski, W. W., Carter, N., Sileo, N., & Prater, M. A. (2012). Communicating and collaborating with families. In N. Sileo & M. A. Prater (Eds.), *Working with families of children with special needs: Family and professional partnerships and roles* (pp. 59–90). San Francisco, CA: Pearson.

Murawski, W. W., & Dieker, L. A. (2004). Tips and strategies for co-teaching at the secondary level. *Teaching Exceptional Children, 36*(5), 52–58.

Murawski, W., & Dieker, L. (2013). *Leading the co-teaching dance: Leadership strategies to enhance team outcomes.* Arlington, VA: Council for Exceptional Children.

Murawski, W. W., & Goodwin, V. (2014). Effective inclusive schools and the co-teaching conundrum. In J. McLeskey, N. L. Waldron, F. Spooner, & B. Algozzine (Eds.), *Handbook of effective inclusive schools: Research and practice* (pp. 292–305). New York: Routledge.

Murawski, W. W., & Hughes, C. E. (2009). Response to intervention, collaboration, and co-teaching: A logical combination for successful systemic change. *Preventing School Failure, 53*(4), 267–277.

Murawski, W. W., & Lochner, W. W. (2011). Observing co-teaching: What to ask for, look for, and listen for. *Intervention in School and Clinic, 46*(3), 174–183.

Murawski, W. W., & Lochner, W. W. (2016, April). *Don't forget the data: Improving co-teaching student outcomes and evaluating program effectiveness.* Presentation at the Council for Exceptional Children Conference, St. Louis, MO.

Murawski, W. W., & Scott, K. L. (Eds.). (2017). *What really works with exceptional learners.* Thousand Oaks, CA: Corwin.

Murawski, W. W., & Spencer, S. A. (2011). *Collaborate, communicate, and differentiate! How to increase student learning in today's diverse schools.* Thousand Oaks, CA: Corwin.

Murawski, W. W., & Swanson, H. L. (2001). A meta-analysis of co-teaching: Where are the data? *Remedial and Special Education, 22*(5), 258–267.

Nash-Aurand, T. (2013). *A comparison of general education co-teaching versus special education resource service delivery models on math achievement of students with disabilities* (Unpublished doctoral dissertation). Liberty University, Lynchburg, VA.

Newton, I. (1676). Letter from Sir Isaac Newton to Robert Hooke. *Historical Society of Pennsylvania.* Retrieved from http://digitallibrary.hsp.org/index.php/Detail/Object/Show/object_id/9285

Nierengarten, G. (2013). Supporting co-teaching teams in high schools: Twenty research-based practices. *American Secondary Education, 42*(1), 73.

Ogle, D. M. (1986). KWL: A teaching model that develops active reading of expository text. *The Reading Teacher, 39*(6), 564–570.

Okes, D. (2009). *Root cause analysis: The core of problem solving and corrective action.* Milwaukee, WI: ASQ Quality Press.

Otsupius, I. A. (2014). Microteaching: A technique for effective teaching. *African Research Review, 8*(4), 183–197.

Pfeffer, J., & Sutton, R. I. (2000). *The knowing-doing gap: How smart companies turn knowledge into action.* Boston, MA: Harvard Business Press.

Pietarinen, J., Pyhältö, K., Soini, T., & Salmela-Aro, K. (2013). Reducing teacher burnout: A socio-contextual approach. *Teaching and Teacher Education, 35,* 62–72.

Prater, M. A., & Sileo, N. M. (2015). Fantastic family collaboration. In W. W. Murawski & K. L. Scott (Eds.), *What really works in secondary education* (pp. 322–334). Thousand Oaks, CA: Corwin.

Ramaprasad, A., & Prakash, A. N. (2003). Emergent project management: How foreign managers can leverage local knowledge. *International Journal of Project Management, 21*(3), 199–205.

Regalla, M., Nutta, J. A., Ashtari, N., & Verkler, K. (2014, May). English learner (EL) avatars for pre-service teachers. In C. Straub, L. Dieker, M. Hynes, & C. Hughes (Eds.), *Proceedings from the 2nd Annual TLE TeachLivETM Conference 2014: Ludic Convergence* (pp. 24–28). Orlando, FL: University of Central Florida.

Rentfro, E. R. (2007). Professional learning communities impact student success. *Leadership compass, 5*(2), 1–3.

Saint-Onge, H., & Wallace, D. (2012). *Leveraging communities of practice for strategic advantage.* New York: Routledge.

Scherer, M. (2001). How and why standards can improve student achievement: A conversation with Robert J. Marzano. *Educational Leadership, 59*(1), 14–18.

Scruggs, T. E., Mastropieri, M. A., & McDuffie, K. A. (2007). Co-teaching in inclusive classrooms: A metasynthesis of qualitative research. *Exceptional Children, 73*(4), 392–416.

Serrat, O. (2010). *The five whys technique.* Washington, DC: Asian Development Bank.

Shaffer, L., & Thomas-Brown, K. (2015). Enhancing teacher competency through co-teaching and embedded professional development. *Journal of Education and Training Studies, 3*(3), 117–125.

Sileo, N., & Prater, M. A. (Eds.). (2012). *Working with families of children with special needs: Family and professional partnerships and roles.* San Francisco, CA: Pearson.

Solis, M., Vaughn, S., Swanson, E., & Mcculley, L. (2012). Collaborative models of instruction: The empirical foundations of inclusion and co-teaching. *Psychology in the Schools, 49*(5), 498–510.

Spencer, S. (2016). Classroom simulation: A new paradigm in teacher education.

CTL on the Cutting Edge. Center for Teaching and Learning, California State University, Northridge. Retrieved from http://www.csun.edu/sites/default/files/CTL-Cutting-Edge-A-New-Paradigm-in-Teacher-Education.pdf

Stoll, L., Bolam, R., McMahon, A., Thomas, S., Wallace, M., Greenwood, A., & Hawkey, K. (2005). *What is a professional learning community? A summary*. Australia Department for Education and Skills. As cited in http://www.ldonline.org/article/31653/

Stoll, L., Bolam, R., McMahon, A., Wallace, M., & Thomas, S. (2006). Professional learning communities: A review of the literature. *Journal of Educational Change, 7*, 221–258.

Stoll, L., & Louis, K. S. (2007). *Professional learning communities: Divergence, depth and dilemmas*. New York: McGraw-Hill Education.

Strauss, V. (2014, March 1). Why professional development for teachers is useless. *Washington Post*. Retrieved from https://www.washingtonpost.com/news/answer-sheet/wp/2014/03/01/why-most-professional-development-for-teachers-is-useless/

Strieker, T., Gillis, B., & Zong, G. (2013). Improving pre-service middle school teachers' confidence, competence, and commitment to co-teaching in inclusive classrooms. *Teacher Education Quarterly, 40*(4), 159–180.

Strogilos, V., & Stefanidis, A. (2015). Contextual antecedents of co-teaching efficacy: Their influence on students with disabilities' learning progress, social participation and behaviour improvement. *Teaching and Teacher Education, 47*, 218–229.

Tague, N. R. (2004). *The quality toolbox* (2nd ed.). Milwaukee, WI: ASQ Quality Press.

Taylor, M. J., McNicholas, C., Nicolay, C., Darzi, A., Bell, D., & Reed, J. E. (2014). Systematic review of the application of the plan-do-study-act method to improve quality in healthcare. *BMJ Quality and Safety, 23*, 290–298.

Tomlinson, C. A., & Murphy, M. (2015). *Leading for differentiation: Growing teachers who grow kids*. Alexandria, VA: ASCD.

Trust, T., Krutka, D. G., & Carpenter, J. P. (2016). "Together we are better": Professional learning networks for teachers. *Computers and Education, 102*, 15–34.

Tzivinikou, S. (2015). Collaboration between general and special education teachers: Developing co-teaching skills in heterogeneous classes. *Problems of Education in the 21st Century, 64*, 108–119.

U.S. Department of Education. (2013). Office of Special Education Programs, Individuals with Disabilities Act (IDEA) database. Retrieved from http://nces.ed.gov/programs/digest/d13/tables/dt13_204.60.asp

Valentine, J. (2012). IPI Research summary B: Strategies for effective implementation of the IPI process. Retrieved from https://ipistudentengagement.com/papers-presentations/ipi-research-summaries

Valentine, J., Cockrell, D., Herndon, B., & Solomon, B. (2006, April). *Project ASSIST: Comprehensive, systemic change initiative impacts school culture, climate, leadership, and instruction*. Presentation at the American Educational Research Association Annual Convention, San Francisco, CA.

Van Driel, J. H., Beijaard, D., & Verloop, N. (2001). Professional development and reform in science education: The role of teachers' practical knowledge. *Journal of Research in Science Teaching, 38*(2), 137–158.

Vaughan, S., & Dornan, T. (2014). Communities of practice. *The Wiley Blackwell Encyclopedia of Health, Illness, Behavior, and Society*. Retrieved from http://onlinelibrary.wiley.com/doi/10.1002/9781118410868.wbehibs261/pdf

Villa, R. A., Thousand, J. S., & Nevin, A. I. (2013). *A guide to co-teaching: New lessons and strategies to facilitate student learning*. Thousand Oaks, CA: Corwin.

Waldron, N. L., & McLeskey, J. (2010). Establishing a collaborative school culture through comprehensive school reform. *Journal of Educational and Psychological Consultation, 20*(1), 58–74.

Walsh, J. M. (2012). Co-teaching as a school system strategy for continuous improvement. *Preventing School Failure, 56*(1), 29–36.

Walther-Thomas, C., Bryant, M., & Land, S. (1996). Planning for effective co-teaching: The key to successful inclusion. *Remedial and Special Education, 17*(4), 255–264.

Weißenrieder, J., Roesken-Winter, B., Schueler, S., Binner, E., & Blömeke, S. (2015). Scaling CPD through professional learning communities: Development of teachers' self-efficacy in relation to collaboration. *ZDM Mathematics Education, 47*(1), 27–38.

Weiss, M. P., & Lloyd, J. W. (2002). Congruence between roles and actions of secondary special educators in co-taught and special education settings. *The Journal of Special Education, 36*(2), 58–68.

Wenger, E. (1998). *Communities of practice: Learning, meaning, and identity.* Cambridge, England: Cambridge University Press.

Wenger, E. (2006). *Communities of practice: A brief introduction.* Retrieved from http://www.ewenger.com/theory/communities_of_practice_intro.htm

Wenger, E., McDermott, R. A., & Snyder, W. (2002). *Cultivating communities of practice: A guide to managing knowledge.* Boston, MA: Harvard Business School Press.

WestEd. (2012). *Becoming a successful community of practice facilitator: Linking learning and assessment in Rhode Island schools.* Retrieved from http://www.ride.ri.gov/Portals/0/Uploads/Documents/Instruction-and-Assessment-World-Class-Standards/Assessment/Formative-Assessment-PD-Online-Modules/Becoming_a_Successful_CoP_Facilitator.pdf

Willett, J. B., Yamashita, J. J., & Anderson, R. D. (1983). A meta-analysis of instructional systems applied in science teaching. *Journal of Research in Science Teaching, 20*(5), 405–417.

Wischnowski, M. W., Salmon, S. J., & Eaton, K. (2004). Evaluating co-teaching as a means for successful inclusion of students with disabilities in a rural district. *Rural Special Education Quarterly, 23*(3), 3.

Wormeli, R. (2006). *Fair isn't always equal: Assessing and grading in the differentiated classroom.* Portland, ME: Stenhouse.

Zigmond, N., Magiera, K., Simmons, R., & Volonino, V. (2013). Strategies for improving student outcomes in co-taught general education classrooms. In B. G. Cook & M. Tandersley (Eds.), *Research-based practices in special education* (pp. 116–124). Upper Saddle River, NJ: Pearson.

Zimpher, N. L., & Howey, K. R. (2013). Creating 21st-century centers of pedagogy: Explicating key laboratory and clinical elements of teacher preparation. *Education, 133*(4), 409.

Index

Note: The letter *f* following a page number denotes a figure.

About the Authors

Wendy Weichel Murawski is the Michael D. Eisner Endowed Chair and Executive Director for the Center for Teaching and Learning at California State University, Northridge (CSUN). She received her doctorate from UC Riverside and her Masters and EdS from the College of William and Mary. She is a tenured full professor in the department of Special Education, a past president of the Teacher Education Division (TED) for the Council for Exceptional Children, a former Teacher Educator of the Year for the state of California, a Division of Learning Disabilities (DLD) research award winner, and the recipient of the outstanding faculty award for CSUN. Wendy previously taught both special education and German and has authored numerous books, chapters, articles, and handbooks on co-teaching, collaboration, inclusion, differentiation, and teaching. Wendy owns her own educational consulting company (2 TEACH LLC), speaks nationally and internationally, and is a frequently requested keynote speaker.

Wendy Whitehair Lochner is a national educational consultant and is a former school improvement and federal programs coordinator for the West Virginia Department of Education, where she led districts and schools in the school turnaround process. She specializes in needs assessments, data analysis, and strategic planning and provides daily technical assistance to districts, superintendents, administrators, and teachers. She designed, developed, and published several software systems for co-teaching observation, lesson planning, Response to Intervention (RTI) and Intervention Tracking, online student assessment, and data and outcomes management that are used statewide and nationally. Wendy was a special educator in two separate schools that successfully went through the school turnaround process, utilizing co-teaching as a strategy for improving achievement for all students, and is the co-founder of the Co-Teach Solutions System.

Related ASCD Resources

At the time of publication, the following resources were available (ASCD stock numbers appear in parentheses):

Print Products

Educational Leadership: Co-Teaching: Making It Work (December 2015/January 2016) (#116031)

Co-Planning for Co-Teaching: Time-Saving Routines That Work in Inclusive Classrooms by Gloria Lodato Wilson (#SF117018)

Reading for Meaning: How to Build Students' Comprehension, Reasoning, and Problem-Solving Skills by Harvey F. Silver, Susan C. Morris, and Victor Klein (#110128)

Teaching in Tandem: Effective Co-Teaching in the Inclusive Classroom by Gloria Lodato Wilson and Joan Blednick (#110029)

For up-to-date information about ASCD resources, go to www.ascd.org. You can search the complete archives of *Educational Leadership* at www.ascd.org/el.

ASCD EDge® Group

Exchange ideas and connect with other educators on the social networking site ASCD EDge at http://ascdedge.ascd.org/.

ASCD myTeachSource®

Download resources from a professional learning platform with hundreds of research-based best practices and tools for your classroom at http://myteachsource.ascd.org/.

For more information, send an e-mail to member@ascd.org; call 1-800-933-2723 or 703-578-9600; send a fax to 703-575-5400; or write to Information Services, ASCD, 1703 N. Beauregard St., Alexandria, VA 22311-1714 USA.